Social Media and Everyday Politics

Tim Highfield

First published in 2016 by Polity Press

Polity Press
65 Bridge Street
Cambridge CB2 1UR, UK

Polity Press
350 Main Street
Malden, MA 02148, USA

ISBN-13: 978-0-7456-9134-3
ISBN-13: 978-0-7456-9135-0 (pb)

A catalogue record for this book is available from the British Library.

Library of Congress Cataloging-in-Publication Data

Names: Highfield, Tim, author.
Title: Social media and everyday politics / Tim Highfield.
Description: Malden, MA : Polity Press, 2016. | Includes bibliographical references and index.
Identifiers: LCCN 2015034090| ISBN 9780745691343 (hardback) | ISBN 9780745691350 (pbk.)
Subjects: LCSH: Social media–Political aspects. | Internet–Political aspects. | Communication in politics–Technological innovations. | Political participation–Technological innovations.
Classification: LCC HM742 .H53 2016 | DDC 302.23/1–dc23 LC record available at http://lccn.loc.gov/2015034090

Typeset in 10 on 12 pt Sabon
by Toppan Best-set Premedia Limited
Printed and bound in the CPI Group (UK) Ltd, by Croydon, CR0 4YY

For further information on Polity, visit our website:
politybooks.com

Contents

Figures

Preface

Social Media and Everyday Politics is an examination of user practices online concerning political contexts, as part of the social mediation of everyday life.

Before We Begin ...

This research comes from a background of Internet Studies and Media and Communication, positioned within a Political Communication context.

More pertinently, though, this book was written by a straight, white, agnostic, middle-class, male academic, at the time of writing approaching thirty, and based in Australia. I have endeavoured in my discussion here to provide a range of cases around different aspects of politics and social media, from around the world. However, my work is also inevitably filtered through a Western context, and through my own background and experiences. While the book addresses various topics, I certainly do not propose that I am the best (or indeed appropriate) voice for going into depth about certain long-debated issues and views, and I have endeavoured to cite and promote scholars and writers who have published extended coverage of these perspectives around politics and media.

This book draws on material from collaborative projects, including *Mapping Online Publics* (with Axel Bruns, Jean Burgess et al.), the ARC Future Fellowship project *Understanding Intermedia Information Flows in the Australian Online Public Sphere* (Axel Bruns), *Mapping Movements* (with Sky Croeser) and *The Ends of Identity* (with Tama Leaver). My continued thanks go to my colleagues for all their support.

The writing of this book was a global undertaking. Sections were written in: Cambridge, MA; Brisbane, QLD; Perth, WA; Adelaide, SA; Melbourne, VIC; Sydney, NSW; Byron Bay, NSW; Munich, Germany; and Tokyo, Japan. Additional prep work took place in: the Forest of Dean, Bristol and London, UK; San Juan, Puerto Rico; San Francisco and Los Angeles, CA; and Queenstown, New Zealand. I acknowledge the traditional, indigenous owners of the lands on which this text was prepared.

Acknowledgements

Thanks, everyone.

Theveryone.

But also, thanks to:

My QUT friends and colleagues past and current, at the ARC Centre of Excellence for Creative Industries and Innovation, the Digital Media Research Centre, the Social Media Research Group and the Creative Industries Faculty: Axel Bruns, Jean Burgess, Jason Sternberg, Peta Mitchell, Patrik Wikström, Ben Light, Stephen Harrington, Darryl Woodford, Katie Prowd, Marcus Foth, Folker Hanusch, Ben Goldsmith, Theresa Sauter, Nic Suzor, Emma Baulch, Brenda Moon, Anne Watson, Terry Flew, Troy Sadkowsky, Jaz Choi, Eli Koger, Brian McNair, Tanya Nitins, Mark Ryan, Stuart Cunningham, Helen Klaebe, Deb Murray, John Keaney, Colleen Cook, Kate Aldridge, Sue Carson and Mimi Tsai.

My Curtin friends and colleagues (including the book proposal support group): Sky Croeser, Tama Leaver, Michele Willson, Mike Kent, Eleanor Sandry, Gwyneth Peaty, Clare Lloyd, Kate Raynes-Goldie, Katie

Ellis, Helen Merrick, Stewart Woods, John Hartley, Henry Li, Sam Stevenson, Ange Glazbrook, Sara Gillies and Sue Summers.

The dream team of Liz Ellison and Lee McGowan.

The peer pressure writing/support group (unofficially known as 'You're Not My Supervisor'): Elija Cassidy, Stefanie Duguay, Sara Ekberg, Kim Osman and Emma Potter.

The QUT Social Media/Creative Industries postgrad (and extended) community, including Ella Chorazy, Ariadna M. Fernández, Annelore Huyghe, Katherine Kirkwood, Morag Kobez, Dan Lynch, Nino Miletovic, Felix Münch, Ellen Nielsen, Dan Padua, Kelly Palmer, Avi Paul, Andrew Quodling, Fiona Suwana, Tess Van Hemert, Portia Vann, Wilfred Wang and Meg Zeng.

All at Polity and their associates, including Elen Griffiths, Andrea Drugan, Clare Ansell, Jane Fricker and Susan Beer.

My friends around the country and around the world, especially Christina, Helen, Hourann, Jessica, Robert, Lisa, Jarrad, Sophie, Cameron, Zoe, Chiara, Alex, Dave, Arron, Martin, Tristan, Agata, Julee, Travis, Kim, Krystina, Jan and Liz. Also, everyone who has hung out, had coffee/tea/miscellaneous drinks, and/or let me crash on spare beds and couches, especially in the midst of my travels. Also, naturally, the Bob Katter Experience and Party Animals soccer teams, the Growl Theatre Company, the Byron, San Juan and Queenstown crews and the Swift Taylors running team.

My academic family, including the Association of Internet Researchers and the alumni of the Oxford Internet Institute Summer Doctoral Programme (2009); special mention goes to academic friends who have provided support, pomodoros, and talked through/made sense of my half-baked ideas and nonsense at various conferences, workshops, colloquia and more, including Matthew Allen, Anders Larsson, Kate Miltner, Amy Johnson, Whitney Erin Boesel, R. Stuart Geiger, Emily van der Nagel, Jonathon Hutchinson, Frances Shaw, Brady Robards, Paul Byron, Martina Wengenmeir, Crystal Abidin, Jenny Kennedy, Sonja Vivienne, Gerard Goggin, Rowan Wilken, Kath Albury, Nancy Baym, Christian Nuernbergk, Sanja Kapidzic, Julia Neubarth, Christoph Neuberger, Hallvard Moe, Eli Skogerbø, Christian Christensen, Bente Kalsnes, Gunn Enli, Sander Schwartz, Yana Breindl, Bridget Blodgett, Eve Bottando, Todd Graham, Scott Wright, Dan Jackson, Ramon Lobato and Greg Elmer; Thomas Nicolai and Lars Kirchhoff from Sociomantic Labs; *Such Parody Much Wow* and its spin-offs (including *Your Parody is Bad and You Should Feel Bad* and *#badscience*); and all involved with #suwtues.

My actual family: Elaine and Tony, Hannah and Jamie, the extended Highfield &c. ensemble and the menagerie accompanying them.

Finally, my unending gratitude goes to the staff of the many cafes and bars at which I wrote this book.

Started: Voltage Coffee and Art, Cambridge, MA: June 2014.
Mostly written: Room 60/The Menagerie, Kelvin Grove, QLD: November 2014–May 2015.
Finished: somewhere over the Pacific between Japan and the US: May 2015.
Revisited: Bespoke Kitchen, Queenstown, NZ: July 2015.

Introduction: Everyday Politics and Social Media

In May 2014, the British Electoral Commission issued advice to polling place staff ahead of the upcoming local and European elections: voters should not be taking selfies while in polling booths. Selfies – self-portrait photos, usually taken with a smartphone and uploaded to social media platforms such as Facebook and Instagram – were deemed to be a threat to the validity and security of the vote, particularly when polling papers were also featured in the images. By posting highly private and confidential material such as a personal vote – potentially identifiable through a user's social media content – and possibly infringing on others' privacy at the same time, voters taking selfies were seen as irresponsible at best, and at worst committing a criminal offence (Press Association, 2014; Wheeler, 2014).

The fact that this activity warranted an official statement also demonstrates the intersection of politics and everyday lives, as documented through smartphones and social media. Voting in an election is a democratic right, an ideal which is not universally realized around the world, and which has a clear, important implication: that a citizen's choice directly contributes to determining how the country will be run. Voting is also, though, just another thing happening on a day, something a little out of the ordinary that encourages being documented and shared with friends and followers online. If we update our social media profiles with details of other aspects of our everyday lives, why not present updates from the polls?

A polling booth selfie is an example of an act that is both personal and political: it is obviously personal in the sense that it is about the individual, their own actions and choices and their unique experience of voting. It is political as it is a clear engagement with a definite political activity. Even if the content of the selfie has no partisan content or commentary, such as promoting a specific campaign, it is still a politically oriented artefact, an image whose meaning is underlined by the election context. If, as in figure 1 I take an election selfie and/or a photo of my ballot paper and upload it to my personal Instagram account, I am demonstrating my engagement with the electoral process (in my case, voting in Australia, I am also possibly engaging with the obligation of participating and the potential confusion of preferential voting). The surrounding photos in my photo stream, or those of the

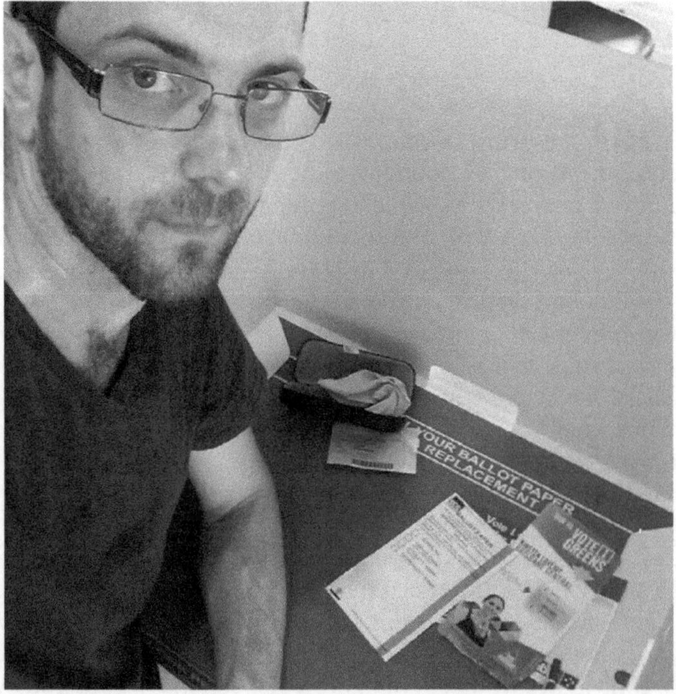

Figure 1: The author's polling booth selfie, as posted to Instagram on 31 January 2015. Moments later I was told off for taking photos inside a polling place.

users I follow, might have no political content whatsoever – but for a moment, the personal and political aligned, and were documented on social media.

However, I'm getting ahead of myself; polling booth selfies and other social media activities involving elections, while political, are examples of how our mundane uses of social media intersect with a particular political event that is not an everyday occurrence. The election context will return at times throughout this book, but not in detail until chapter 7. The purpose of introducing the selfies here, though, is to put forward two key ideas that guide this work:

First, that the personal and the political are highly interlinked, and that social media are platforms which can bring about the further personalization of politics – not in terms of parties or politicians tailoring their messages to individuals, but in how we discuss and document our experience of political issues.

Second, that for many people, political topics are not a major interest or a regular feature in their shared content. We might engage with a wide range of issues, but these are not necessarily constant concerns, and they coexist on social media with baby photos, music videos, comments on who just died in *Game of Thrones* and updates from nights out. That is not to say that social media are primarily made up of photos of cats and coffee, of friends and brunch: it is more that political discussions may be fleeting but recurring for many people, part of more extensive activity shared online. Politics is not solely the domain of 'political junkies' for whom such topics are their primary subjects of conversation (S. Coleman, 2006) – those individuals just have long-term, sustained interest in continuing political discussions. For others, engagement and reaction come tangentially, through particular events or issues, not in response to every little aspect of politics.

What this means then is that when we look at how politics and the internet intersect, at how social media might change patterns of political and media power alike, at how individual citizens use the internet for political involvement, we cannot and should not look solely at contexts such as elections, for they present one specific – and artificial – arena for political engagement. Social media, as I will demonstrate throughout this book, have fostered a wide range of political actions and functions, across numerous contexts. By taking all of these into account, we can arrive at a clearer understanding of the impact of social media on the political and media ecosystem. To do so, though, we need to consider not just 'Politics' – the work of politicians, the coverage of major government events, elections – but the *everyday* politics, how political themes are framed around our own experiences and interests. As highly personalized spaces, social media would appear to be clearly suitable for the discussion and promotion of everyday politics, and this idea is examined in depth here.

A secondary theme running through this book is a consideration of the evolving uses of the internet for political discussions by citizens, politicians and journalists. The empirical research carried out for this book took place between 2009 and 2015, drawing on blogs, Twitter and Instagram, and supplemented by observations and secondary research on further platforms and cases. This is not a book just about, for example, Twitter and politics (and there are some highly detailed studies of individual platforms or formats – see, for example, Burgess and Green, 2009; Massanari, 2015; Walker Rettberg, 2008; Weller et al., 2013). While Twitter is heavily featured in my previous research, it is not the only platform used to discuss politics. An individual's online activity encompasses multiple social media platforms, often simultaneously, and our practices on one platform can inform how we behave on others. My research considers the changing patterns and functions around different platforms, as internet-mediated communication moved from 'Web 2.0' to 'social networking sites' to 'social media' and beyond. While not organized chronologically, this book treats blogs, Twitter and other platforms not as examples used in isolation, but as part of an ever-evolving mediasphere.

This book comes out of my PhD and post-doctoral research into social media, politics and other topics between 2008 and 2015. Yet this is not just an account of what has occupied my time over this period. There is far more to the discussion of social media and political talk, reflecting the everyday in both contexts, than is found in my datasets alone. My work is subject to my own situation, background and perspective, and there are many elements of this topic, and numerous platforms, that I have not addressed – directly or indirectly – in my studies thus far. In the following discussion, I also draw on many examples that are – at the time of writing in early 2015 – recent, but which, like so many previous cases, might fade in relevance and memory over time. My rationale for choosing these very current examples is not that they are especially exceptional, but that they are emblematic of evolving and recurring practices. Ritualized social media behaviours coincide with politics, and while the specific outputs and contexts for them will change, these practices are established parts of political discussion and engagement online.

My interest here is in social media practices around politics, across platforms as well as on individual sites. While aspects like hashtag politics and activism are obvious starting points, they are not the be-all and end-all. This is also not intended to be a data dump; I am less interested in how many tweets contained, for instance, #illridewithyou, #JeSuisCharlie, #GamerGate, #ICantBreathe or #ruddmentum, than in *why* and *how* these markers arose and persisted, including the external factors beyond the social media context. The extent of hashtags is not unimportant, but it can also be misdirection, as can an endless series of network maps visualizing connections between sites, users or themes. Of course, I do quantitatively study hashtags and networks at points, but I have not used this approach for every single case because there are many other ways to interrogate and study social media practices. The limitations on data collection from the Twitter application programming interface (API) mean that, without Firehose access, complete archives of relevant Twitter activity around major topics are an extreme improbability at best (González-Bailón et al., 2014; Morstatter et al., 2013). For this reason, I argue that gaps in my data are not a limitation, since I am not claiming to be presenting the entirety of social media activity around everyday politics. Practices, themes and approaches of interest are identified here, but this is just one of the more visible – and public – sides of the story.

As a general methodological overview, my analyses have drawn on digital methods approaches and provocations (Rogers, 2013b). The cases I study feature data captured using automated processes, crawling from seed lists of blogs and using tools to query Twitter and Instagram APIs, including yourTwapperKeeper, Archivist and NodeXL, and supplemented with tools like Issuecrawler. From datasets organized around defined populations, users, keywords or hashtags, I have filtered relevant content to focus variously on overall patterns, time-specific periods, topical discussions (see Highfield, 2012) and networked communication, using software including Gephi, Tableau and Leximancer to aid these analyses, and drawing on and adapting scripts developed for processing Twitter datasets (see Bruns and Burgess, 2011b). For the *Mapping Movements* research into Occupy Oakland and anti-fascist activism in Greece, the social media analysis supported ethnographic fieldwork and interviews carried out by Sky Croeser and outlined in our relevant publications. Citations are provided as appropriate to cases that are covered in depth in previous publications.

Key Concepts

Social media

Because this book is in part a historical treatment of how political discussions online have changed over time, the term 'social media' is used differently here from its standard definition in much Internet Studies research, primarily for internal continuity. I take an expansive, inclusive approach to 'social media'. Terminology changes often, particularly within fields of constant development like Internet Studies, and 'social media' is both a successor to and replacement of 'social networking sites' (see boyd and Ellison, 2008), which in part overlapped with the idea of 'Web 2.0' sites (Allen, 2012). As technologies and uses continue to evolve, 'social media' itself will be replaced by other terms, which might reflect the growing importance of mobile devices, apps and ubiquitous media. Here, then, 'social media' represents a moment in time but is also a catch-all term, covering blogs and blogging platforms, social networks such as Facebook, content-sharing sites and apps including YouTube and Instagram, and forums and communities like reddit and 4chan. This also includes platforms set up for (or originating from) different national, cultural and linguistic contexts, such as Weibo, Line, Orkut and CyWorld.[1]

A critical element of this definition is that while these are all forms of internet-enabled communication, they are not solely websites. In particular, social media include mobile apps, which have website presences and profiles that are not the primary means for users to access and share content. Even platforms that were not initially launched for the mobile web, such as Facebook or Twitter, have shown the importance of mobile technology in the user experience, especially in integrating and connecting to other services, as users share updates and content wherever they are and whenever. Similarly, users do not access these media through a computer or even a single device (although some may be primarily accessed through one device, users are not limited to just a computer, tablet or smartphone). Many of these services also privilege and promote 'small' data, where users share short messages (Twitter), images and time-limited videos (Instagram, Vine) or highly ephemeral media (Snapchat) – but are encouraged to continually use these services and add to their content. While there are niche and topical apps and websites which serve specific purposes, rather than the more generic nature of Facebook, Twitter, blogs, YouTube, Instagram and so on, the focus here is on these popular social media with myriad functions and uses, which were not explicitly developed for political purposes but where politics is a regular and emergent topic.

It goes without saying that social media are not separate, disconnected phenomena. There are practices specific to individual platforms and reflective of social media cultures, but these are also rooted in wider social, political and technological contexts and norms (among others). These predate and extend beyond social media, and the influence of external factors that are not online-only is important to remember. The offline and the online are closely interlinked and impact upon one another; for this reason, delineating between the two is rather redundant, especially in considering the various aspects of the political featured here. As Whitney Phillips (2015) argues,

> so-called real life necessarily bleeds into online life, and vice versa. Our raced, classed, and gendered bodies are encoded into our online behaviors, even when we're pretending to be something above or beyond or below what we 'really' are IRL (in real life). (p. 41)

For this reason, while I refer to social media activity and practices directly in this book, I am not claiming that they are divorced from the wider contextual factors which affect individuals' and groups' experiences of politics and the internet.

Everyday politics

This book also considers politics as not solely what is presented through elections, politicians' speeches or protests. The adoption of different politically relevant practices by increasing numbers of social media users highlights the importance of digital platforms as arenas for politics in addition to, and alongside, other personal concerns. Such practices further underline the importance of *everyday* politics to online discussions, where ongoing political concerns that affect education, welfare, immigration, relationships or families, for instance, are discussed, debated, critiqued, supported and challenged.

Everyday politics, as described by Boyte (2005), is populist and civic: of the people, not of governments or campaigns. Politics then is not just formal, as shaped and discussed by established political actors and the mainstream media, but highly informal. Everyday political talk features occasional contributions by individuals who are loosely connected (if at all), but who have their own personal interests, perspectives and issues of importance. In this book, I extend this idea by treating everyday politics as a lens through which to obtain a further understanding of how politics is discussed online, beyond the heightened interest surrounding elections and other major events.

In particular, I argue that the everyday informs how people cover politics, including both the mundane and the more extraordinary and artificial settings like elections. This view is substantiated by examining what people are doing in relation to social media – their practices (Couldry, 2012) – within political topics and contexts. Politics is also an emergent topic within other discussions; conversations about different subjects, however banal, may include political themes. Social media users discuss both the explicitly and tangentially political, and the overlap between various topical discussions and common practices is apparent throughout this book. A recurring element of this discussion is the idea of the ritual – patterned and repeated actions that demonstrate socially mediated phenomena and behaviours (see Couldry, 2003, 2012) – as a part of how individuals use social media platforms for everyday communication and contribute to political discussions. The everyday is also an increasingly critical provocation for social media research: Brabham (2015) argues for more research into 'normal, everyday topics' in the field, as 'very few social media users use social media tools to coordinate revolutions'. While I am still focused on discussions that might not involve the majority of social media users – and which are certainly not representative of wider populations – the consideration of the everyday here, for political talk and for the practices accompanying it, is a step towards more research into the mundane activity taking place on Facebook, Twitter and their ilk.

Publics

A guiding concept for this book is publics. The underpinnings for this I have drawn from Warner (2002), especially the idea of publics as 'the social space created by the reflexive circulation of discourse' (p. 62). While publics are self-organized spaces formed between strangers and featuring personal and impersonal discourses, there are differences between often-transient, topically specific issue publics (Dahlgren, 2009) and longer-term publics (as part of, or in place of, a public sphere in the Habermasian sense; Habermas, 1989). Publics on social media, whether predefined or ad hoc (Bruns and Burgess, 2011a, 2015), reflect the convergence of different groups of actors in these spaces – within these assemblages, there are politicians and media as well as 'the public', although these topical groups involve different combinations of members of these groups in different roles. Further conceptual publics within this analysis include networked publics (boyd, 2011), personal publics (Schmidt, 2013), calculated publics (Gillespie, 2014) and affective publics (Papacharissi, 2015): these are variously shaped by and respond to affordances of social media platforms, and by practices and styles of communication on the likes of Twitter and Facebook.

The concept of hybridity – seen as traditional and newer media intersect, overlap and in combination shape political coverage and action – has guided further research in this field (Lindgren, 2013, 2014). Chadwick (2013) argues that media logics in the hybrid media system are created by media, political actors and publics, where power is held not just by the first two groups (p. 20). An addition to this argument made in this book is that there are participants here which are variously members of the media, political actors and publics at different times, and that these 'publics' may extend to encompassing the other groups too. Social media also bring their own further concerns of power and influence, such as the politics of social media platforms: how information is presented, how people are able to use these platforms, what these actions represent (and what they do not), how individuals' data are used and the algorithms behind these platforms as well as methodological questions around 'big data' analysis (boyd and Crawford, 2012; Bucher, 2012a; Gillespie, 2010; Langlois and Elmer, 2013). As will be seen in the following chapters, these considerations add new dimensions to the discussion of social media and politics, which overlap and influence one another through questions of surveillance, privacy, consent and more.

Everyday social media practices

In this book, I explore the everyday coverage of politics on social media, through mundane practices on different platforms. How social media users employ Twitter, Facebook, Instagram, Vine, Tumblr and other platforms and apps for interactions, information-sharing and -sourcing and communication shapes how these same users discuss and participate in political issues. Everyday practices are commonplace in politically relevant social media activity, including @mentioning other users, retweeting and sharing others' comments, replying and liking, posting and creating memes and using markers like hashtags for topical, structural and emotive purposes alike. Politicians and journalists are tagged and @mentioned, in response to their social media comments but also at times when talking *about* them as well; user accounts become shorthand and a direct reference to these public figures, in the same way that users tag friends and celebrities.

Everyday social media practices can be specific to political themes. The day-in, day-out discussion of politics on Twitter is reflected in the creation of standardized hashtags for such topics. Markers from #auspol to #dkpol and #cdnpoli are employed to denote tweets about Australian, Danish and Canadian politics respectively – any outcome of general, civil discussion from their use is debatable, with #auspol tweets highly polarized and vitriolic (Jericho, 2012) – while state, province and city-specific hashtags are also apparent (such as #qldpol for Queensland, Australia). The thematic scope of these hashtags is seemingly limitless. Beyond the context of Danish politics, a #dkpol tweet might dwell on health, economics, foreign policy, immigration and refugees, religion or particular political actors, among other potential topics. Such standardization also applies to particular political events which, while not everyday, are recurring: #ausvotes for Australian elections, #SOTU for the annual State of the Union presidential address in the US. However, of course, it is essential to remember that hashtag use is neither universal nor a requirement; it is a user's choice to include, or to refrain from featuring, topical markers in their social media comments.

The political can be present within the personal, without needing to be framed as explicitly political (see also Papacharissi, 2010a). The principles behind mundane forms of social media communication, from selfies to memes, intertextual references through animated GIFs and checking-in to particular locations, are also applicable to political themes both directly and tangentially. Understanding the personal uses and everyday practices of social media (Baym, 2010; boyd, 2014; Walker Rettberg, 2014) provides us with insight into the diverse ways that politics is realized, discussed, challenged and participated in online. As Rogers (2013a) has explored for Twitter research, debanalizing platforms and studying mundane communication practices are 'a means to study cultural conditions' (p. xiv). To understand everyday politics *on* social media, we also need to understand the practices, logics and vernacular *of* everyday social media. Whether through selfies and their various sub-genres (Senft and Baym, 2015), tweets about trending topics (Papacharissi, 2015) or image macros mixing photographs with topical captions (Shifman, 2014b), everyday and banal communication online is extended to, remixed and appropriated for political themes.

Social Media and Everyday Politics

These ideas are explored through different practices around political discussions on social media, across seven chapters which each focus on specific aspects of everyday social media and politics. My argument guiding this analysis is that social media afford the opportunity for different groups, including citizens, traditional political actors and journalists, to contribute to, discuss, challenge and participate in diverse aspects of politics in a public, shared context. In doing so, social media centralize and demonstrate the overlap between different political practices and topics. If ultimately they do not lead to increased formal participation, then they still reshape and facilitate new, informal ways of political talk and action.

The behaviours, topics, groups and discussions facilitated on social media platforms reflect various elements of formal and informal politics, and the application of everyday social media practices to politics. From ad hoc responses to breaking news, to ritualized irreverence fuelled by ongoing political intrigue, the coverage of political themes on social media takes many forms and involves diverse participants who bring with them their own personal and professional perspectives and motivations. In this book, I do not argue that any one way of political talk on social media is the right and only approach, or indeed that any of these practices alone will change our political and social institutions, norms and behaviours. What happens on social media is one part of our everyday lives and experiences; what this offers, though, is a lens for examining the ways that individuals engage with political and personal issues as part of everyday social media activity, and by extension what this means beyond the social media context.

The structure of this book is designed to support this argument, with each chapter focusing on specific practices and contexts that build on one another to detail how politics is featured on social media. Starting with the personal and the not obviously political, the subsequent chapters move from individualistic irreverence, humour, play and ritualized styles of political engagement to the intersections and overlaps between social media users and established political actors (representing formal political institutions, including the mainstream media and politicians themselves). Collectively, the practices and examples highlighted across the seven chapters demonstrate some of the extensive ways in which the political and the personal, the formal and the informal, the everyday and the extraordinary, are intertwined on social media.

Chapter outline

The everyday context means that the personal is closely interlinked with the political. **Chapter 1** examines this in more detail, exploring the personalization of politics and the emergence of political themes from seemingly unrelated topics and spaces. Issues that can be deemed *political* affect our everyday lives without needing to be framed around presidents or prime ministers, monarchs or ministries, while the politics *of* social media platforms informs how everyday practices can become politicized.

Personal and everyday social media practices, including the coverage of political themes, often take ritualized forms. **Chapter 2** examines political and media rituals as standardized practices in response to various types of news event, which may from time to time take on political dimensions.

Chapter 3 considers what the adoption of social media means for the mediasphere at large, discussing how media politics has changed through the introduction of blogs, Twitter and other platforms. In particular, the chapter explores the intersections between mainstream and social media, which have taken both contentious and collaborative positions.

The flows of information around political topics are examined further in **chapter 4**'s consideration of flashpoints of activity and interest: breaking news, scandals and crises. The importance of social media as a practical, and mobile, means for quickly communicating to a large population is explored here – as well as the potential pitfalls and issues accompanying such communication.

Chapter 5 studies social media within collective action, including the integration of social media into movements with strong physical components, such as Occupy, and the development of social media-driven (or -only) campaigns. Although the use of social media for collective action may go beyond the 'everyday politics' marker, these cases also tie in with more quotidian discussions and practices examined in the preceding chapters.

The focus turns in part to traditional actors and structures in **chapter 6**, exploring politicians, their parties, and how partisan politics plays out on social media. The analysis considers how politicians make use of online platforms, including their styles of use and their choice of social media. The chapter also examines the partisan side of political discussions, and the deliberate incitement of others in order to get a reaction as part of the everyday coverage of politics online.

Chapter 7 brings the main ideas and themes featured in the previous chapters together within an election context. Elections are treated as a microcosm of everyday practices around politics and social media, highlighting the different practices outlined in the rest of the book. These include election-day rituals carried out on social media, party and politician strategies and the interlinking of traditional and social media as results are made available.

Finally, the **Conclusion** collects the book's various threads in summarizing the evolving uses of social media around everyday politics. The conclusion outlines future directions for research in this field, and for how the mediasphere will continue to evolve with new technological, social and political developments.

1

Personal/Political

There is plenty of content on the internet that is objectionable, illicit, disgusting and just plain awful – often deliberately so. There are practices around the abuse of strangers and acquaintances alike, of attempting to ruin others' lives (and of this being achieved without that specific aim), of racism, sexism, homophobia and general intolerance, of being mean and antagonistic for the 'lulz' and of sharing material like child pornography where 'illegal' does not even begin to cover it.

And then there is content shared online that is not necessarily any of these things, except it is apparently offensive enough to register complaints about inappropriate material and for platforms to remove said content: such as, for example, images of women that also feature visible nipples (Esco, 2014), pubic hair (Hinde, 2015; Vagianos, 2015) or menstrual stains (Brodsky, 2015).

I will come back to the former type at points during this book, but it is the latter that I am initially focusing on here. A photograph posted to Facebook promoting public breastfeeding, an arty Instagram image of a woman who happens to visibly be on her period, or a selfie that features, among other physical attributes, the subject's nipples are perhaps not obviously political artefacts in themselves. They are highly personal but also mundane, depicting everyday scenes and experiences, not necessarily anything extraordinary.[2]

However, the personal becomes politicized in these examples. The political is seen in the response of other users to flag content as inappropriate, and the ways that platforms deal with such content, especially in comparison to posts or pages perpetuating rape culture or racism, or inciting violence against individuals or groups. It is also apparent in the riposte to these responses: countering the platforms and their users directly, more content is shared featuring or addressing breastfeeding (especially as outright lactivism – see Boon and Pentney, 2015), nipples and aspects of menstruation. Hashtags are established, helping to boost these movements' visibility, and to draw attention to related protests and approaches. From #freethenipple to #PadsAgainstSexism, the personal takes on political and social media dimensions as part of its wider context.

These examples are not restricted to social media, and certainly did not originate with Facebook or Twitter, Instagram or Tumblr. Part of the reason for the opposition to images of nipples or menstruation is long-established social norms that have consolidated stigmas, conservative attitudes and taboos. Of course, the responses and policing of this are not consistent or equal, for images of topless men cause less outcry than women in similar states of undress – #notallnipples, if you like (and the problematic part is not the rest of the breast beyond the areola). The question of inappropriate nipples and the period dramas incited by social media platforms reflect wider debates that play out around feminism, sexism, misogyny and gender (Tolentino, 2015; Williams, 2015).

Such cases illustrate the intersection of the personal and the political, which is the focus of this chapter. The politicizing of everyday experiences through platform policies about acceptable content and practices extends to representations of motherhood (Duvall, 2014; Jin et al., 2015), or acknowledging the mundaneness and normality of menstruation, or indeed the female body (Olszanowski, 2014; Tiidenberg and Gómez Cruz, 2015). Everyday life becomes politicized in other ways, too, in order to counter inconsistencies, conservatism and the apparent platform view that menstruation, pubic hair and nipples are far more problematic than, say, the perpetuation of rape culture. #PadsAgainstSexism was initially an art demonstration where menstrual pads with slogans written on them were posted in public places to highlight the hypocrisy and social taboos causing more uncomfortable objections around periods as opposed to rape (Bassily, 2015). The social media element to this campaign came first through the sharing of images of the pads on Tumblr and other platforms, and then in the adoption and participation in the project by other, unrelated people around the world. Similarly, #freethenipple is both a social media phenomenon, with hashtagged content posted on Instagram and other platforms, and a wider movement that has included a film and topless marches (freethenipple.com).

In the following discussion, I examine the intersection of the personal and the political on social media from several perspectives, as politically themed activity is variously explicit, emergent, affective and tangential (see also Papacharissi, 2010a). This chapter covers practices that are not unproblematic, such as revenge porn and doxxing, as well as contexts that are perhaps not obviously political, such as the Eurovision Song Contest. Together, these examples serve to underline how everyday personal social media use is impacted upon by elements that can be seen as political, and how the political overlaps with mundane contexts.

Personal Politics and Politicizing the Personal

Social media, as with other preceding online platforms, provide individuals with the opportunity to post their thoughts and media content, without requiring extensive technical literacy or qualifications; with blogs and citizen journalism, much conjecture surrounded whether the ability for amateur voices to broadcast themselves to a large audience online would be a threat to – or even actively replace – traditional journalism (detailed by Wall, 2015). Yet even without any intent or desire to cause seismic change to the media industry, commentary on blogs, Facebook, Twitter and more has underlined the personalization of politics in the form of political talk that draws upon an individual's own perspective and experiences, particularly around issues of personal import.

The personal and the political are not mutually exclusive, and separating the two is both impossible and impractical: they are closely interlinked, encouraged by the conventions and norms of social media. This can be seen in the topics discussed, the framing and presentation of these topics and how messages are tailored to individuals. The influence of the personal and the everyday is also seen, at its most basic, in patterns of activity: politically oriented social media discussions, from political blogging to hashtagged discussions, occur less frequently on weekends than on weekdays. This may be partly in response to fewer overtly political stimuli on weekends, but is also perhaps reflective of personal lives, of having a weekend that does not necessarily revolve around posting about politics online (Highfield, 2011; Smyrnaios and Rieder, 2013).

The everyday and the personal also influence the framing of the political. For example, and as will be discussed further in chapter 3, the concept of 'political blogs' is a descriptor that is both informative and rather vague: political blogging encompasses a vast range of approaches and topics, specializations and perspectives (Highfield and Bruns, 2012; Lehti, 2011). While some bloggers will comment on the major 'Political' topics of the day, others will focus on economics, polling data, particular parties and politicians, environmental issues or other foci. Communities of interest form, connected by shared views and an appreciation of different perspectives or analyses. Such groups then provide their own framing of particular issues, news and events, positioned around their interpretations and backgrounds; this extends to the everyday or more mundane, including identifying secondary political themes within these contexts.

For example, feminist bloggers in Australia and New Zealand formed an interconnected community, enhanced by a monthly 'carnival' wherein a different blogger would curate submissions from other members of the community (Down Under Feminists' Carnival, n.d.). While a part of the Australian political blogosphere, the bloggers here did not solely cover 'Politics' in its traditional form, but discussed domestic and everyday issues, long-running social debates that might especially have personal relevance and decidedly non-political topics. This separation from bloggers dedicated to 'Politics' at times led to them being overlooked; Frances Shaw (2012b) notes a case when a prominent (male) Australian political blogger asked 'where are the female political bloggers?', to which the feminist blogging community, and connected bloggers, responded that they were present and active, but they were not just talking about 'Politics'.

The formation of communities of like-minded individuals, around shared interests and beliefs, is a recurring element online, from the blogosphere to social networking sites and social media. This is not new or surprising: the difference is in the ability for these individuals to be geographically distributed, connected through digital technologies both synchronously and asynchronously. As I set out in the introduction, this does not mean that these are online-only communities, or that they are not shaped by their physical and local contexts. What is of interest here is that social media offer opportunities for the further construction and articulation of identity, of individuals and of groups.

The presentation of identity on social media, and the documentation of experiences, is a contested process, though: at the time of writing, the prominence of hashtags like #GamerGate, #BlackLivesMatter and #WomensLivesMatter demonstrates debate (or a certain value of 'debate') around issues challenging (and being challenged by) dominant social attitudes around sexism, racism, feminism, class and privilege. While the catalysts and contexts for these specific tags are contemporary, the wider issues they pertain to are not new. Instead, they take new dimensions and directions in a socially mediated form, shaped by the wealth of platforms and voices (supportive and antagonistic) able to participate. The political and the personal are in concert on social media, as platforms are used to document experiences which are everyday for some – whether this is desired or not – and to present users' identities, lifestyles and interests. The articulation of gender, race, sexual orientation, religion and other aspects of individuals' lives and their communities can make for a politicized life, by design or necessity.[3]

Voicing (in)difference and (in)tolerance

So, let's talk about sexism.

Social media are, variously, platforms for revealing experiences of sexism, including assault and abuse (Bates, 2014), and platforms that enable further attacks perpetuating sexist attitudes and/or promote misogynistic practices (Manivannan, 2013). The former features in chapter 5; the latter is at the crux of contexts like Gamergate, and symptomatic of toxic gamer culture in general (Chess and Shaw, 2015; Consalvo, 2012). These settings, which are typically (but not necessarily accurately) seen as predominately male environments, have been criticized for the sexist and misogynistic tropes and attitudes that pervade. Projects like Anita Sarkeesian's *Feminist Frequency* (which provides feminist critiques of various media, including films and books as well as video games) analyse the treatment of women within popular culture: Sarkeesian's 2012 series of YouTube videos on 'Tropes vs. Women in Video Games', for example, identified and critiqued recurring gendered elements of video games.

The response to this series included support and critiques, but also harassment, abuse, stylized and explicit violence through games and personal threats directed at Sarkeesian (Consalvo, 2012; Higgin, 2013) – and, as Chess and Shaw (2015) note, this was not the first example of attacks on women with some connection to gaming or on individuals trying to challenge dominant (white male) attitudes (see also Salter and Blodgett, 2012; Tomkinson and Harper, 2015). This abusive style of response escalated in 2014 with Gamergate. Initially a campaign directed at game developer Zoe Quinn (who had been accused of trading sex for reviews), 'gamergaters' justified their socially mediated abuse, claiming they were trying to protect the ethics of video game journalism, and confronted attempts by feminists to challenge the industry. This led vitriolic and threatening attacks made through platforms like Twitter (and beyond social media) to also target Quinn's supporters and defenders, and, by extension, basically anyone trying to argue for diversity and attitudes that did not conform to the dominant masculine and heteronormative gamer culture. These included Sarkeesian and, indeed, academics, as noted by Chess and Shaw (2015).

While extreme and highly problematic, the sexism apparent on social media in Gamergate comments is not the sole example of such attitudes. They might not take such threatening forms (or actually realize threats through hacking and doxxing, more on which soon), but responses to, and harassment of, women sharing opinions, perspectives and experiences on social media (and in general) can still demonstrate ingrained sexist and misogynistic norms (Sarkeesian, 2015; see also the feminist strategies of online resistance, outlined by F. Shaw, 2013a).

Language is a key element of these social media phenomena – partly because of the geographic dislocation between the parties involved, and also because on Twitter, for example, the character limit for tweets has obvious impact on what can be said. Loaded terms and swearing accompany threats and obscenities through tweets, comments on statuses and news articles, emails, forum posts and other online outlets – what Emma A. Jane (2014) describes as 'e-bile'. Jane notes that abuse, attacks and threats of sexual violence in this form are not just directed at women. However, the hostile messages sent to women are of a kind where 'Such discourse has become normalized to the extent that threatening rape has become the *modus operandi* for those wishing to critique female commentators' (p. 535; see also Rentschler, 2014).

The political significance of language can be perfectly apparent to the people employing it. Whitney Phillips (2015), highlighting the everyday racism of online trolling, examines the use of particular terms with loaded racial meanings. Including these words in messages is a deliberate act:

> trolls are fully aware that this word [n–] is the furthest thing from a floating, meaningless signifier. In fact they depend on its political significance, just as they depend on the political significance of all the epithets they employ. (p. 96)

As with sexism, racism plays out on social media in everyday contexts – an issue or topic like Gamergate is not necessary for intolerant speech online, although such examples amplify the visibility of these actions. Social media can also be used to counteract this (successfully or not), and to provide the individuals and communities that are subject to such attitudes platforms to develop their own political and cultural identities.

Race and Black Twitter

Various online technologies have been adopted for the articulation of identity, and for the creation of communities of users with common interests and experiences. From early websites to blogs, social networking sites and contemporary social media, the opportunities and affordances provided by individual platforms have encouraged particular practices and user bases, from the collegiate roots of Facebook and photo-sharing focus of Flickr to the international origins of Orkut and Chinese microblogs like Sina Weibo. Diverse patterns have been apparent, around gender and sexuality, class and race. For example, as MySpace and Facebook attracted attention from young Americans in 2006, different experiences around these social networking sites – and which sites were likely to be adopted, or abandoned – had links to race and class, via friendships and personal tastes (boyd, 2012a).

Research into race and the internet, especially in the US, has been led by scholars including André Brock (Brock, 2009, 2012; Brock et al., 2010), Jessie Daniels (Daniels, 2009, 2012; Hughey and Daniels, 2013), Lisa Nakamura (Nakamura, 2008, 2012, 2014; Nakamura and Chow-White, 2012) and their colleagues. Their work notes not just the historical use and non-use of digital technologies by particular communities, and online forms of racism, but also the other elements that contribute to these behaviours and practices beyond a simple distinction of 'race'. As outlined in the introduction, there are a multitude of interconnected factors influencing what a person does online, how they engage with political themes and present themselves, and how social media are used in general: external personal, cultural, social, political and economic aspects, among others, all contribute. At the same time, though, it is also the case that some perspectives, factors and experiences are overlooked or under-represented in social media research.

Jessie Daniels's (2012) examination of how Internet Studies treats race and racism highlighted three primary themes represented within the literature: around the internet as infrastructure (including discussions of the digital divide), online practices and identity and legal perspectives. In reviewing the state of the field, Daniels argued for 'a strong theoretical framework that acknowledges the persistence of racism online while simultaneously recognizing the deep roots of racial inequality in existing social structures that shape technoculture' (p. 711). Events in the US in late 2014 and early 2015 provide a clear backdrop to current uses of social media in response to racism and in the formation of identity: in Ferguson, Missouri, Staten Island, New York and Baltimore, Maryland, protests and demonstrations showcased public ire and discontent following the controversial deaths (in separate incidents) of several Black Americans at the hands of police, the judicial responses to this, and the wider issues of racial, economic and social inequality. Hashtags like #BlackLivesMatter accompanied these protests, documenting what was happening on the streets and facilitating a wider discourse around race and inequality in the US[4] (Bonilla and Rosa, 2015; Kang, 2015).

The use of social media by Black Americans has attracted attention for its specific practices and topics of interest which have been treated as different from the 'usual' activity on Twitter or Facebook. Central to the articulation of racial identity in the context of Black American uses of Twitter is language, and especially its application and adaptation in response to the affordances of social media platforms. The use of hashtags and their promotion to trending status enable particular performances of identity, and reveal 'alternate Twitter discourses to the mainstream' (Brock, 2012, p. 530; see also Sharma, 2013). Within tweets, too, the practice of signifyin' – conceptualizing Black Americans' inclusion of several levels of meaning within a single comment – is well-suited for Twitter: the limit of 140 characters per tweet makes an approach that deftly and concisely constructs multiple meanings invaluable structurally and in the performance of identity (Florini, 2014).

The umbrella term of 'Black Twitter' describes 'a temporally linked group of connectors that share culture, language and interest in specific issues and talking about specific topics with a black frame of reference' (Clark, in Ramsey, 2015). Yet this term is also highly problematic, since it can be interpreted as assuming – and imposing – a homogeneity that, as with social media at large, is not present. Instead, 'Black Twitter' features diverse users, practices and interests, rather than a single, unified or 'monolithic' group (Brock, 2012; Florini, 2014). Indeed, both Brock (2012) and McElroy (2015) argue that treatment of 'Black Twitter' as singular and a generalization of 'Black America' 'speaks to the power of American racial ideology's framing of Black identity as monoculture' (Brock, 2012, p. 546).

LGBTQ stories

In their examination of the mainstream media's treatment of 'Black Twitter', McElroy (2015) argues that 'the construction of media content in the digital age shapes and distorts racial and gendered narratives in the twenty-first century'. The construction and challenging of narratives are also apparent in the social mediation of lesbian, gay, bisexual, trans* and queer (LGBTQ)[5] experiences and identities. Digital media have been adopted for the presentation (and self-representation) of identity: Vivienne and Burgess (2012) examine the 'everyday activism' apparent in the digital curation of mundane experiences by queer storytellers, politicized in the face of heteronormative attitudes. Such practices are not platform-dependent; however, LGBTQ experiences have varied over popular social media in response to the platforms themselves and the wider user bases present.

Stefanie Duguay (2014) raises issues of context collapse (see also Marwick and boyd, 2011a) on Facebook for LGBTQ students. Here, the performance of identity is affected by the different audiences represented on Facebook. With multiple social and professional contexts colliding, gender and sexuality diverse identities are accompanied by careful selection of audiences. Facebook here is reflective of social media platforms where users are encouraged to employ their real names and reaffirm their interpersonal connections, bringing together an individual's different social contexts that might not otherwise intersect.[6]

Various social media platforms have become openly adopted by LGBTQ users due to their affordances for different types of community and expression (see, for example, the study of drag communities and social media by Lingel and Golub, 2015). Tumblr especially has witnessed popular communities around different gender and sexual identities, including asexuality and polyamory as well as trans* users (Cho, 2015; Fink and Miller, 2014; Renninger, 2015). Here, groups may share characteristics with the networked publics described by boyd (2011), although Renninger's (2015) study of an asexuality community on Tumblr is framed instead as a networked *counterpublic* differently experienced in comparison to publics that might be considered more dominant. As with other communities and conversations, though, the autonomy and support fostered through personal and shared expressions of identity and experiences can also be subject to antagonistic disruption from others outside the community.

Where the articulation of identity within 'Black Twitter' makes notable use of hashtags and wordplay through signifyin', LGBTQ communities showcase the importance of visual social media as a means of identity formation and expression.[7] A platform like Tumblr, where the visual is a significant communication device, fosters the sharing and adaptation of selfies, memes, GIFs and other curated and constructed visual media by LGBTQ users. This includes the documentation of personal and everyday experiences, including sexual and not-safe-for-work (NSFW) content (Tiidenberg, 2015), as well as appropriated and shared media from other sources, cross-posted or embedded from platforms such as Vine and Instagram. The popularity of Tumblr (especially pre-Yahoo!'s acquisition of the platform) is particularly noteworthy; Marty Fink suggests that:

> To appreciate the impact of queer trans tumblr production, it is important to consider the acute need for new media spaces for trans cultural production, given the long history of obstacles to self-representation that transgender, gender nonconforming, and gender variant people have faced. (in Fink and Miller, 2014, p. 615)

The visual here can enable new and alternative expressions of identity and sexuality, utilizing the affordances of different platforms for creative and interactive practices. As with other personal and political contexts online, LGBTQ activity on Tumblr, Vine or Instagram is not restricted to these platforms. Nor are these practices online-only: different media are employed as is deemed appropriate, available or sympathetic by individuals and their own purposes and intents (Cassidy, 2015; M. L. Gray, 2009; Mowlabocus, 2010; Renninger, 2015). Support and community are also encouraged through common social media cultural forms and logics. The 'It Gets Better' campaign on YouTube, launched in 2010 in response to gay teen suicide and bullying, started with a video sharing the personal experiences of two gay men and how their lives did 'get better' from their teens to adulthood (Yep et al., 2012). This message sparked responses from other LGBTQ individuals, uploading their own videos and in turn provoking 'a negotiation over LGBTQ collective identity' (Gal et al., 2015). The campaign expanded through memetic practices (see chapter 2), adopting the tone and format of the original video in the creation of new contributions, although not all content cohered to the original sentiments, instead offering subversion and defiance in documenting further personal LGBTQ stories.

Subversive practices

Visual social media are also a key form for practices that go against dominant societal and platform norms. Challenging attitudes towards identity and sexuality is carried out directly through the presentation of explicit and personal images, videos and mixed-media. On Tumblr, the sheer volume of erotic and pornographic material, in GIFs, videos, text and mixed formats, is not just a means for curating and consuming sexually explicit material (for the platform's attitudes to this, see Gillespie, 2013); trans* Tumblr users, for instance, maintain blogs around porn and x-rated content that flout:

> the limitations within rigidly gendered categories of 'female' and 'male.' ... Posts featuring self-shot porn are routinely accompanied by commentary that creates new discursive terrain for trans subjectivity, through kinky and gender queer reconfigurations of dominant discourses. (Fink, in Fink and Miller, 2014, p. 622)

The presentation of explicit and erotic material, whether personal or a priori, enables social media users to challenge ideas of sexuality and identity, of societal norms and attitudes. A framing like NSFW attempts to balance what is and is not 'accepted' in society and on platforms, acknowledging its inappropriateness for conservative environments but still sharing the content. This can be realized through particular media forms as well as by user communities: Paul Booth (2014) outlines the subversive potential (including articulating and confronting gender roles and norms) of slash fiction and porn parodies – media that are not specific to social media, but are shared through these platforms.

Katrin Tiidenberg's (2015) study of Tumblr users who create and repost NSFW content also examines how their blogs and images act both as 'embodied performances' and as demonstrations of social and cultural capital.[8] Crucially, the perception of the performative and capital-carrying aspects to NSFW content differs between users: Tiidenberg notes that users creating this content see their images primarily as performances, whereas those who curate and reblog others' content are motivated to do so for reasons of cachet and prominence. This leads to conflict within NSFW communities around practices and content, from photoshopping appearance (where the community sees itself as a 'unique, body-positive environment') to content-stealing, authorship and attribution. These conflicts – and general practices of sharing – can also result in the highly personal content, shared in ostensibly a safe space, circulating through different networks of users; this includes the appropriation of imagery on sites promoting identities and behaviours which are seen as controversial, subversive, unhealthy, or go against traditional norms – see, for instance, the pro-anorexia (pro-ana) blogging community (Yeshua-Katz and Martins, 2013).

The contestation and conflict apparent in these communities and their practices are reflected in platforms' treatment of their content, and in how other users also respond. The examples I noted at the start of this chapter, such as #freethenipple, are in part reactions to what platforms allow and do not allow, and the contradictions inherent in what the user base at large might flag as inappropriate or offensive (Crawford and Gillespie, 2014). The masking of problematic content by social media platforms is also demonstrated by policies like

Instagram's banned hashtag list: explicitly sexual, fascist, racist and obscene (including inciting violence) hashtags can be included in comments and captions, but searching for them will not return results. Also on the list are tags promoting self-harm pro-ana views, and this highlights an uneasy negotiation of subversion and resistance: social media users can employ platforms for their own ends, including for particular personal and politicized purposes, but how the platforms support this will vary. The filtering of search results based on content or apparent tone and intent by Tumblr and Instagram alike highlights this: the platforms will not necessarily take down pornographic material or block pro-ana users, but they will also make it harder for other users to find this content.

Users can subvert markers through hijacking and spamming. This is particularly apparent as movements and hashtags gain in popularity or promote specific, potentially controversial views: trending topics on Twitter are regularly subjected to an influx of spam comments. Campaigns like #freethenipple have also witnessed a proliferation of content that goes in perhaps unintended or unwanted directions. At the time of writing, much of the latest content tagged with the #freethenipple hashtag on Instagram contains pornographic imagery. The intent here may not be a direct response to questions of the female body and what is 'appropriate', instead, such content might be hooking into a popular (and semi-related) tag to automatically and deliberately circulate explicit material whether in opposition to the movement or to hijack a hashtag.

Callout culture and shaming

Social media and online platforms are employed for articulating identities, for challenging and subverting societal norms and for providing a voice (and safe spaces) for individuals and groups who might variously be marginalized, ignored or under-represented elsewhere. These are not uncontested, though: as noted above, racism, sexism, misogyny and various forms of discrimination and hatespeech are apparent on social media. Online prejudice can arise from everyday discussions without referring to anyone in particular, reflecting a general level of casual racism. These messages can also be directed explicitly at others, whether in response to other comments and behaviours, or completely unsolicited.

The experience of abusive and offensive messages on social media has led to users documenting this as part of a 'callout culture'. In the US in 2012, in the wake of a rape incident at Steubenville High School, Ohio (which was itself socially mediated), 'social media sites become aggregators of online misogyny' through screenshots and archiving posts published by the assailants (Rentschler, 2014). Sexism in everyday life – not just online – is highlighted by projects like *Everyday Sexism* (Bates, 2014), including actively confronting sexist advertising and behaviours on social media. On Tumblr, among other platforms, 'people of color can draw awareness to and effectively critique daily practices of racism and cultural appropriation that often go unchecked' (Fink, in Fink and Miller, 2014, p. 616).

The scale of callout culture, and of online shaming, extends from the individually public (or semi-public), posting screenshots of abusive or offensive messages to a user's own profile and shared just with friends and followers, to the widely public. Identifying and confronting toxic activity on apps and social media are the rationales behind repository sites like *Douchebags of Grindr*, where

> the rudest, most offensive, or downright hateful MSM-specific [men who have sex with men] social networking profiles are screen captured and posted to the web with the goal of highlighting issues such as ageism, femmephobia, racism, and 'arrogance' (among others). (Miller, 2015)

The political element here is perhaps minimal, yet the practices are consistent with more politics-explicit contexts, callout culture and shaming: the difference here may be in content, but not form.

The basic existence of shaming and callout culture, and its immediately defensive and antagonistic overtones, also makes these practices politicized, especially when they pass comment on or attempt to construct humour out of situations that are steeped in debates around class, race, gender and sexuality (among others). A website like *People of Walmart*, for instance, is predicated on differentiating between the observers and the subjects they are documenting: the appearance and behaviours of other shoppers at Walmart are used to discriminate with classist, gendered, racist and ableist overtones. The intent here may be humorous, but the content of such sites also reflects wider political and societal divisions. These practices are used to share outrage and disapproval, simultaneously shaming others and positioning the user as 'better'. During the Sydney siege in December 2014 (see chapter 4), reports of people taking selfies at the exclusion zone were accompanied by umbrage and images of the individuals and groups in question (White and Di Stefano, 2014): it is also important to note, though, the clickbait framing of such coverage, which may be used to fuel further outrage.

Of revenge porn and slut-shaming

Callout culture is, at times, intended to highlight behaviours without necessarily focusing on the individual concerned (although making them potentially identifiable), drawing attention to prevalent or emergent attitudes. At its most extreme, though, these practices lead to individuals being targeted, in response to their personal views and comments, for revenge or to publicly humiliate someone. The ability for internet users to spread information and content quickly and widely is discussed – in admittedly mostly optimistic framing – in chapter 4; the flipside, though, is that the same mechanisms can be used for sharing any kind of content, which can be copied infinitely.

Personal uses of social media, and other online technologies such as instant messaging, become politicized further through the consideration of surveillance, privacy, consent and an individual's data. Practices like account hacking, surreptitious recording and uploading highly private and personal content as an act of revenge all take advantage of these channels of distribution. The mass hacking and leaking of nude photographs of (female) celebrities in September 2014 is purely the most visible example of this – and an extension of a tabloid media culture and readership that thrives on celebrity gossip, sexism, misogyny, the male gaze, scandal and sensationalism. Such trespasses are not limited to celebrities; whether famous or not, though, the victims of these actions are predominantly female (van der Nagel and Meese, 2015). The taking of creepshots, and the surreptitious recording of others in public, over video chat, by hacking webcams and taking screenshots are a violation of consent at the very least, an invasion of privacy and an abuse of trust (issues also raised in Milner, 2013; Tiidenberg, 2015).

Anne Burns's (2015) study of 'involuntary porn', where personal, sexually explicit images, videos and texts created privately with consent are later posted publicly without authorization or awareness, highlights the role played by social media in facilitating the instant sharing – and ongoing production, replication and circulation – of private content (p. 94). This is also, again, a highly gendered process: the majority of people humiliated by the public distribution of involuntary porn are female, and victims are further shamed by other social media users criticizing them for consenting to being recorded in the first place. Such attribution of blame is emblematic of 'slut-shaming', decrying female promiscuity and autonomy (Shah, 2015; Webb, 2015). The role of male participants here is essentially excused: female victims of revenge porn or the public sharing of private sexting are instead shamed and humiliated further (Oravec, 2012; Ringrose et al., 2013).[9]

The recording and sharing of personal activity and ostensibly private communication on social media underlines how users are subject to multiple levels of surveillance. These are both overt and covert, by governments, platforms, individuals, groups and more, and take place with and without consent. The monitoring of a user's location as they use Facebook, Uber or Tinder, for instance, is in principle done with consent, since it is an accepted term of use for the app (and mobile operating system, and service provider) to work – even if the terms and conditions are objectionable, a user still has to actively accept them (even if they do not read them).

Doxxing and cybervigilantism

The illicit distribution of involuntary porn, creepshots and sexts, and practices like slut-shaming make use of the same affordances and mechanisms of social media platforms that allow users to call out sexism and misogyny and document the pervasiveness of these attitudes. At their most extreme, these practices are realized through cybervigilantism, doxxing and swatting. These again arise in part from the visible and public calling-out of behaviours that others deem inappropriate (for whatever motivation, including an inherent delusion by some men that women should find them sexually irresistible). Cybervigilantes take advantage of the availability of information online – both what the individual provides themselves and the digital shadow following them, of information about them but not necessarily provided by them. These practices are, as Quodling (2015) puts it, 'born of a perfect storm in personal data insecurity and easily-abused systems for reporting crime'.

Doxxing – wherein personal and ostensibly private information about an individual is shared publicly, including their 'real-life name, phone number, address, and/or workplace' (W. Phillips, 2015, p. 78) – is a response to social media users actively pursuing an agenda that others feel very strongly about (and against), and so resort to making their personal details public. The recipients of doxxing cover a range of contexts and topical inspirations, from vocal feminists and their supporters, social justice activists, abusive trolls, individuals posting offensive content, journalists, police officers and Minnesotan dentists and other hunters of endangered animals (and those carrying out the doxxing also vary depending on the target). Harassment and abuse, including rape and death threats, are directed at the subject of the doxxing online, at home and at work. Within the Gamergate context, prominent feminists criticizing the toxicity and masculinity of gamer culture were doxxed (see also Jenson et al., 2015), and this also morphed into 'swatting': where the personal information revealed by doxxing is used to target individuals by making false reports to police, with the aim of armed responses causing harm or even death (Quodling, 2015).

While platforms closely associated with trolling, like reddit and 4chan (Manivannan, 2013; W. Phillips, 2015), are visible proponents of doxxing, these behaviours are not limited to this space (and not everyone on reddit or 4chan is a troll or carries out doxxing). Activist and protest movements will also share extensive information about persons of interest, particularly those deemed responsible for injustice or opposition, and these can occur alongside the organizational, strategic and solidarity-oriented communication concerning the movement. In March 2012, activists within Occupy Oakland posted tweets highlighting personal information about a police officer alleged to have assaulted a pregnant protestor: building from the original information of badge number and name, the details shared publicly also included the officer's address, phone number, family members, online profiles and church (Croeser and Highfield, 2014).[10]

Cybervigilantism may arise in response to problematic behaviours, but can be offensive and abusive itself. The practice of scambaiting aims to entrap internet users responsible for scamming schemes, including attempts to extort money from susceptible individuals. Scambaiters 'identify themselves as protective vigilantes who help keep the internet safe, and have a "bit of fun" at the same time' (Nakamura, 2014: 261). In targeting scammers from Western Africa, for example, scambaiters obtain revealing and incriminating images (without the scammers necessarily realizing what they are being asked to do), using visual media practices and memetic logics in order to create and circulate this content. In doing so, Nakamura finds that scambaiters perpetuate racist and colonialist attitudes, revelling in the exotic by 'requiring Africans to perform primitivism' (p. 262). These underline continued issues – on social media and elsewhere – around power and privilege, of identity, race, class, gender and sexuality: exploitation on social media takes many forms within everyday experiences and practices.

Combating problematic behaviour on social media can also be unfortunately fruitless, as again people with opposing views can use the same devices that enable collective and connective action online. People who regularly post about social justice issues and attempts to change attitudes and behaviours already get labelled with the pejorative term 'Social Justice Warrior' (see, for example, Chess and Shaw, 2015; Deller, 2015). The contestation between 'Social Justice Warriors' and users antagonizing and deriding them plays out across, and responds to, activity on multiple platforms. Renninger (2015) identifies the highlighting of oppressive and offensive reddit posts through the /r/ShitRedditSays subreddit; this practice is mocked by users on rival subreddit /r/TumblrInAction, which 'exists to rip apart political correctness they see as laughable on Tumblr'.

The politicized personal experiences of everyday life and social media, from the articulation of identity to the directed attacking and shaming of individuals, demonstrate some of the many ways that the personal and the political coincide. The intensity of feeling here – whether challenging social attitudes, developing safe spaces and communities for marginalized and alternative identities, or engaging in vitriolic abuse of others – underlines the importance of social media platforms in these contexts. The problematic elements should not be ignored or accepted, particularly systematic public harassment and humiliation of individuals. What I have attempted to outline here, though, is just how everyday social media and everyday politics are extensively intertwined, experienced and framed through the personal.

Affective Publics and Personalizing the Political

Everyday practices around identity and community invoke the use of personal elements to describe and engage with the political. The consideration of personal politics, in both framing and topic, has clear overlaps with the affective publics described by Papacharissi (2015). Examining the role of affect in social media discussions, Papacharissi focuses on Twitter, within Occupy, the Arab Spring and more mundane trending topics. Affective discussions of unrest in Cairo in 2011 combined the personal with the political: Twitter users reporting from protests and demonstrations incorporated their own experiences and stories in their updates. Individuals provided unique takes on the events of the Arab Spring, personalizing the political in creating an affective form of storytelling for those following developments online. The importance of affect and personal resonance is not limited to the political on social media. Nahon and Hemsley (2013) identified resonance as a key contributing factor in determining themes and content that might get traction and go viral by attracting extensive attention in a short period of time and spread beyond an initial audience to a mass public. Critical for provoking widespread awareness and recognition of the content is the salience of content for audiences, where media content has personal relevance or interest (pp. 65–7).

Everyday politics can be seen as 'everyday' in part because it has a direct, personal impact or connection that is not fleeting, even if the issue or topic at hand is not 'Political' in the sense of budget negotiations or election debates. Debates around vaccination, refugees and asylum seekers, or climate change are demonstrative of topics that receive long-running coverage and campaigning, and where levels of engagement may be variable dependent on current events and catalysts for new discussions. Online platforms are used by those holding the various views represented in the debates. These contexts are often not single-issue discussions, either, but feature various overlapping topics (related or not to the main theme). Even when using a marker like a hashtag to denote an explicit overarching issue or setting for comments, a diversity of topics, interests and practices remains apparent. This includes the framing of commentary that reflects affective and personal contributions in addition to, and alongside, the explicitly political.

Political talk in non-political spaces

Politics on social media can be explicit and implicit, affective and personal, and reflect many practices, communities and issues. What is notable though is that these discussions are taking place on platforms which were not designed with such purposes in mind; Twitter and Facebook, like LiveJournal and MySpace before them, are not political social media, but are relatively generic channels enabling a wide range of topical coverage, of which politics is just one example.

This is in contrast to niche social networks, forums and websites set up around particular communities of interest. Yet even on these specialist sites everyday political talk emerges. Wright (2012) describes the evolution of 'Third Spaces', where communities on messageboards and discussion forums engage in conversations beyond the topical remit of the site. The hierarchical folder structure of messageboards can allow for 'off-topic' sections, where miscellaneous subjects outside the specific niche interest of the messageboard can be introduced. These are not the raison d'être for the boards, and not the factor inciting individuals to create accounts and participate in discussions, but they remain popular and recurring topics in these non-political spaces.

It can be argued that the most popular social media platforms reflect this kind of phenomenon, although their status as a 'Third Space' may be disputed. While politics is again not the reason behind the platforms' existence, there is also no one single topic that is the focus of Facebook or Twitter; rather than niche spaces from which political talk emerges, they are more generic and universal in scope. This also means that rather than having its own delineated space, such as its own section on a forum, political discussions appear more haphazardly on popular social media

– and to a more diluted extent than might be the case for messageboards. Political discussions are not visible to all registered users on Twitter or Facebook, purely because of the sheer volume of material as well as the follower/friendship networks shaping what can be seen. Politics is still an emergent topic, though, especially since it can hook into other discussions, appears alongside posts about unrelated subjects and may be a topic only occasionally mentioned by users. The likes of Facebook and Twitter then promote various elements of 'Third Spaces', demonstrating the emergence of political discussions on sites not initially set up for that purpose.

Emergent, Tangential and Overlapping Publics

This idea of emergent politics connects to the personalization of politics through the ways that individuals present and draw out political themes in their discussion of issues, events and subjects. Politics can be tangential, a sub-theme within more mundane and everyday subjects, yet not unimportant. The users discussing tangential politics may also be peripheral to the majority of the topical coverage, but they remain part of the surrounding context and perspectives on social media. Media events and spectacles have many aspects and dimensions to them that receive attention; a music contest is not just about the music, a sporting event is not just sports, and audiences engage with them for a variety of reasons, including as social and cultural phenomena.

The social media politics of Eurovision

The Eurovision Song Contest is an annual competition, held since 1956, broadcast across Europe and to which European nations send a musical act and song to represent them in the hopes of winning from a popular vote (combining the broadcast audience and national juries). As a production that has been running for sixty years, Eurovision is a media, cultural and social institution, occupying a particular part of multiple national and subcultural psyches; it is more than a cult phenomenon, though, for its fandom takes many forms across the continent (and beyond). Despite presenting itself as apolitical, however, emergent and tangential political talk is still apparent within the Eurovision context, on social media and beyond.

The perception of Eurovision by participants and audience alike varies across Europe (and beyond). In the UK, the contest is treated primarily as kitsch and a camp irrelevance, engaged with ironically or indeed as active anti-fandom (S. Coleman, 2008). In other parts of Europe, though, Eurovision is a serious proposition: to win potentially means acceptance on the way to joining the European Union, or the added prestige of hosting a major European cultural event. The contest is also popular among LGBTQ audiences and performers (Lemish, 2004; Singleton et al., 2007); in 1998, Eurovision was won by Israel's Dana International, a transsexual performer, while second place in 2007 went to Verka Serduchka, the drag persona of Andriy Danylko, representing Ukraine.

Eurovision then takes place at the confluence of many different interests, including cultural and social issues, geopolitics and gender politics. This can lead to various tensions, since Eurovision does not occur in complete separation from its national and pan-European contexts; the European Broadcasting Union (EBU), which runs the event, bans explicitly political songs.[11] However, political messages still make their way into the broadcast – and certainly appear within the social media coverage of the contest.

The 2012 Eurovision Song Contest was held in Baku, Azerbaijan, following the Azerbaijani victory in 2011. It was the country's first victory, in its fourth appearance at Eurovision, and the first of the Caucasus former Soviet republics to win the contest. Before the contest, Azerbaijan was criticized for its poor human rights record and the tensions between it and Armenia. Entrants in the 2012 contest were requested not to speak to activists and demonstrators; one performer, the eventual winner Loreen, representing Sweden, ignored this. Similarly, while political comments and partisan messages are not permitted in the broadcast, a thinly veiled reference to Azerbaijan's human rights record, political corruption and freedom of choice was made by the German presenter Anke Engelke when giving the results of the German vote (stating that 'It is good to be able to vote, and it is good to have a choice... Europe is watching you').

In the Twitter coverage of the 2012 Eurovision Song Contest, such themes did not account for the majority of tweets; rather, the #eurovision hashtag was a backchannel for providing live commentary, engaging genuinely, ironically and irreverently with the performances (for extended analysis of Eurovision as a case study for social media audiences and fandom, see Highfield et al., 2013). Yet this does not mean that the political was completely absent. Indeed, Eurovision commentary (both on television and on social media) often deals in political and cultural stereotypes (and casual racism) (Georgiou, 2008). Popular retweets during the 2012 contest, for example, discussed the Greek entry through the lens of Greece's dire financial situation and the German-led economic bailout it had received. The overall #eurovision activity also saw discussion of human rights issues as a secondary, tangential theme, symbolically connected to the spectacle-specific coverage by @ mentioning Loreen. By using the common #eurovision marker, the explicitly political tweets were still part of the wider, denoted discussion, just as the Azerbaijani political context was part of the Eurovision setting even if the majority of the audience did not obviously engage with it (or was unaware of it).

During the broadcast, additional political themes emerge, and these can be specific to individual contests and the contemporary context, and recurring tensions. The trend of bloc voting, or political voting, where nations give preferential treatment in their votes to their neighbours (a country's Eurovision *euro-voisins*), is an established trope of the contest; while seen as problematic for the 'authenticity' of the contest in some countries, it is established to the point of cliché (and a recurring feature of Eurovision drinking games/bingo) that Cyprus will give Greece 12 points, the Balkan and Scandinavian countries will share votes among themselves and the spectre of Russia continues to haunt many former Soviet republics (Fenn et al., 2006; Ginsburgh and Noury, 2008). Such ritualization, around social media practices and media and political phenomena alike, is discussed further in chapter 2; within the Eurovision context, the recurrence of bloc voting is frequently commented upon during the Twitter coverage of the broadcast.

The Eurovision audience – including but not limited to its social media coverage – encompasses numerous overlapping publics, representing different perspectives, national groups, fandoms, languages and topical interests. During Eurovision 2012, the human rights discussion was more peripheral to the live commentary on the contest itself, and to sub-topics such as the devoted fandom dedicated to hyperactive Irish twins Jedward (see also Deller, 2011) – especially since it was not an obvious feature of the broadcast itself. Other political themes can become dominant, particularly around LGBTQ cultures and gender and sexuality politics. This was apparent during the 2014 contest, won by Austria's Conchita Wurst. The drag persona of Thomas Neuwirth, Wurst was a different proposition to the outrageously camp Serduchka; in particular, Wurst sported a beard as part of her appearance. The combination of drag and the presence of a 'bearded lady' meant that the entry was not viewed positively in some participating countries, where alternative sexualities and gender roles are not established, tolerated or legally permitted (Miazhevich, 2015).

The topical centrality of Conchita Wurst to Eurovision 2014 – online and in the contest itself – encourages a strong interlinking and overlap of Eurovision publics. Those present include the casual Eurovision viewer, the dedicated fan, the anti-fan and ironic viewers (for more on anti-fandom, ironic detachment and snark around popular content, see J. Gray, 2003; Haig, 2014; Harman and Jones, 2013), LGBTQ audiences, those opposed to alternative sexualities, transvestism, drag and so on (and these groups are obviously not mutually exclusive). On social media, this plays out through a combination of approaches. Live-tweeting may take different perspectives, depending on the individual and their own views and contexts, with pro-, anti-, neutral, amused, bemused and confused messages co-occurring in backchannels. Viewers also provide visual displays of their attitudes and beliefs: again, as an event with an extensive LGBTQ fanbase, Eurovision is regularly accompanied by associated imagery, such as rainbow flags (online and in the crowd at the event itself). Visual social media content on platforms such as Instagram also feature these aspects in users' depictions of their Eurovision experiences. The political, personal and social become further entwined here, as the social event of hosting Eurovision parties, for example, includes pro-tolerance signs and LGBTQ iconography. This is also reflected in the use of memes and image macros to provide supportive and irreverent commentary about Eurovision, LGBTQ issues and fandom.

The coverage of Eurovision on social media serves as an example of fan practices and audiencing online, where political elements feature as emergent topics. Eurovision then provides a clear example of topical diversity and tangential politics, where such topics are related to but not necessarily the primary focus of an event's discussion – see also the various political themes during the 2014 Winter Olympics in Sochi, Russia, around LGBTQ rights and the feminist punk rock group Pussy Riot (Burchell, 2015). Politics also occurs concurrently in fan communities on social media, such as those for *The Sims* or Korean pop music, with emergent political discussions found alongside the subject of the fandom (Deller, 2015; Jung, 2012). Within these settings, tangential political topics are found within an individual's own interests, reflecting their personal views and issues which may be relevant to their particular fandom.

The diversity of personal experiences present within social media politics is further recognized through initiatives like rotation curation, where individuals temporarily take over the running of institutional or organizational social media accounts. Examples can be national, such as the @sweden Twitter account, curated by a different Swedish person each week and providing their own perspective on life, culture, politics and more (C. Christensen, 2013a). Rotation curation can also promote marginalized and under-represented voices, giving them individual and collective platforms for sharing their own views and experiences; the Australian @IndigenousX and its Canadian spin-off @IndigenousXca, for example, feature different indigenous voices each week. What is important and noteworthy about these accounts is the promotion of voices – with free rein, content-wise and tonally – through a more widely followed outlet than they might have individually. By offering a social media dais around specific groups, identities, communities or issues, rotation curation accounts provide a banner under which individual perspectives can be centralized, and which a wider audience can follow to discover and read their stories.

Tangential and overlapping topics are also apparent within the content denoted by a common, overarching hashtag. Hashtags demonstrate linguistic flexibility, variously serving informational, emotive, commercial and structural purposes (Zappavigna, 2015). Burgess et al. (2015) describe the 'hybrid forum' of hashtagged content, wherein different issues, publics and voices (expert and everyday) coincide. They use the example of markers like #agchat or #agchatoz, which designate a specific focus – in this case, agriculture – and promote a central time and theme for conversation, but where the ensuing tweets still demonstrate a miscellany of less prominent but related topics. These include the elements of the mundane and the everyday, documented through personal imagery and affective framing: whether discussing politics in general or specific topics, social media commentary and participation are filtered through personal experiences of issues and platforms.

Politics and Platforms

Consideration of the personal and the political of social media – and the internet in general – should not ignore how the platforms used are themselves parts of political debate. The questions of privacy and surveillance raised earlier in this chapter are connected to issues around digital rights and digital liberties. The corporate ownership of the major social media platforms, their commercial interests, policies and the lack of transparency in how they use and present individuals' data also feed into recurring concerns for social media users (for more on platforms, see van Dijck, 2013). While attempts have been made to establish open and alternative platforms, browsers and other online technologies, these have had varying degrees of success and have generally not yet attained the critical mass or popular momentum to compete with the likes of Facebook and Twitter (explored further by Gehl, 2014).

Digital rights, digital liberties

How social media users employ their platforms of choice, including the content that they create, share, consume and appropriate in their everyday activities, is part of a long-running debate about participatory cultures and digital technologies. The issue of digital rights, including policies and policing of copyright and piracy, has variously focused on the illegal sharing of music, film and television shows online, through peer-to-peer networking and streaming sites, on copyrighted material uploaded to sites like YouTube without permission and on the creation of new content from previous media and questions of 'fair use'. Related debates predate popular online communication, and these have clear links to everyday practices on social media. Postigo (2012) highlights how creative, participatory practices like remixing and mash-ups may be used for political critique, but are also 'a complicated array of potential copyright law violations' (p. 1178). Indeed, several of the ritualized practices that I discuss in chapter 2 make extensive, unauthorized use of copyrighted material, for political and non-political purposes alike. While I do not go into detail in this book about the policing of digital rights, the fight against online piracy and protecting copyright and how users subvert and hack platforms, media and devices, such topics are extensively featured elsewhere (Lobato and Thomas, 2015; Meese, 2015).

Postigo's (2012) examination of digital rights activists notes related issues pertinent to the movement, including 'privacy, net neutrality, bloggers [*sic*] rights and expanding access to digital content' (p. 1167). Also overlapping here is what Croeser (2012, 2014) refers to as the 'digital liberties movement'. Their research employs this label as distinct from – but connected to – digital rights and other civil liberties groups, as the term 'digital liberties'

> encapsulates both the grounds of battle (including hardware and software) and the general disposition of the movement (which highly values individual autonomy, and is often inclined towards liberal or libertarian principles). (2014, p. 78)

Sharing concerns with groups promoting free/libre and open-source software and net neutrality, the digital liberties movement is identified by Croeser (2014) through participants' 'understanding that citizens (or, often, "users") – rather than corporations or governments – should control digital technologies, with this control tied to democratic principles and ideals of personal freedom' (p. 77). Such freedom is contested by surveillance of online activity, by corporations and governments (pp. 87–9), and by the tracking and sharing of user data by the popular, everyday social media platforms and providers like Facebook and Google.

Questions of privacy and data retention are ongoing concerns, debated on social media and elsewhere at the personal and mass levels, including government policies (Moe, 2012) and the response to the leaking of

National Security Agency (NSA) data by Edward Snowden in 2013 (Lyon, 2014). The social media platforms discussed here are free to use, but with the caveat that the platforms are commercial undertakings – what they do with your data is essentially up to them. Users can control their personal privacy settings, in terms of who can see their posts, but at the same time Facebook has access to everything posted on it (and sometimes more, with linked accounts and access options). The move towards connected profiles and single-platform authentication – where apps like hook-up and dating service Tinder use Facebook accounts to create user profiles – has further implications for this data privacy, particularly when these apps make use of, and share, additional, personal information. Similarly, investigations into the 'quantified self', of apps and wearable devices tracking location, health and movement, and of immense amounts of personal data being shared, raise further questions about user privacy, surveillance and identity (Crawford et al., 2015; Jethani and Raydan, 2015; Walker Rettberg, 2014).

Because algorithms?

At the start of this chapter, I introduced projects that use imagery of the female body and its functions to counter societal attitudes and platform policies about what is and is not appropriate. The flagging of content as offensive by individual users, and the approaches of platforms like Facebook and Instagram (which is owned by Facebook) to removing content with visible nipples or menstrual stains, is a process that is rife with abuse and inconsistencies (Crawford and Gillespie, 2014) – giving the impression that platforms are more okay with racist hatespeech, abuse, harassment and trolling of individuals and rape jokes than with nude and semi-nude images of the female body (posted with consent). Similarly, how different platforms respond to reports of harassment and doxxing, and the transparency of their processes, is an ongoing and critical debate at the time of writing (see, for example, the report about abuse on Twitter by Matias et al., 2015). The question of what social media platforms deem to be political or appropriate is especially pertinent, for it leads into considerations of what activities platforms will allow and what might be censored.[12] Manipulation of platforms, their policies and user base is apparent within trolling, as users attack and abuse others for their own pleasure. Whitney Phillips's (2015) study of users trolling the memorial pages of deceased Facebook users described the process as one of amplification, in which trolls would get a reaction from others, which further inspired trolling. This amplification encouraged (or forced) a swifter response from Facebook itself, as the groundswell of attention from multiple parties meant it could not remain silent or passive regarding what was or was not allowed on its platform. The inconsistencies here remain concerns, especially when content like revenge porn and personal and explicit material posted without consent are shared widely but not removed by the platforms in question (see Anne Burns, 2015; Citron, 2014).

In cases of civil unrest and protest, social media platforms have been suspected by activists of censoring messages; as will be seen in chapter 5, the research that Sky Croeser and I carried out on Occupy Oakland found that activists at demonstrations and on Twitter were wary of the surveillance and policing of their comments and online organization (Croeser and Highfield, 2014). There were also accusations that the algorithms determining trending topics were being manipulated so that Occupy-related hashtags and keywords were not showing up, reducing the visibility and downplaying the presence of the movement. Such concerns reflect an awareness of both the power of social media platforms' algorithms, and of their inscrutability. The logics behind algorithms influencing what users see within Twitter's trending topics or Facebook's news feed are not made public, and are changed in response to user experiences and behaviours (Bucher, 2012b; van Dijck and Poell, 2013).

There is also a gamification angle here, as social media users – reflecting different motivations, whether commercial, activist or humorous – attempt to get particular topics or issues to reach 'trending' status (explored in part in Sharma, 2013). Tarleton Gillespie (2014) has argued that, in addition to the various publics users form on social media, algorithms help to shape 'calculated publics' based on patterns around interests, connections, interactions, clicks and purchases. Such publics are constructed from a platform's user base and content, without their members knowing the specific processes and choices at play, for 'These algorithmically generated groups may overlap with, be an inexact approximation of, or have nothing whatsoever to do with the publics that the user sought out' (p. 189).

The policies and politics of platforms shape and are shaped by the personal: the results of algorithms are in part guided by past personal behaviours and choices. Platforms respond to informal practices, too. Social media behaviours created by users and gradually adopted en masse, despite not being part of a platform's initial architecture, may become supported by the platforms. The evolution of the hashtag on Twitter demonstrates an informal practice designed for information coordination eventually morphing into a key, defining feature of the platform with its own traits (Halavais, 2013). Facebook, Twitter and Google change their algorithms, terms of use, design and functionality at will and without transparency or consultation, as is their wont – and this has raised concerns by communities that use the platforms, such as when ownership changes (for instance, the response by trans*, queer, asexual and other communities to Tumblr's acquisition by Yahoo! in 2013: Fink and Miller, 2014; Renninger, 2015). What happens on their platforms, though, is dependent on – and responds to – the personal and the mundane.

Conclusion

The overlap between the personal and the political is extensive, on social media and in general. This is seen in both how the political is framed, around individual interests and experiences, and how the personal becomes politicized. These are realized on social media through everyday practices. Politics emerges out of the presentation of the mundane, and the extraordinary is documented using the same approaches as a user might share media about their lunch, their cat or their pop culture tastes. These discussions also coexist and overlap with the coverage of emergent, explicit and non-political topics by social media users.

The personal and the everyday are critical lenses for examining social media overall, not just the political. By debanalizing platforms (Rogers, 2013a), we can treat the everyday and the mundane not as trivial but as the context for understanding the logics and practices of social media. The banal uses of the social then extend to, are appropriated by and encourage the political, among other topics. Crucially, the coverage of the political on social media makes use of the same practices as the mundane: the social mediation of both politics and everyday experiences employs the same mechanisms, vernaculars and logics.

In the following chapter, I explore the intersection of the political and the everyday on social media by analysing ritualized practices. These include political rituals responding to particular figures or events, and social media rituals that will at times have political relevance. These can variously take serious and silly forms, and in concert are examples of a social media culture that uses the affordances and vernaculars of platforms to engage with politics.

2

Political Rituals of Social Media

July 2013 was a momentous month for the United Kingdom. On 22 July, Prince George was born, automatically becoming third-in-line to the throne. On 7 July, professional tennis player Andy Murray won the men's singles championship at Wimbledon, the first British man to win Wimbledon in 77 years. And on 21 July, Chris Froome won the men's Tour de France cycling race, achieving back-to-back British victories following Bradley Wiggins's triumph in 2012. Throughout, Queen Elizabeth II tweeted her thoughts, providing regular updates as the world waited for the birth of her great-grandson and showcasing the monarch's sense of humour and awareness of popular culture.

Well... this was obviously not the real Queen Elizabeth II tweeting. These comments were instead the work of Elizabeth Windsor, @Queen_UK, one of many social media accounts parodying figures from political, pop culture, sports and fictional contexts. Their tweets mix the topical, whether major news headlines or the daily work of being the Queen, with the mundane and the humorous, including regularly commenting about the 'monarch's' love of gin and sharing a dislike of Mondays with many. Topical comments in particular attract widespread attention from Twitter audiences; tweets framed within the world of the parody have also been found to attract greater attention, and possibly have more appeal or salience for a wider audience, than their more mundane, everyday posts (Highfield, 2015a).

Topical commentary by parody accounts, and the creation of new parody accounts in response to breaking news and unexpected developments, are examples of social media practices that demonstrate ritualized behaviours. In this chapter, I examine rituals around the political and around social media. These include political rituals on social media, and social media rituals that may take on political dimensions. In addition to everyday political talk, the activities featured here are instances of everyday social media practices which are adaptable for politically relevant subjects. Irreverent and playful practices, from memes and image macros to parody and satire, are recurring elements of social media activity in general, including political coverage.[13]

Practices which are not necessarily political in themselves can be adapted for political commentary, and those practices which start off as political may over time move towards the irreverent, offbeat and generic. In general I am focusing here on what could be considered as 'nice' irreverence. Similar approaches are used for antagonistic and bigoted content, as noted in Whitney Phillips's (2015) examination of race, trolling and Photoshop regarding Obama, and these are mentioned in later chapters. This is not to say that focusing on the light-hearted is the right, or only, approach: Nakamura (2014) rightly points out that 'Because memes are often defined by their humor and whimsical nature – indeed, they circulate because of these very traits – they are seldom analyzed from the perspective of racial and gender critique' (p. 260).

Humour is a key factor in determining the spreadability and salience of online content (Jenkins et al., 2013; Nahon and Hemsley, 2013). Playful practices online exemplify 'vernacular creativity' (Burgess, 2008), where users create and share content in response to previous instances and variations, adapting and altering social media logics and cultures in the process. Users are not only aware of the social media context in which they find themselves, though, incorporating this understanding into their online activity; they are also cognizant of the logics and affordances of the platforms they are using. Gibbs et al. (2015) identify a 'platform vernacular', examining how content is shaped by practices specific to individual platforms (in their study, Instagram) and what can and cannot be done here.

The platform vernacular is also a response to standardized practices. For example, the diversity of discursive functions for which hashtags can be adapted (Page, 2012; Zappavigna, 2015), and varying practices across platforms which support hashtags, encourage irreverent hashtaggery. These jocular responses become ritualized in themselves. Similarly, users make use of devices appropriate to chosen platforms – such as text-based wordplay, including punning, on Twitter, or visual media with intertextual references on Tumblr – to frame politically themed content (and these of course will also cross platforms).

The Irreverent Internet and Social Media Culture

The context for this chapter is the 'irreverent internet' (Highfield, 2015a), where play and silliness are common approaches to topical and mundane activities. The importance of playful engagement with issues, breaking news, unfolding events, entertainment and everyday discussions is perhaps under-valued in current research; yet irreverence, sarcasm, irony, satire and (humorous) cynicism are popular framing devices for social media commentary.

Silly citizenship and commentary through comedy

The prevalence of witty and pithy remarks on Twitter especially, and the audience for such content, are explored later in this chapter. However, the trend towards comedic coverage of politics and other topics is not a social media-only phenomenon. Hartley (2012) describes 'silly citizenship', wherein engagement with public debate and issues occurs through the creation and consumption of humorous and irreverent media. The popularity of comedians such as Jon Stewart, Stephen Colbert and John Oliver as political commentators is, for Hartley, emblematic of the rise of silly citizenship, moving beyond traditional sources of political opinion leadership to new and alternative presentations of content.

Satire and humour have been long-standing means for expressing political views and interpreting news and culture. Mainstream and alternative media alike have employed these devices for decades, from print (the UK magazine *Private Eye*; the French *Charlie Hebdo* and *Le Canard Enchainé*), to radio (*On the Hour* in the UK) and television (*Newstopia* and *The Chaser* in Australia; *Spitting Image*, *The Day Today* and *Brass Eye* in the UK; *Les Guignols de l'Info* in France), among many examples (W. Doyle, 2012; J. Gray et al., 2009; Harrington, 2010, 2012; Meikle, 2012). The internet has provided the opportunity for further means of lampooning political figures, events and topics: *The Onion* is just one prominent and long-running example (Berkowitz and Schwartz, 2015).

These examples, though, are all professional and institutionalized to some extent, with corporate backing and sponsorship. Hartley (2012) also notes that silly citizenship is carried out in mundane contexts, as amateur productions by citizens using online technologies. Assuming access and digital literacy, theoretically anyone could participate in politically oriented activity on social media, from creating YouTube videos to sharing and reinterpreting political memes on Facebook. The participatory culture described by Jenkins (2006) illustrated the potential for internet users to engage with media content by creating, distributing, remixing and spreading it among others as well as simply consuming it. Political participation – in the sense of actively engaging with political material, figures or themes on social media, however briefly – is one aspect to this culture, but it also employs practices associated with other media content and internet culture (see Zittrain, 2014).

Irreverent deviations

The importance of humour and satire to political commentary is not new to social media, then. It has also been realized in strategies for improving audience engagement with journalistic content, both in how stories are presented and how journalists themselves use social media (Holton and Lewis, 2011). With the unrelenting news cycle of social media and 24-hour news channels, original takes on news are critical for attracting and maintaining an audience.

If social media such as Twitter can be seen as 'always-on' for covering news – what Hermida (2010) dubs 'ambient journalism' – then, I argue, these platforms could also be viewed as 'always off-topic'. This is not to say that all content is 'off-topic', but rather that social media discussions around a given subject do not follow one sole narrative trajectory. This was seen in chapter 1 in the discussion of tangential and overlapping politics and publics, such as in the context of Eurovision, and can reflect the evolution of news stories and unfolding events. Irreverence and ritual also prompt tangents and deviations, though; silliness, satire and mockery can arise from serious political subjects and campaigns, reflecting the interests of the participants and the social media culture present on individual platforms.

For example, online protests against the Stop Online Piracy and PROTECT IP Acts (SOPA/PIPA) in the US in January 2012 included blackouts of major websites as a form of demonstration (Croeser, 2014, pp. 105–6). Wikipedia was one of the sites taking part in the blackout, and had notified users of its intentions prior to the protest. In addition to support among social media users for the protests, the political context was accompanied by socially mediated irreverence. During the period that Wikipedia was theoretically inaccessible, #FactsWithoutWikipedia trended on Twitter, as users tweeted 'facts' that could not be verified due to the blackout (N. Ross, 2012); the hashtag made the comedic intentions obvious, although there was also clear trolling potential for the discussion, and the actual success of any humour is a matter of debate and taste.

Ritualized Social Media Practices and Politics

The #FactsWithoutWikipedia irreverence demonstrates the willingness of a subset of social media users to engage with the anti-SOPA/PIPA campaigns in silly, rather than serious, ways. Such approaches take many different forms, and in the following sections I focus on four ritualized social media practices which are adapted for political purposes, but which are not explicitly political in themselves: memes, wordplay, parody and intertexts.

Memes as participatory politics

Memes are a central component of internet culture, reflecting elements of participatory and convergence cultures (Jenkins, 2006). In their extensive research into memes, Shifman (2012, 2014a, 2014b) highlights key attributes that lead content to become memes, including its replicability and mutability. While popular content shared widely in its original form is described as viral (Nahon and Hemsley, 2013), memes spread as both initial and adulterated content. Users remix content, adding in new elements to images or videos to create new meanings and commentary by using humour and playful practices. While image macros – offering a common template of image, font and writing style with the caption decided by the user – are particularly commonplace and diverse meme forms, they are not the only types apparent (Nooney and Portwood-Stacer, 2014): related practices around visual media include inserting public figures or characters into new settings and contexts (Bayerl and Stoynov, 2014). Memetic practices are also apparent through primarily textual means, as users on Twitter adopt, appropriate and ritualize behaviours variously serving informative purposes, sharing mundane comments and featuring irony and parody (Leavitt, 2013). As will be seen later in this chapter, too, hashtags offer a marker for memes, and can follow memetic logics in themselves (Thrift, 2015).

Can haz politiks? LOLCat framings

Image macros and memes have their own vernaculars and templates: from Imminent Ned ('Brace yourselves…') to Rage Face, there is a structure to these forms that is emphasized through repetition. Adhering to the structural and linguistic rules of individual memes helps to determine their success, particularly among early-adopters. More variation – and disregard or ignorance of the rules – has followed the mainstreaming of meme culture as it spread beyond its origins on reddit's /b/ forum and 4chan to everyday and popular contexts (see Miltner, 2014; W. Phillips, 2015, pp. 137–45).

The language of memes can be a key memetic element. Cat macros, commonly referred to as LOLCats, invert the typical image macro form by making the visual content a more variable component: different pictures of cats (and later other animals, people and things) were overlaid with text that followed rules of typeface and dialect. Sites like *I Can Has Cheezburger* streamlined these processes, as users could upload images and add captions that cohered to the visual template of LOLCats. Appropriate text for LOLCats, using its own brand of 'LOLspeak' (Miltner, 2014), has an enthusiastic but haphazard writing style, with abundant misspellings ('iz', 'nao', 'teh', 'ur' and so on) and captions like 'I made you a cookie but I eated it', while other memetic grammars include the very words and much vernacular of doge (Esteves and Meikle, 2015).

The LOLCats template also extended to non-feline subjects (including other animals, such as the elephant seal dubbed 'Lolrus'). The approach was applied to politicians, with LOLpolz markers and repositories for this content. The original cat context though was also employed for political commentary: representing political topics with topically captioned LOLCats enabled irreverent interpretations of current events through the medium of pictures of cute animals. In mid-2009, Australian politics was inflicted with the 'Utegate' non-scandal (for more, see Highfield, 2011): as the government introduced bills responding to the Global Financial Crisis, Prime Minister Kevin Rudd was accused of preferential treatment for a car dealer who had provided a utility vehicle ('ute') during Rudd's 2007 election campaign. The accusations were denied, but Leader of the Opposition Malcolm Turnbull alleged that he had proof, in the form of a leaked email which was eventually found to be a fake. The debacle reflected poorly on Turnbull especially, but the general political event was mocked through a retelling of the story through a series of LOLCat images ('Utegate, as told by LOLCATS', 2009). The political commentary and irreverence were not limited to simply reporting the key events of the scandal: representing key media commentators in animal form too, the format also poked fun at the media rituals of Australian politics as well as the personalities of the main players.

Political memes and macros

Other memes and macros reflect more explicitly political settings. Images of politicians are adapted and coopted into new templates: 'Texts from Hillary', for example, presents a two-frame dialogue between Hillary Clinton and other (political) actors, established by adding invented captions to two images: first, a variable picture of the person texting, and then the response, added to a 2011 photograph of Clinton (then US Secretary of State), in sunglasses and looking at her phone (Anderson and Sheeler, 2014). Similarly, images of Russian President Vladimir Putin have begat their own templates ('Sad Putin', as promoted by *BuzzFeed*) and motifs that are incorporated into Photoshop mash-ups and collages (such as shirtless Putin on a horse). Flippant and potentially disrespectful reimaginings of politicians and other public figures have received varying responses from their subjects. Anderson and Sheeler (2014) note that Hillary Clinton made her own meta-commentary using the 'Texts from Hillary' style when she joined Twitter. Conversely, reports in April 2015 suggested that Russia was preparing legislation that would outlaw the use of images of celebrities, politicians and public figures in memes (Rothrock, 2015).[14]

Politicians are also the subjects of memetic practices, inspiring repeated forms rather than remixed content. A series of politician-specific Tumblr blogs simply present undoctored and unadorned photographs of the corresponding politician. No real commentary is provided, or even necessary. The sites are predicated on the mundane, highlighting the banality and ridiculousness of political media opportunities by framing their content as '[person] [verb]ing things'. Starting with a tumblr dedicated to then-North Korean leader Kim Jong-Il 'looking at things' (kimjongil-lookingatthings.tumblr.com), the template has since been used to showcase often-staged images of leaders like Kim Jong-Un and Tony Abbott (both 'looking at things'), or Vladimir Putin ('doing things').

Political memes focusing on individual politicians are not always playful. As a prominent example, Barack Obama has been the subject of multiple racist meme forms and visual hatespeech (Burroughs, 2013). The application of forms such as memes and macros to political themes is not unproblematic; the variable success of humour – and different political and comedic tastes – means that not everyone will react the same way to a politically motivated meme. Similarly, humorous intent does not mean that concurrent racist, sexist or otherwise prejudiced overtones will be universally accepted

As with other social media practices, platforms can be used for inclusive and intolerant communication alike. Facebook groups sharing visual content perpetuating racist stereotypes, such as 'Aboriginal memes' in Australia, are reported and campaigned against, but they continue to reappear (Oboler, 2012). These image-based forms of hatespeech were even standardized through the creation of macro templates on sites like MemeGenerator, further promoting prejudiced and uninformed comments. Furthermore, as noted by Oboler, platforms and meme creation sites did not immediately respond to requests to take down offensive material (even when it infringed on copyright).

Emergent political memes

Political memes also emerge in response to specific events or figures, as ad hoc content. In April 2015, memes accompanied an ill-advised social media strategy intended to commemorate the centenary of the Gallipoli campaign during the First World War. The failures of the Gallipoli campaign had a noticeable legacy in Australia and New Zealand, with both nations making 25 April the ANZAC Day public holiday, and Gallipoli considered a key element within the idealized notion of the Australian identity.

To commemorate the centenary of Gallipoli, the Australian supermarket Woolworths launched a website branded as 'Fresh in our memories'. Sharing images and stories of Australian veterans, the website offered users the opportunity to contribute their own stories. Users could create their own user icons and header images for their social media profiles, with suggested uploads including photographs of relatives who had served. Images then featured captions of 'LEST WE FORGET – ANZAC 1915–2015' and 'FRESH IN OUR MEMORIES', complete with 'Woolworths' logo.

The 'Fresh in our memories' campaign backfired almost immediately. The commercial interests involved in the campaign were criticized for prominently promoting themselves both through logos and implicit sloganeering (Woolworths market themselves as the 'fresh food people', making the use of 'fresh' rather questionable). Commercializing past conflicts was seen as crass, and initial responses on social media expressed disbelief about the campaign.[15]

The outcry took a further form, though, as Woolworths had essentially provided social media users with its own branded meme generator. Uploading ANZAC-unrelated images and adding the slogans encouraged additional commentary about the campaign's lack of subtlety and awareness (Sainty, 2015). Spread using hashtags including #freshinourmemories and #freshmemes, pointedly irreverent takes included images of Will Smith as the *Fresh Prince of Bel-Air*, photographs of Australian Prime

Minister Tony Abbott and screenshots of news stories about Woolworths' problematic history with ANZAC Day (such as not paying its staff at public holiday rates).

The appropriation of the campaign, transforming it from commemorative, commercially instigated social media strategy to emergent and mocking meme template, increased its visibility and critiques. Within hours of the campaign's launch, the website was taken down, at the behest of the Minister for Veterans' Affairs (ABC News, 2015d); inevitably, a final reinterpretation of the meme featured a screenshot of the 404 Not Found error in place of the website, framed by the 'Lest we forget' and 'Fresh in our memories' text.

The emergent memes of #freshinourmemories were short-lived, but act as an example of how topical irreverence can briefly obtain resonance. This behaviour accompanies other breaking news contexts and new developments, as detailed further in chapter 4. Such memes are not the full story, but highlight different interpretations, focusing on particular themes within a wider topic. #freshinourmemories memes accompanied discussion of commercial interests and the repurposing of ANZAC Day, and these were denoted using the #brandzacday and #brandzac hashtags. These served as markers concisely denoting multiple subjects, and also highlight a further ritualized practice: that of portmanteaugraphy – the creation of portmanteaux – especially within hashtags.

Hashtaggery and portmanteaugraphy

The strictness of the 140 character limit on tweets has helped foster a social media culture that places importance on concise flippancy. One does not simply try to be funny on Twitter; rather, there is a craft behind creating a one-liner that combines irreverence and topicality in a single tweet. Comedians – professional and amateur alike – make use of Twitter to share their takes on current events with their followers (and to attract new audiences), and also as a training exercise; the British comedian Peter Serafinowicz (@serafinowicz), for instance, asks for questions (tagged with #PSQA) from followers on a given theme for which he then provides unscripted joke answers.

At the centre of this craft is the embrace – and ritualization – of wordplay. From punning to juxtaposition and double entendre, packing multiple levels of meaning into a tweet can be realized by playing with language, as noted in Florini's (2014) study of signifyin' on Twitter. Portmanteaux, the combining of two words to create a new linking concept, are particularly appealing for ironic discourse and for adhering to a strict character limit. Similarly, adopting social media conventions for humorous purposes is also a common practice. Providing playful inversions of hashtags, as well as dedicated comedic tags, demonstrates the audience's awareness of social media forms and practices in presenting their comments.

Such approaches then lead to ritualized portmanteaugraphy and hashtaggery, at times in tandem. These are not unique to political themes. Instead, they are everyday practices that can be applied to political contexts. During 2012, social media buzz around a rumoured challenge to the leadership of the Australian Labor Party (ALP) by former Prime Minister Kevin Rudd attracted commentary using hashtags like #kevenge and #ruddmentum. These markers, used alongside less overtly punny tags like #respill (a reference to the leadership spill which had seen him replaced as leader by Julia Gillard in 2010, denoted by the #spill hashtag), did not dissipate when Rudd lost the ballot; rather, #ruddmentum in particular became a recurring, irreverent hashtag offering ironic commentary on any topic vaguely connected to Rudd, Gillard or the ALP's fortunes. Even though Rudd ruled out running against Gillard – declining to run in a leadership ballot in March 2013 before deciding to do so in June 2013, ultimately reclaiming the leadership and becoming Prime Minister for a second time – #ruddmentum remained part of the background noise among the tweeted coverage of Australian politics.

The recurring mention of #ruddmentum reflects a narrative, not restricted to social media, dedicated to the instability of the ALP. This theme, heavily featured in conservative media as well as on social media, was promulgated (inadvertently or otherwise) by the ALP itself, especially by Rudd and stories about his micro-managing and destabilizing presence. Social media speculation did not cause Gillard to be replaced by Rudd, nor did it bring about the victory by the Liberal Party, led by Tony Abbott, in the subsequent federal election; the commentary here was reflective of a wider media and social attitude towards the ALP. However, the hashtaggery at play provided a socially mediated interpretation of an ongoing political topic. That #ruddmentum was often used sarcastically, or as a punchline added to seemingly unrelated comments, does not diminish from its political origins and its presence within the social media consciousness (and its tropes). Indeed, this application of the hashtag underlines the ritualization and repurposing of political elements on social media.

Intertexts

As with other social media activity, political commentary online also makes uses of repurposed media from other sources. These can be political in origin, but are often unrelated to the specific context for which they are being employed until appropriated for this purpose. The use of animated GIFs as punchlines, illustrations and for tonal emphasis is a practice dependent on intertexts: texts making explicit connections to other texts (McKee, 2003). The importance of intertextuality is apparent within social media (and internet) cultures, where memes and irreverent content respond to previous examples, expanding the lexicon of their particular form (see the examination of LOLCat intertextuality by Miltner, 2014).

Intertexts adapted for political topics include reaction GIFs, where popular culture sequences are appropriated to illustrate ideas or sentiments, from expressing disbelief or joy to underlining sarcasm. Social media audiences create and circulate content, often reflecting texts or individual characters which have extensive fan communities online, particularly on Tumblr (Petersen, 2014; Thomas, 2013). While the explicit political content of these sources may be limited, the GIFs they inspire provide affective responses and visual means for social media users to respond to different themes and events.

More obviously political GIFs and intertextual media are also drawn from popular sources to highlight choice quotes, actions and sentiments. These further complement political commentary, adding feminist statements to posts, for example, by using relevant captioned GIFs of Leslie Knope (played by Amy Poehler) from *Parks and Recreation*. The practices of creating GIFs extend to non-fiction political programming as well; funny, salient and bemusing comments from talk shows, speeches and news reports are ideal candidates for engifulation. The adoption of the GIF for depicting short comments demonstrates several affordances of the format: they are smaller files than full video of the same content, embeddable and sharable across multiple platforms, and their looping presentation can powerfully reiterate their points through repetition (see also Poulaki, 2015).

Further popular culture appropriation and memetic framings of political talk are seen in the creation of parody videos utilizing the 2004 German film *Der Untergang* (*Downfall* in English-speaking countries). *Downfall* parodies make use of the same scene in its original German, and the dialogue and action remain unchanged throughout the numerous reinterpretations. The subtitles, though, are modified to make it appear that Adolf Hitler, played by Bruno Ganz, is infuriated by an incongruous and contemporary topic rather than Nazi Germany's imminent defeat. *Downfall* parodies form a long-running memetic practice, covering topics that reflect both global and highly local and individual issues. Examples of subjects that Hitler has apparently become angry about include sports and election results, the break-up of the band Oasis and meta-commentary on his memeification.

The *Downfall* parody as a reaction to unfolding events became established to the point of ritual within internet culture, with breaking news being accompanied by the obligatory video. Versions continue to be created, even if not to the same extent as its peak between 2008 and 2011. The eventual decline in *Downfall* parodies is both a reflection of the constant development of new memetic forms and practices, and also perhaps an outcome of the one-time ubiquity of the parody, the removal of videos from YouTube for infringing copyright in 2010 and the time involved in creating and uploading a new video (and the possible lack of originality or comedic success, since the same beats need to be hit in each parody). There is also the political context of the *Downfall* source text, too; even though the film is a fictionalized piece, the representation – and humanization – of Hitler in both film and parody was not without its criticisms (as noted by Gilbert, 2013). Here, as with other intertexts, it is impossible to entirely divorce politics from everyday social media practices and internet culture.[16]

Parody accounts

The ongoing creation of *Downfall* videos reiterates how parody, satire and spoofing are popular strategies for communicating online. Internet users have developed various formats for these practices, such as the creation of spoof trailers and videos on YouTube (Rodríguez Ortega, 2013), and these do not need to have political connections. Individual social media platforms have their own approaches to policing parody and satire: Twitter's explicit policy about parody accounts both sets guidelines and serves as an endorsement of the practice. This has led parody accounts to become 'part of the fabric' (Vis, 2013, p. 35) of Twitter.

The creation of parody accounts on Twitter is a ritualized practice, following what Shifman (2014a) describes as 'hypermemetic logic' (p. 4): media events are inevitably accompanied by a raft of audience responses, encompassing textual, image, video and audio (and blended media) contributions, from updated image macros to recut videos and individual opinions recorded via webcams. For unexpected and unintentional media events, including gaffes and general weirdness, the creation of topical parody accounts is almost obligatory: see, for example, the immediate influx of accounts acting as the empty chair addressed (as 'President Obama') by Clint Eastwood at the 2012 Republican National Convention (for more, see Highfield, 2015a).

Regardless of the topical context of parody account or of media event, it is important to note that neither context limits the contribution of parody accounts to political or news-oriented discussions. Established parody accounts with wide followings cover a variety of topics in their tweets, relevant to their audience's interests (in order to maintain their audience and cultivate further followers), with the hook being the framing of these topics within the world of the specific parody. Accounts satirizing or spoofing individual politicians would be expected to have some comment when the subject of the parody is in the news, but seemingly unrelated parodies will also participate and may become regular commenters on such topics (and thus more visible or continued contributors to ongoing political discussions than other, topically specific accounts). These accounts demonstrate their creator's social media literacy as well as political understanding, integrating relevant hashtags into their topical tweets. The popularity of these accounts, and the recirculation of their views through retweets, also identify an audience for original interpretations and, especially, irreverent takes on news and politics. In addition to noting topical tweets by journalists, there is a section of the social media audience promoting and following the satirical and dry, the understated and outrageous responses to unfolding events.

While there is humour in the incongruity of fictional characters irreverently engaging with contemporary news topics, other parody accounts are more directly politically motivated (Wilson, 2011). Parody is also a means for expressing opposition and resistance to dominant political groups and regimes, as studied by Amy Johnson (2015) within the Middle East, focusing on an account satirizing Bahraini Prime Minister Khalifa bin Salman Al Khalifa. Johnson's study also highlights that parody is not restricted to the content of tweets. Rather, the performance of the parody extends to the account's presentation, through user icons and names. These semi-permanent elements of a Twitter parody, accompanying each tweet and the account profile, can be used to provide visual and textual expressions and extensions of the parody.

While parody accounts usually clearly identify themselves as not the real thing, both in name and in practice, some accounts encourage fuzziness between joke and subject. The InfoSecTaylorSwift Twitter account (@SwiftOnSecurity) positions itself as the real Taylor Swift providing genuine commentary about internet security-related matters. The parody extends to a tumblr mixing pictures of Swift with topical quotes, presented as Swift making genuine and accurate statements about privacy and digital rights (swiftonsecurity.tumblr.com). InfoSecTaylorSwift does not just make use of humour; its content is on-topic and educational about information security. The dedication to positioning the account as a legitimate expert in the subject while simultaneously arguing that this expert is Taylor Swift, international pop superstar, sets out a different approach to parody than the more obviously broad comedic stylings of Elizabeth Windsor. Humour for InfoSecTaylorSwift (beyond initial incongruity) might be more of a long-game strategy (and the author might continue to argue that humour is not the aim); what this example demonstrates, though, is further variety in topical scope for parody accounts, and the mixture of a niche focus with a parody of a well-known public figure.

Parody accounts of fictional characters can be overtly political, too. Kalviknes Bore and Hickman (2013) studied Twitter accounts acting as characters from the television series *The West Wing*, which ran between 1999 and 2006. Predating Twitter, the show was no longer an active concern for its cast or creators, but fans adopted social media to further engage with their favourite characters, extending the fictional universe and narrative of the show and providing commentary on contemporary politics. These accounts are forms of fan fiction, offering non-canonical interpretations of characters and their interactions beyond the timeline of the series itself – although the fans attempt to keep their activity faithful to the original characterizations (see also *Mad Men* parody accounts, discussed by Jenkins et al., 2013). The explicit political context complicates the commentary from these accounts, though, for they attempt to balance the fictional timeline of *The West Wing*, where the US President between 1999 and 2006 (and beyond) was a Democrat, with the very real American political experience.

Appropriating the Non-Political and Adding the Political

Digital expressions of fandom (Booth, 2010; Jenkins, 2006) also appropriate specific popular cultural texts, and other media, in order to challenge and participate around political issues. The Harry Potter Alliance, for example, uses the fictional wizarding world of *Harry Potter* (created by J. K. Rowling) to frame real-world issues, including social justice, human rights, anti-slavery, digital rights and fundraising for disaster relief (Jenkins, 2012; Rosenberg, 2015; Terrell, 2014).

By using the *Harry Potter* setting for responding to contemporary political issues, the Harry Potter Alliance appropriates the non-political in its civic engagement. Its activism has clear goals and results, and utilizes different channels for its campaigns, of which digital media (from blogs and podcasts to social media and online video) are just one part (Jenkins, 2012). Its longevity – the Alliance was founded in 2005 – makes it an established example of fan activism, but also sets it apart from more fleeting and ritualized approaches to mixing the non-political and the political. Drawing on practices highlighted in the first half of this chapter, such as image macros, the transformation of the non-political to political contexts and the insertion of political elements to unrelated material, can offer simple punchlines rather than extended commentary or campaigning. However, the recurrence of these practices, and the understanding implied by their use and logics, reflect a social media culture that frequently brings the political into irreverent and irrelevant contexts.

Occasional and fleeting politics can be unexpected. In March 2015, photographer Martin Le-May captured an image of a green woodpecker flying through a London park with a weasel on its back. Shared on Twitter, the photograph went viral, as a highly unusual and remarkable example of wildlife photography, and it was soon accompanied by the inevitable portmanteaunic, concatenated hashtag #WeaselPecker. The memetic potential of #WeaselPecker, though, was also instantly noted, and soon after the original image spread, adaptations and additions started to proliferate online (Romano, 2015). As a shot of a woodpecker and a weasel, the photograph contained no political content, but elements of the political were inserted in the irreverent, user-generated follow-ups: an early enhanced #WeaselPecker image featured a shirtless Vladimir Putin riding on the back of the weasel.

What is also interesting in the case of #WeaselPecker is that as well as presenting variations on a theme, popular images formed a chain: new content built on previous versions such that the scene became more and more ridiculous. The #WeaselPecker-riding Putin was then trailed by characters from *Return of the Jedi* and *The Lord of The Rings*, while older meme forms were also included such as Bubble Girl. These were by no means the only #WeaselPecker images – or the most popular ones – but they highlight further the memetic logic and social media practices apparent in these spaces, and how the political is not absent from these contexts, even if it is only tangential. The inclusion of Putin makes sense because of his personally constructed public image of a rugged, 'wild' man who hunts bears and rides horses while shirtless – *of course* social media irreverence would present him riding a #WeaselPecker.

Tangential political irreverence: #JeSuisNico

Political narratives are malleable and mutable. During crises, protests or breaking news, the tenor of the coverage changes as new information comes to light and in response to new developments. No one theme might dominate. The tragedy in Paris in January 2015, where gunmen entered the offices of the satirical magazine *Charlie Hebdo* and shot several cartoonists, as well as other employees and police officers, received commentary covering a number of themes, including but not limited to religious extremism and intolerance, free speech and a free press, satire, solidarity with *Charlie Hebdo*, racism and xenophobia. The mass outpouring of support through the 'Je suis Charlie'/#JeSuisCharlie slogan – and its critiques – I will return to later in this chapter. Several days after the tragedy in the *Charlie Hebdo* offices, though, its coverage had continued to diverge along several thematic paths, and ongoing events led in part to irreverence.

On Sunday 11 January 2015, millions marched in solidarity through the streets of Paris and in other cities, bearing signs reading 'Je suis Charlie', 'Freedom' and similar messages. In Paris, protestors were joined by political leaders including French President François Hollande and German Chancellor Angela Merkel. Also present was former French President Nicolas Sarkozy, and his prominent appearance in the group of current leaders, captured in press photographs, was subsequently mocked on social media. Playing on the #JeSuisCharlie and #JeSuisAhmed tags prominently used – for far less flippant purposes – immediately after the attack, social media users adopted #JeSuisNico to circulate images inserting the visual of Sarkozy at the march into other contexts (Kirkland, 2015). Examples included Sarkozy being added to artworks (from Escher's 'Hand with Reflecting Sphere' to Seurat's 'Un Dimanche Après-midi à l'Île de la Grande Jatte'), stills from films (such as *E.T. the Extra-Terrestrial* and *Return of the Jedi*) and historic images (including the group selfie from the 2014 Academy Awards), collected on the *Je suis Nico* tumblr (je-suis-nico.tumblr.com).

The creation of a Sarkozy meme follows the conventions of previous topical examples. Most obviously, #JeSuisNico shares traits with similar photoshoppery-based forms like 'McKayla is Not Impressed', which saw the image of American gymnast McKayla Maroney, seemingly perturbed after winning the silver medal at the 2012 Olympic Games, integrated into other visual media (Leaver, 2013).[17] Such forms use juxtaposition and incongruity, mixing together contexts that are otherwise unrelated. They play with the media literacy of their audience, in the creation and understanding of the meme form, and also the comprehension of its social media context. These can take more obviously political forms: the memeification of images of police officers carrying out violence and prejudiced actions towards protestors, for instance, serves to highlight injustice and intolerance through visual commentary (Bayerl and Stoynov, 2014). Similarly, visual mockery of government officials in China reflects international meme cultures, specific practices on platforms like Sina Weibo and the importance of humorous devices for Chinese internet users in posting political views (Poell et al., 2014).

However, the image of Sarkozy at the march is not particularly extraordinary; he is just one figure among a group of (predominantly male) politicians in suits and overcoats at the front of a large crowd. There is no strange facial expression, no small child making a grimace, nothing that appears obviously meme-worthy. The political context, though, explains the #JeSuisNico response. Sarkozy had been French President between 2007 and 2012, from the centre-right Union pour un mouvement populaire (UMP), and had recently returned to political prominence as the chair of the UMP in late 2014. As President, and indeed previously as Minister of the Interior, Sarkozy had been the subject of criticism from left-leaning commentators, including online, for political reasons and for his personal style (see Campus, 2010 for more). The start of Sarkozy's presidency in 2007 was a flashpoint for the French political blogosphere: numerous blogs opposing Sarkozy were started in response to the result, including the *Sarkofrance* series of blogs, set up using multiple blogging platforms, styled essentially as Sarkozy's watch-dogs. These blogs also formed part of a network dubbed *les vigilants*, which surveilled and resolutely opposed Sarkozy through analytical, partisan and humorous posts (see Highfield, 2011).

This prior, prominent resistance directed specifically at Sarkozy among an internet-literate audience, then, suggests that later attempts by Sarkozy to appear within the spotlight would not pass without comment. Posting mash-up images featuring Sarkozy in unexpected contexts is not the same type of response as a vitriolic blog post – let alone starting a blog explicitly responding to one political figure. The #JeSuisNico images have a level of irreverence and mockery underlining that, regardless of the dislike of Sarkozy, he is no longer President. Extended commentary is perhaps unnecessary; it is enough to momentarily have fun at the expense of a political figure, and then move on to other, more pressing issues. #JeSuisNico is not the main story – it is a tangent several steps removed from the *Charlie Hebdo* attack – but the mere presence of the meme indicates that, regardless of the seriousness of the context, ritualized social media practices will still continue if the moment and inspiration – and popular sentiment – arrive.

From mischievous to misleading

It of course needs to be noted that these means and conventions are also used to share malicious and inaccurate information. Memes, their tropes and their creation, are successful in part due to their appropriation and repositioning of visual content into new contexts, divorced from their original setting. A drawback of this approach, though, can be the lack of attribution and source for the initial media. This missing information is critical for fact-checking and verification: its absence means that content which presents particular popular and compelling political views and which acts as a successful memetic form can be spread widely before its hoaxing or imprecisions are noted.

The implications of erroneous and unverified user-shared content are not necessarily profound. This was seen in March 2015 when an image claiming that IKEA had introduced a rainbow-coloured pillow named 'Putin' to its range went viral on social media (Pramlady, 2015). However, IKEA had not actually manufactured a 'Putin' pillow: in fact, the image was of a pillow recently removed from the IKEA range, with the label doctored so that it read 'PUTIN' rather than 'SKARUM' (Campbell, 2015). The effectiveness of the image, and the (Western) public mood that it played towards (given the Russian President's lack of support for LGBTQ groups), made it a successful example of spreadable media with a political subtext – indeed, it may be that the unverified image was more popularly shared than any subsequent corrections or debunkings (examined further within a crisis communication context in chapter 4).

The potential political impact of the fake pillow story was fairly minimal: while the image might have been a popular item in the US, the UK or Australia, there is a negligible (at best) effect that users in these countries might have on Russian policy or electoral results. More potentially damaging, though, are erroneous media that are directly linked to local political contexts and contests, and which again present effective uses of memetic formats. A blog post on *The Spectator* by Isabel Hardman (2014) decried the ongoing creation of viral images that erroneously presented the attendance for parliamentary debates in the UK Parliament. These juxtaposed a largely empty chamber with a packed one, captioning the images with dates and debate topics to present particular arguments about what elected representatives actually deemed important. As Hardman notes, though, many of these images were misleading, giving the wrong dates or topics in their not-so-subtle commentary.

The simplicity of the message, though, can account for its success, since it has high affective impact for a disgruntled electorate. Intentionally misleading presentation and spin are apparent and problematic in social media spaces as well as in other political media settings. The spreadability of content through social media can also mean that mechanisms for publishing corrections and apologies – and sharing these to the same extent as the original media – are under-developed or haphazard. Even though fact-checking is possible for these images to determine their actual contexts, the erroneous and uncorrected media might continue to be shared and interpreted without users realizing the mistakes or provenance.

Social Media Rituals in Political Commentary and Solidarity

While I have focused primarily on irreverent applications of social media rituals for political participation, engagement and commentary, these same practices are also apparent within contexts that are less frivolous or flippant. Shifman (2014a) notes the hypermemetic logic at play with regard to Occupy and, especially, the 'We are the 99%' campaign responding to the disparate economic inequality within US society (protesting against the concentration of wealth among the top-earning 1% of Americans). Tumblr was used to collate and reblog primarily visual content sharing stories from individuals self-identifying as part of the 99% (Bennett and Segerberg, 2013). Such approaches make use of social media logic – the norms and affordances of platforms and the cultures that have arisen around these – to promote their campaigns and to humanize them. By featuring individual stories, and giving them a visual face, the 'We are the 99%' campaign had added resonance, making its experiences relatable to others.

The social media logics of #JeSuisCharlie

There are elements of ritualization and social media logic – and everyday social media practices – in the coverage of, and response to, breaking news and emerging political topics. The public reaction to the shooting of multiple cartoonists and employees at the French satirical magazine *Charlie Hebdo* in Paris in January 2015 took many forms: from outrage and condemnation to confusion, disseminating live updates from confirmed and unconfirmed sources alike, sharing video from the scene and expressions of shock and solidarity with those affected. The fact that the killings were carried out by two Muslim men added a further political dimension to the commentary, as other Muslim voices (in France and externally) took to social media to condemn the actions, while jihadists added their support (Hubbard, 2015). In addition, these responses came within a context of ongoing racial and religious tensions in Europe and beyond, including the rise of the Islamic State in Iraq and Syria (ISIS, also variously IS, ISIL and Daesh) and the use of digital technologies for recruitment by terrorist groups (see Callimachi, 2015; Klausen, 2015). Breaking news and the overlap between social media and everyday politics are covered further in chapter 4. What I want to focus on here, though, is a few sub-themes within the *Charlie Hebdo* tragedy. These cover different aspects of the shootings, and demonstrate the advantages – and problems – of viral and memetic logics within social media culture.

As the manhunt unfolded, footage from bystanders appeared online. This included video of an injured police officer, Ahmed Merabet, being executed by one of the gunmen. As a document providing evidence of the crimes and atrocities committed in this event, such material is unfortunately necessary – yet its presence online, being shared through social media at the height of the manhunt, was not met with universal approval (Cormack, 2015; Dearden, 2015). Not only did the footage show a man being murdered while carrying out his job, but it was shared without social filters or empathetic norms – for instance, the confirmation of the officer's identity and whether or not his family (and colleagues) had been informed. The choice made by social media users to share the link to the video, including retweeting links, was also criticized by others – just because the material is there and you can link to it does not mean that you have to. Obviously not all users who saw the link in their social media feeds would share it further (although there are additional critiques and questions here about embedded videos and autoplay functions, where even if a user did not want to see the video, it might be displayed to them automatically). However, the affordances of platforms which enable material to be shared widely and instantly in this particular instance could be both help and hindrance: giving updates from the scene and affected arrondissements, but also providing the unnecessary and uncontrollable distribution of an execution at point-blank range.

The public response to these events saw an outpouring of social media solidarity which took the form, in essence, of a viral campaign: Twitter users adopted the #JeSuisCharlie hashtag in the wake of the shootings, to show their support for the victims of the tragedy, for *Charlie Hebdo* and for freedom of expression in general. The hashtag was not limited to Twitter. Social media users changed their profile pictures and banner images to prominently display the hashtag, while images containing the 'Je suis Charlie' message were created and circulated across platforms, including Instagram and Tumblr (ABC News, 2015a). These strategies are in keeping with other campaigns, at the French and international levels, such as internet 'blackout' protests (see chapter 5; Breindl and Gustafsson, 2011).

The public declarations of 'Je suis Charlie', though, were also contested. The narrative put forward here was challenged for multiple reasons (including mixed feelings about defending *Charlie Hebdo*'s freedom to satirize politics without necessarily endorsing the way it chose to carry out its satire) (Bajekal, 2015; L. Phillips, 2015). An alternative solidarity hashtag was promoted, #JeSuisAhmed, for the police officer killed during the attack (Lexpress.fr, 2015; Lin, 2015). The fact that Merabet was an innocent victim executed in the course of his job prompted this alternative narrative (whereas *Charlie Hebdo* had attracted outrage and opposition in the past from its cartoons depicting the prophet Mohammed [Berkowitz and Eko, 2007]). Critiques of ongoing #JeSuisCharlie activity – including using #JeNeSuisPasCharlie – also demonstrated a desire to focus on other topics following the initial wave of outrage; reports that the militant Islamist group Boko Haram had committed a massacre in Baha, Nigeria, did receive attention in Western mainstream, alternative and social media – but the ongoing coverage of *Charlie Hebdo* and its associated topics featured more prominently in the news agenda (Shearlaw, 2015).

These responses underline the importance of the visual to the socially mediated coverage of breaking news and unfolding events (Vis et al., 2013). The *Charlie Hebdo* context promoted the visual, since political and satirical cartoonists were targeted. In the days following the attack, social media disseminated responses from other cartoonists, circulating the images of their work as well as reporting their reactions. The imagery of the pencil as powerful tool for political expression, and its reusability, was featured in cartoons and artworks shared online, and #JeSuisCharlie also begat its own memes appropriating popular culture texts like *Where's Wally?* (published in French as *Où est Charlie?*; for extended analysis of the visual tropes of #JeSuisCharlie and related activity, see Abidin, 2015a, 2015b).

The responses to the *Charlie Hebdo* shootings, in the form of hashtagged solidarity through #JeSuisCharlie/Ahmed and the creation and sharing of viral and memetic imagery, demonstrate social media users' 'vernacular creativity' (Burgess, 2008). These also show awareness of the vernacular of each platform (Gibbs et al., 2015), and the overlaps and flows between individual platforms. A hashtag can be used on Facebook, Twitter, Instagram and more, with different structural and functional implications (Highfield and Leaver, 2015; Zappavigna, 2015). It can also be adopted for different forms, from textual content to image-based macros. The resulting media can be shared across the wider social media ecology, limited in theory only by visibility and public/private settings. Social media users take advantage of the conventions and affordances of their chosen platforms to create content, share media and connect with others – and these approaches can become standardized and ritualized – but these are not occurring in isolation or restricted to a single platform. In the response to the *Charlie Hebdo* attack, everyday social media practices were applied to an extraordinary political context, following established social media and internet logics. These responses also underline the importance of the visual for providing context and commentary: from memes to photographs taken from crises and protests, visual social media are crucial components of the everyday and the political alike online.

Conclusion

This chapter has outlined how mundane and ritualized social media practices are variously employed for direct and tangential political purposes. From image memes to punning hashtags and other forms of wordplay, everyday practices inform how social media users engage with and participate in politically themed activity online. These are not necessarily reflective of explicit or long-lasting civic engagement; what such practices demonstrate is the further intersection of the banal and the political, extending the personal of the previous chapter to how individuals employ their social media platforms of choice.

These practices reflect changing patterns of social media use. By posting commentary, whether irreverent or serious, or appropriating existing media content for political purposes, social media users make use of capabilities that have developed over time. The ritualized practices and logics of a platform like Tumblr are not the same as those of Instagram or Twitter, despite the presence of common structural elements, content and users. Similarly, these are not the same as those apparent on older platforms like LiveJournal, MySpace or Blogger. The adoption of different platforms for political and news-related themes, and the ongoing dynamic between traditional and new media organizations and actors, are the focus of the following chapter, examining the evolution of social media and their connections to politics.

The examples featured in this chapter have highlighted some of the evolving practices around political commentary and framing on social media, and indeed the longevity of forms like image macros or specific texts like *Downfall* parodies. Further ideas about media politics are raised by extreme cases like the sharing of video footage of the *Charlie Hebdo* attack on social media: the availability of the material to share, through non-traditional channels, and the gatekeeping-like decision of whether or not to share the video, demonstrate possible changes to our understanding of media power, particularly within a political context. In the next chapter, I explore this topic further, examining how social media – and their precursors – have impacted upon the creation, presentation and distribution of news and political media content.

3

Media Politics

In season 1 of *The West Wing*, White House Deputy Communications Director Sam Seaborn (played by Rob Lowe) tells President Josiah 'Jed' Bartlet (Martin Sheen) that the defining issue that will shape American society, and thus be the biggest challenge for Bartlet's presidency, is privacy: 'I'm talking about the internet. I'm talking about cell phones.' The year (of broadcast) is 1999.

In the seventh and final season of *The West Wing*, Democratic presidential nominee Matt Santos (Jimmy Smits) is introduced by campaign manager Josh Lyman (Bradley Whitford) to a blogger named Atrios (although not the actual Atrios, author of *Eschaton*), described as a major campaign fundraiser with a readership comparable to *The Philadelphia Inquirer*. The year is 2006.

In season 3 of *The Thick of It*, Malcolm Tucker (Peter Capaldi) gets increasingly sweary when he discovers that the shambolic goings-on around the party convention speech have been live-tweeted by a member of the public receiving an award from Minister Nicola Murray (Rebecca Front), and none of Murray's team had realized. The year is 2009.

In season 2 of *Veep*, Vice-President Selina Meyer (Julia Louis-Dreyfus) attempts to counteract a popular meme that inserted an image of her on her cell phone into other photographs[18] by showing her sense of humour at a political dinner. However, her song parodying Paul Simon's '50 Ways to Leave Your Lover' and poking fun at election pandering, goes viral on reddit and Tumblr, causing further problems for Meyer and her team. The year is 2013.

In season 1 of the Netflix remake of *House of Cards*, up-and-coming *Washington Herald* journalist Zoe Barnes (Kate Mara) takes advantage of her raised profile due to a major scoop by joining online-only news site *Slugline* instead of any of the *Herald*'s traditional print or television rivals. The year is 2013.

In season 3 of *Veep*, White House staffer Jonah Ryan (Timothy Simons) loses his job after his unauthorized 'gossiptainment' blog *WhiteHouseMan* inadvertently upsets the planning of major announcements. Ryan starts his own political opinion site ('*Ryantology*'), which has a brief moment of prominence before crashing and burning, while VP Meyer's new web presence (meetmeyer.com) receives a porn parody (meatmeyer.com). The year is 2014.

In season 2 of *House of Cards*, reporter Lucas Goodwin (Sebastian Arcelus) tries to dig up dirt on Vice-President Frank Underwood (Kevin Spacey) by accessing the 'deep web', entering a world of encryption, rerouting, hacking and surveillance. The year is 2014.

In season 7 of *Parks and Recreation*, the question of privacy raised by Sam Seaborn in 1999 is reframed and realized anew in the future vision of tech company Gryzzl and its invasively data-rich relationship with the people of Pawnee, Indiana. The year is 2015.

The above paragraphs demonstrate a few things. First, of course, is the realization that I probably watch too much politically themed television.[19] Second, and more pertinent, is the acknowledgement of the role of the internet and online technologies as a subject of public policy, civic engagement, news and commentary and the political process – and in everyday situations. Third, these scripted programmes are very much 'of the moment': they show their contemporary media situations, and the rate of change over the past fifteen years is reflected in the mention of platforms and internet terminology. The writers of these programmes were not aiming to create a historical overview of the intersection between politics and the internet, and their personal experiences shape their presentation of the internet and its contribution to contemporary media and politics; a season 3 episode of *The West Wing* saw Deputy Chief of Staff Josh Lyman become embroiled in a war of snark with a fan site, '*Lemon Lyman*', ostensibly based on writer Aaron Sorkin's own interactions with the recap site *Television Without Pity* (S. Doyle, 2011).[20]

The rate of change is such that political and news-related dramatic programming can become instantly dated; the 2003 drama *State of Play* (an otherwise thrilling and highly recommended show) is almost quaint in its depiction of relevant technologies and apparent disregard for the internet as its journalists try to investigate and break a major political scandal. The film remake in 2009, while less successful dramatically, did at least include blogs as part of the journalistic arsenal, although this also fell into a wider but tired debate of old vs new media, and resistance from the former towards the latter.

The point here is that popular culture uses contemporary cues for contextualizing its content, and we can get a sense of the perceptions around social media for political talk through the television, film and other entertainment media of the time. The varying institutional and popular views towards digital technologies depicted here then set the scene for this chapter's examination of the changing roles of social media and related platforms (and, on an associated note, mobile telephony) within the political and media landscape. In the process, analysing the evolution of the mediasphere also provides the opportunity to explore how political and media power is challenged, confronted and disrupted by new and alternative voices.

Media/Politics Power

The impact of the internet on established ideas of power, within the realms of media and politics, has been the subject of much theorization and empirical research. Castells (2007) has explored the possibilities – and limits – to changing structures of power and counter-power in a networked society, arguing that 'politics is dependent on media politics': traditionally, it is the mass media environment 'where power is decided' (p. 242). What has changed with the internet becoming embedded within politics, media and society, for Castells, is an increased multiplicity and diversity of networks in which power is exercised. Within the context of online communication there is still evidence of power for its traditional holders – states and governments, mass media, who determine access, control and information – and for those controlling the networks, including the owners and developers of popular social media like Facebook and Twitter. Media politics represents, then, the 'dynamic interface between political networks and media networks' (Castells, 2011, p. 783): for individual actors within these networks, though, their own choices and interests help determine the scope and form of the networks, and power is variable within the multitude of networks.

How individuals and new actors within media politics exercise power, through their participation and contributions within debate and shaping and disrupting flows of information, is empirically investigated by

Chadwick (2013). His conceptualization of a 'hybrid media system' is supported by analysis of politically oriented traditional and social media in the UK and the US. The impact of digital communication upon traditional media and politics has varied over time in response to new formats, actors, technologies and political and social catalysts, each offering different contributions to the mediasphere. Within a setting that reflects various elements of a networked public sphere (Benkler, 2006), a network society (Castells, 2007), networked publics (boyd, 2011) and issue publics (Dahlgren, 2009), critical aspects here are the structural and social attributes of networks and information flows, topical interests and new and alternative voices.

In the following sections, I explore the evolution of the relationship between social media and established political and media actors. From the early work of citizen journalists and political bloggers to the use of Facebook and Twitter for the 'social infomediation' of news (Smyrnaios and Rieder, 2013), and the adoption of new formats by news audiences, journalists and politicians alike, the trajectory of social media within news and politics has taken a meandering course with fluctuating fortunes of acceptance and resistance.

Alternative Media, Citizen Journalism and Blogs

The early examples of online sources, including new actors, to break news, provide alternative reporting and organize social movements, are well documented, and I do not want to dwell too long on the overly familiar (and, in a sense, the outliers). The successes of individuals like Matt Drudge, who in 1998 scooped the allegations of an affair between then-US President Bill Clinton and White House intern Monica Lewinsky on his political gossip and news curation site *The Drudge Report*, demonstrate new media upsetting established models. They are also extreme cases, though: the allegations published by *The Drudge Report* represent the 'first occasion on which a web-based news outlet set the agenda for the media as a whole' (McNair, 2006, p. 119), but similar levels of agenda-setting or major scoops did not necessarily follow.

This is perhaps ascribing intentions to new media that were not the actual goals of individuals, treating them as homogeneous rather than taking into account the wealth of interests and practices apparent. Some forms of alternative media online incorporated journalistic aims in providing non-professional reporting, commentary and analysis, like the South Korean *OhMyNews* and the US *Huffington Post*. The creation of *Indymedia*, too, was in part aimed at providing a platform for reporting on events likely to be subject to biases (or ignored) by the mainstream media – the anti-World Trade Organization (WTO) protests in Seattle in 1999 (Meikle, 2002).

Indymedia, alternative media and citizen journalism projects were employed in response to major breaking news and crises, such as the September 11 terrorist attacks in New York City and Washington, DC, the Boxing Day 2004 tsunami in Southeast Asia and the London bombings in 2005. These outlets presented amateur documentation of the events, reports from the scene and commentary and conjecture (S. Allan, 2014; Gillmor, 2006; Tynan, 2008). Accompanying these discussions were blogs, a further case of the personal approach to political and news-related coverage. While the earliest blogs were predominantly personal diaries, with entries organized in reverse-chronological order (Blood, 2002), the topics of interest to individual (and group) bloggers varied extensively, and numerous sub-genres of blogs developed and overlapped. Politics was both a dedicated focus for a growing population of political bloggers, but also an emergent and occasional topic for many others as they discussed their own interests and personal experiences.[21]

While not the same as citizen journalism, politics and news blogging shared characteristics and practices with this approach (see in particular Bruns, 2005). Bloggers, including military personnel, offered reports and commentary from war zones from Afghanistan to Iraq, as part of a growing sub-genre of war blogs (Wall, 2005). Such reporting might take more personal and affective dimensions than would be expected for citizen journalism, though: the sudden international audience for Salam Pax's blog – intended initially for a friend overseas – as he blogged through the invasion of Baghdad in 2003 demonstrates the appetite for original, alternative and personal framings of breaking news (Zuckerman, 2008).

Political bloggers, in the US particularly, had some early successes in breaking news and impacting upon the coverage of politics, which are well documented elsewhere (Drezner and Farrell, 2008). It is also notable, though, that the likes of the Trent Lott/Strom Thurmond remarks (2002 – Gillmor, 2006), 'Rathergate' (2004 – Munger, 2008) and Howard Dean's rise and fall as potential Democratic presidential candidate (2004) remain some of the most prominent examples of bloggers having a significant impact on news or politics (see also Hindman, 2009). However, a direct sacking or scandal is not the only way that bloggers and citizen journalists participated in and changed the dynamics of media and politics.

Bloggers, citizen journalists and social media users play various roles in presenting, reframing, critiquing and sharing news. Bruns (2005) described the work of the emerging collection of citizen journalists and bloggers as 'gatewatching': if mainstream media are the gatekeepers of news and politics, determining what is to be reported and how, then gatewatchers monitor 'the output gates of news publications and other sources in order to identify important material as it becomes available' (p. 17). Serving as corrective, respondent and endorsement of mainstream media coverage, the blogosphere and its ilk were also considered to represent part of a digital 'Fifth Estate', extending from the view of journalism as the 'Fourth Estate' reporting on the three contemporary estates of the legislative, executive and judiciary systems (Dutton, 2009; Jericho, 2012). These practices continued to diversify and evolve: within the political blogosphere, individual bloggers carried out different functions in collectively covering particular topics. From focusing on their own specialty subjects to adopting practices like link/filter blogs (curating lists of links of interest, with minimal commentary from the blogger themselves), bloggers found their own niches within networks (Vanbremeersch, 2009).

The thematic variation and specializations of bloggers led to the emergence of distinct and diverse approaches to political blogging (Lehti, 2011). Similarly, networks of political blogs reflected partisan interests, but also numerous topical and structural factors; where political blogging was originally studied from the point of view of ideological divisions (for example, Adamic and Glance, 2005), in the Australian and French political blogospheres outright partisan support was only part of the collected blogging experience. Instead, bloggers clustered together around common themes (focusing on economics, polling analysis or feminist issues, for example), and through common affiliations (including through blog collectives). This thematic distribution is apparent in figure 2, which depicts a selection of the Australian political blogosphere as it was in 2009,[22] based on connections within blogrolls.[23]

Bridging international blogospheres

The Western focus of my research here puts a particular spin on the 'everyday': quotidian blogging is in general a fairly mundane and *safe* practice (especially in Australia, the US or the UK) – although this has not always been the case. Tensions between public communication through blogs, surveillance and users' data have been a factor for international bloggers, from French bloggers being arrested on suspicion of posting messages to their Skyblog blogs inciting violence during riots in 2005 (Allard and Blondeau, 2006; Russell, 2007), to bloggers – and other prominent voices on social media – being targeted and arrested during the Arab Spring series of uprisings in North Africa and the Middle East in 2010 and 2011 (Howard and Hussain, 2011). This experience is

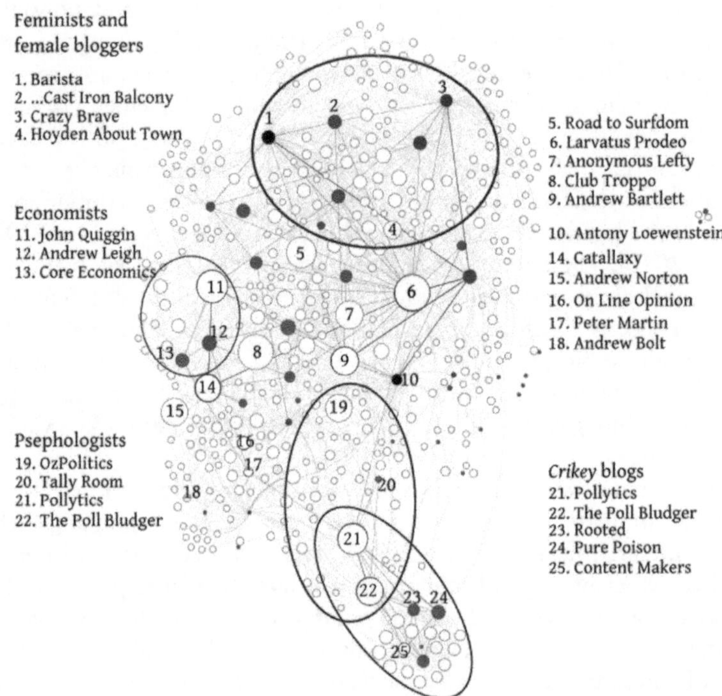

Figure 2: Australian political blogosphere (selection) (from Highfield, 2011).

an ongoing reality for bloggers in countries with oppressive or restrictive regimes and limits on press and personal freedoms. As *Global Voices* continues to highlight even in 2014 and 2015, bloggers (as well as journalists) globally are arrested and killed in response to their reporting and commentary, from Bangladesh (Sanyal, 2015) to Ethiopia (Macha, 2014).

In drawing attention to the plight of bloggers and citizen journalists around the world, *Global Voices* also brings together the collected outputs of international writers reporting on and challenging governments and regimes, and circumventing surveillance. Here, *Global Voices* fulfils a centralizing role, making diverse international experiences available for a global readership. Other sites, including individual and group blogs, might also perform similar functions, providing overlaps and connections with international audiences. Ethan Zuckerman (2008) studied blogging in various African and Asian contexts, finding that while regional blogospheres overall may write and comment in local languages, there are also bridge-bloggers who connect these communities to external readers.

Bridge-blogging practices encompass collating content from various regional bloggers and writing in other languages (including English)[24] to make this work accessible to a new audience (see also MacKinnon, 2008).

International blogospheres feature diversities of practices and interests, as seen in the US or Australian contexts (Russell and Echchaibi, 2009). While political issues are of varying importance for bloggers around the world, they are not the only topics featured, and continue to be emergent and tangential themes as well as specialist subjects. Topical variety is apparent among bloggers in Iran, Egypt and more, as bloggers write about such themes as politics and poetry concurrently (Etling et al., 2010; Kelly and Etling, 2008). International bloggers also made use of platforms specific to their regions and languages (especially those developed prior to local versions of English-language blogging platforms), and this has continued with social media platforms. Such developments are also responses to local contexts: the popularity of WeChat and prevalence of *weibo* (microblogs, offered by various providers including Sina Corp) among Chinese internet users also reaffirm that popular Western social media like Facebook or Twitter are blocked by the Chinese government (Gleiss, 2015; Tong and Zuo, 2014). In other cases, international bloggers have taken extensively to older platforms: the popularity of LiveJournal among Russian bloggers reflects Russian-language interfaces and the advantages of user data not being stored in Russia (Alexanyan and Koltsova, 2009).

The Evolving Mediasphere

The freedom promoted by blogging – where running your own blog meant that you could potentially talk about whatever you wanted – was not universally seen as a positive. From outright decrial of the 'cult of the amateur' online and its negative and deceptive contributions to contemporary culture (Keen, 2007) to critics like Geert Lovink (2008) and Matthew Hindman (2009) noting their reservations about the political and social potential of blogs, the value of online communication has long been disputed. Fears around the negative effects of political blogging, and other alternative sources of news and politics online, were also raised in response to theories of cyberbalkanization (Sunstein, 2008), where internet users would form their own like-minded groups and did not experience opposing views or critiques (Meraz, 2011). Ideological clustering was apparent at times within the blogosphere (Adamic and Glance, 2005; A. Shaw and Benkler, 2012), although not to the extent of realizing these echo chamber effects. Instead, even if structural connections such as ongoing links did not connect bloggers with different partisan views, members of these different groups were still aware of what the others were posting (if only to denigrate and mock it).

The criticisms directed at bloggers were particularly prevalent within the political and news contexts, as elements of the mainstream media became concerned that blogging was going to replace journalism. While some journalists and news organizations quickly adopted online platforms for presenting news and engaging with audiences, others took a more confrontational approach to new media. Between 2007 and 2010, several incidents involving representatives of *The Australian* newspaper highlighted an antagonistic relationship in which traditional media were suspicious of blogging and directly attacked individual bloggers. The endorsement of bloggers' commentary by other media organizations, and bloggers' rival interpretations of polling data which went against *The Australian*'s own analysis, were sufficiently threatening to warrant reactions which included publicly revealing the identity of a previously anonymous blogger (see Highfield and Bruns, 2012; Jericho, 2012; Young, 2011).

Part of the rationale for confronting bloggers was their apparent pretence to journalistic aims without the same standards or qualifications; political bloggers in the US were given press credentials for the 2004 Democratic convention (Carlson, 2007), while concerns about the lack of a code of ethics – and whether bloggers and their sources were protected in the same way as journalists – remain current debates in 2015 (Owens, 2015). Yet this still implies an ambition that might be loftier than many bloggers would have considered; rather than seeking to replace the traditional media system, blogging served to complement and extend coverage of news and politics, offering new perspectives and analyses that took advantage of individuals' own expertise.[25]

Despite the various reservations about the value of blogging, collectively the blogosphere (and later social media) was used by mainstream media as 'a finger on the pulse of the people' (Papacharissi, 2010b, pp. 237–8). Adoption of blogging by journalists themselves was inconsistent but demonstrated different ways that mainstream media responded to the changing mediasphere: blogs dedicated to specialist subjects and commentators enabled detailed coverage of related topics and, at times, interaction between writers and audience through comments (Garden, 2014; Singer, 2005). Topical discussions evolved across the extended mediasphere, incorporating traditional and alternative outlets, mainstream and online media, including blogs. Bloggers linked to, and responded to, the work of their peers and of journalists, drawing together diverse sources to build up their own commentary and analysis.

As more centralized platforms, from Facebook to Twitter, became popular means of sharing and commenting on everyday experiences, including news and politics, the place of blogging within the mediasphere changed. Blogs remain relevant sources, but in countries like Australia greater representation of traditional political actors, including journalists and politicians, has occurred on Facebook and Twitter than happened within the blogosphere. What this means is that the contemporary mediasphere incorporates extended analysis and commentary from blogs and opinion sites like *The Conversation* and *Medium*, short remarks on Twitter, statuses and comments on Facebook, the collected outputs from journalists in their own publications and on social media, and related content on platforms from YouTube to Tumblr.

Engagement with politics and news does not happen on one single platform, and the adoption of everyday practices across social media at large has allowed for further means of framing political coverage, from the serious to the seemingly flippant and sarcastic. These encourage the use of different media in discussing news and politics, embedding videos, tweets, images and GIFs into articles posted on blogs and mainstream news sites alike. The popularity of platforms like Twitter as channels for commenting on news as it happens and sharing instant reactions has also had an impact upon how politics and news are presented online. Smyrnaios and Rieder (2013) describe the 'social infomediation of news', where Twitter and other platforms are used for news-sharing, with a variety of styles of news engagement and content apparent. Social media users engage with a diverse range of news sources and topics in the curation and consumption of current affairs. Most crucially, this is not happening on Twitter alone, since this platform is 'inextricably linked to other so-called Web 2.0 services, as well as to the information and media sphere in general' (p. 360).

Hermida's (2010) notion of 'ambient journalism' on Twitter explains social media as an 'always-on' outlet, where reporting and commentary do not stop. Social media are, in a sense, the first channel of response for media organizations and journalists – the immediate, salient details are posted to social media with the full story available on organizational websites (and through their other channels). The implication here, then, is that if journalism has been previously seen as 'the first draft of history', then Twitter (and other social media used for these purposes) is host to 'the first draft of the present' (Bruns and Highfield, 2012, p. 25). Social media are an arena for collective sense-making of news and politics as they happen, including sharing materials as they become available, and professional and amateur research and analyses. This influence of social media on the coverage of politics and news is explored further in the next chapter's examination of breaking news and crises, where the coverage of unfolding events and controlling messages is critical and contested.

Traditional Actors, New Formats?

The move from confrontation to acceptance of new platforms and opportunities by traditional media organizations and journalists has proceeded unevenly. Prominent alternative media sites, such as *Crikey* in Australia and *Rue89* in France, were established by former journalists taking advantage of the potential for reporting and presenting news afforded by the internet. Other commentators went the other way: mainstream media organizations invited successful bloggers to write for them, through their own institutional blogs and through opinion and commentary sections of their websites. This recognition of renown and popularity among bloggers also extended to other, non-political contexts. Lifestyle bloggers and popular Instagram or YouTube users may become professional social media creators, with commercial backing and promotional posts (Abidin, 2014; Hopkins and Thomas, 2011; Marwick, 2015; Sinanan et al., 2014). Celebrity status could also happen within a blogger's own circle, with bloggers becoming micro-celebrities (Marwick and boyd, 2011b; Senft, 2013) due to their status as influencers for their readers.

Traditional media have varyingly incorporated digital technologies and new media affordances into their own publications and web presences. Major titles like *Le Monde* launched their own blogging platforms, offering bloggers a lemonde.fr address for their content. Blogs became channels for journalists to post material on their personal sites and as part of their professional work for their parent organization (Garden, 2010; Singer, 2005). These spaces could also draw upon the resources – and audience – available to these institutional undertakings, incorporating supporting media into posts and extending coverage to formats like video and audio podcasts. The visibility of blogs on traditional media sites also invites comments from readers, to a potentially greater extent than on other, personal blogs (see Lovink, 2008). However, the resulting comments threads vary in scope and civility: while discussions 'below the line' can offer extended analysis and tangents beyond the scope of the original article, with productive interaction between readers (and occasionally the authors of the article), they can also devolve into antagonistic, circular and offensive arguments (see variously Garden, 2010, 2014; Graham and Wright, 2015).

Podcasts and the sound of political media

Other established formats for presenting news and politics have also been adapted for a new media environment. Podcasting demonstrates the audience for audio (and video) material delivered in delimited, episodic files rather than through radio broadcasts. Podcasts are available from mainstream media publications and these are not restricted to those with radio backgrounds. The BBC offers podcasts drawn from its extensive radio programming, while the likes of the *Guardian* employ the form for journalistic roundtables and discussions around various features, from sports news to books. Podcasts are also an option for other, non-traditional media voices, and feature a diverse range of topics beyond news and politics.

The 'social' media aspect of podcasting can be argued – social discussions and activities inspired by podcasts take place in discussion boards, forums, commentary sites and the usual popular platforms, with listener feedback and correspondence sometimes featured in the podcast's episodes. Podcasts are demonstrative of an asynchronous broadcasting model, adapted in response to user choices and devices. I mention them here in passing, though, because they provide a further example of traditional and alternative voices being able to engage in political and news-related talk, as well as different means of presenting and consuming these discussions. Furthermore, at the time of writing podcasting is experiencing a resurgence in popularity. Findings from the Pew Research Center in early 2015 underline the growing audience for podcasting, even if the term is perhaps now a misnomer with the iPod being replaced as device of choice by smartphones (Vogt, 2015).

While Chadha et al.'s (2012) survey of podcast users found the consumption of podcasts to be a predictor of political participation, they also note that entertainment was a more popular genre than news: while podcast users are engaged media consumers, they are not necessarily using the format for political information or news. However, the evolution of podcasting and its growing popularity has helped the format to realize other approaches to covering related topics. In late 2014, the WBEZ podcast *Serial* employed the format for long-form investigative reporting, re-examining a murder case from 1999. Produced as a spin-off from the WBEZ radio show and podcast *This American Life*, *Serial* attracted extensive attention and audience engagement, as social and participatory elements emerged from a non-interactive text. Listeners shared their theories about the case online (see, for instance, the *Serial* subreddit: /r/serialpodcast, 2014), and the conjecture inspired its own meta-podcast from *The A.V. Club* (*The Serial Serial*: Eakin, 2014).

Political commentary through podcasting can also be found through comedic framing, where the performative aspect of comedy is maintained in the audio format. *The Bugle* by John Oliver and Andy Zaltzman, for instance, is the product of two British comedians whose topical work appears in other venues – Oliver is a former *Daily Show* correspondent and host of the HBO series *Last Week Tonight*, while Zaltzman has featured on BBC radio in addition to his stand-up shows. The podcast format is not highlighting otherwise unheard voices in this case, and indeed was distributed by *The Times* until 2011 (Goodman, 2011). However, *The Bugle* exemplifies a different form of presentation of satirical analysis of news and political subjects. Podcasts from comedians also focus on other issues: Meserko (2014) explores the use of the format for providing support for sufferers from mental illnesses, for example.

Jarrett's (2009) analysis of the talk presented in three Australian podcasts highlights the further messiness of the format in how it engages with its audience and its topics. Finding a 'complicated layering of both lay/mundane talk with expert/institutional forms' (p. 130), Jarrett notes that banal styles of framing and conversing are inconsistently employed, impacted upon by the status and background of presenter and show. However, podcasting offers a further platform through which engagement and participation with political and news topics can be realized, through listening and creating, and through audiencing.

As with the other platforms studied in this book, podcasting as a singular format is not representative of all social media users or political discussions. Instead, it is part of an evolving and emergent mediasphere, where the choice of platforms for everyday practices (including political talk) is subject to a variety of social and technological factors particular to an individual. The 2015 report from Pew suggests that part of the reason for podcasting's increased popularity is 'the rapid growth in use of smartphones and mobile devices in addition to the increased ease of in-car listening' (Vogt, 2015). Technological improvements, such as increased capabilities for creating, sharing and accessing rich, non-textual media via mobile devices, are also apparent in further trends around social media and politics. Visual media and mobile apps around images and video, such as Instagram and Vine, are popular means of documenting everyday life; these same platforms can also find themselves adopted for the coverage of news and politics, and for professional journalistic content.

In which the Prime Minister eats an onion

During a visit to a Tasmanian onion farm in March 2015, Australian Prime Minister Tony Abbott was handed an onion. Having contemplated the bulb, he bit into it, skin and all, making appreciative nods as he chewed. This was an unexpectedly weird move from the Prime Minister, especially in front of reporters, although as Wilson (2015) argued a week later, it was not exactly out of character.

What is particularly interesting about this case is not the onion-eating especially (*although* ...) but more how this was reported. The Australian Broadcasting Corporation (ABC) released a video of the moment where Abbott took a bite of the onion, making it immediately available online. Rather than an edited video within a prepared news story, though, the content was presented on Vine in its raw form – just like the onion (ABC News, 2015c). This was an ideal match between footage and platform: additional commentary and framing were not required to ground the story; more than six seconds of footage would perhaps have overdone it. Indeed, the endless six second loop of the Prime Minister willingly biting into a whole onion adds to its impact: the recurring sight underlines its surrealism, warranting repeat viewing without making it any less inexplicable. Within a month, the video had, according to the statistics on its Vine page, been looped over 4.5 million times. This translates to over 7,500 *hours* of Abbott's onion-munching – on its way to nearly a year's worth, and this does not take into account any offline viewing. Obviously no one person accounts for all of these loops, but these figures serve to highlight the audience for this footage (from explaining the role of Vine in the news process to telling friends about how *weird* Australian politics can be).

Visual content like Vine loops can be appropriated and embedded into new settings, and provide punchlines and commentary themselves. The shortness of the onion loop and its instant impact encourage sharing, across multiple platforms; in its own right, too, Vine also offers journalists (and other users) with an even more immediate mechanism for sharing footage from the scene, in a complete form. Unlike streaming from a press conference using ustream, Periscope or Meerkat, where the footage is ongoing and audiences may continue to join mid-stream, a Vine loop is a finite construct, six seconds in length and ready for repetition upon publication.

Short looping videos will not be the most appropriate vehicles for presenting all news, of course. However, the suitability of Vine for the Abbott video, and a trend at the time of writing of testing Periscope for journalistic streams shared through Twitter, demonstrate an increased awareness of the alternative options for providing and formatting news content. Even more so, these moves underline the integration of the new into the work of established media and political actors. This may just be a desire to maintain an advantage over competitors or an attempt to expand audiences – and a part of a greater reciprocal relationship between journalists and audiences (Lewis et al., 2014). However, it also confirms the change in perceptions and beliefs regarding newer media from those held in the mid-2000s by traditional media; even if arguments about the value of social media persist, the platforms are still being used by these organizations.

Backchannelling and New Ways of Gatewatching

The adoption of new platforms for engaging with and sharing political commentary, news stories and media events has been accompanied by evolving practices that build on the uses of older channels. Gatewatching (Bruns, 2005) described contemporary new media, such as blogs, as responding to the work of the mainstream media, challenging and correcting them as required. Although bloggers and citizen journalists could present their own original reporting and analysis unprompted, this definition establishes a reactionary role for new media, with mainstream media the catalysts for gatewatching. This is not to downplay the work of bloggers, but underlines that at the crux of debates around new and old media and politics, there is a dynamic where one influences the other (and vice versa, over time) rather than a narrative of replacement.

Mainstream media coverage of news and politics remains important to social media activity around these topics. The use of Twitter as a backchannel for media events, including televised political programming, clearly highlights this dynamic. Mainstream media sources have the resources, contacts and capabilities to provide this programming and feature prominent political actors. Social media afford the audiences for this content the opportunity to comment and critique, discuss and debate what is being presented. Anstead and O'Loughlin (2011) describe the emergence of a 'viewertariat' on Twitter, who regularly engage with political television content by posting commentary online. Weekly programming like the BBC's broadcast of Prime Minister's Question Time in the UK, Anstead and O'Loughlin argue, encourages the development of the viewertariat, for it provides a recurring context for discussion and invites a returning audience.

These regular catalysts for social media audiences can strengthen the sense of the viewertariat by making participants aware of other returning commentators, and by establishing the 'rules' and rituals of the broadcasts and their associated backchannel. Not only does watching a broadcast become a media ritual in itself, but secondary rituals develop around the backchannel; indeed, it may be that some participants engage solely in the backchannel without actually watching the programming that is ostensibly shaping the discussion. The Australian political panel discussion show *Q&A*, broadcast weekly on the ABC, is accompanied by social media commentary through the #qanda hashtag (Given and Radywyl, 2013). This hashtag has multiple purposes: it is a mechanism for centralizing commentary about the show; it is a device enabling the social media audience to participate by asking questions which could then be relayed through to the panel discussion; and it is a source for on-screen commentary, as selected #qanda tweets will appear within the broadcast itself.

For the *Q&A* viewertariat, engaging with the show and its backchannel may reflect different motivations. For some, it may be a means to participate in ongoing political discussions, focused on the topics of the particular episode but featuring users who regularly comment on Australian politics in general as part of the wider social media commentariat (Highfield, 2013). For others, though, there may be a self-promotional intent behind their tweets, as they attempt to get their comments featured in the broadcast – and, indeed, individual users posting many times during a broadcast might variously demonstrate both of these practices and more. As with other elements of political activity on social media, these reflect everyday practices which are also applicable to other contexts, with backchannels key elements of regular television programming (Harrington, 2013): 'social tv' extends from dramatic and comedic series (Everett, 2015) and infotainment and documentary programming (Sauter and Bruns, 2014), to talk shows (Giglietto and Selva, 2014), reality television, sports, contests and special events (Deller, 2011; Highfield et al., 2013). Broadcasters also incorporate and encourage social media activity around their programming, as a means for sourcing content and opinions, voting in competitions and for audience research. The dynamic then works both ways: the social media commentary is responding to what is seen on screen (or on second screen), and the broadcasters are taking note of this activity (at the very least quantitatively, if not taking into account every individual tweet).[26]

The use of social media as a backchannel for televised media also extends to other news and political formats. In a sense, the backchannel function overlaps with the gatewatching role identified by Bruns (2005): mixing irreverence, critique and analysis, social media users draw attention to the incorrect, the unusual and the offensive. A misprinted front page of the *Australian Financial Review* in 2014, which prominently featured unedited headlines, blank spaces and placeholder text instead of the final version, was rapidly shared and deconstructed on social media. This page offered a wealth of material for user-generated humour, including a story about Prime Minister Tony Abbott investing in new planes for the Royal Australian Air Force highlighted by a teaser headline that, in its misprinted form, read: 'Buys planes. World is fukt [*sic*]' (McDonald, 2014). Unsurprisingly, this translated into its own #worldisfukt hashtaggery, and into visual memes mixing images of Abbott with a superimposed 'World is fukt' caption (documented by Crerar, 2014).[27]

The mixed backchannel/gatewatching role can also take serious forms, circulating critical responses to news and political stories and opinions through the extended social mediasphere. This expands upon the initial definition of gatewatching, which focused on blogging and citizen journalism as the principal outlets for such practices, to note their applications for multiple platforms and their mundaneness. Engaging with news and political media, by reading, sharing or critiquing content, is an everyday occurrence on social media. The sources might variously be mainstream and alternative, professional and amateur, social and paywalled: the social media commentariat draws on and responds to the wider mediasphere, where traditional and newer voices are present. From critiquing gender inequality and representations in media and popular culture (F. Shaw, 2012a) to sharing journalistic content (Smyrnaios and Rieder, 2013), social media users collectively act as audience, producers, contributors and critics.

Social Media Power

The diverse roles and practices around social media users and political and news media engagement illustrate that the impact of social media on power within political and media contexts is not a simple case of replacing voices or organizations. While theories of media power within a mass media setting such as agenda-setting (McCombs, 2005; McCombs and Shaw, 1972) establish the power of the news media in how politics – and *which* politics – are covered, online platforms like social media complicate this idea (Meraz, 2011). From challenging the work of professional journalists through fact-checking, critique and alternative interpretations (Bruns, 2005; Bruns and Highfield, 2012) to sharing content from a diverse range of sources, social media users have the potential to reshape agendas and information flows – at an individual level and within groups, at least, even if not completely altering a large-scale, public agenda.

Social media users create curated and cultivated information networks, through their friendship and professional connections and their personal interests. They may variously serve as opinion-leaders for others in their networks, sourcing information and commentary and sharing it through their own social media accounts, and have their engagement with politics and awareness of issues shaped by what others share. As Smyrnaios and Rieder (2013) demonstrate, social media users draw on a wide range of sources for their news and political information, and will share accordingly. Research into news-sharing on Twitter has found that, for Australian news and opinion sites, while overlap is far from universal there is a sizeable population on Twitter that does actively and repeatedly share links to articles from sources representing each of the major media organizations (Bruns et al., 2013).

Providing links and responses to traditional media content online does not translate into an endorsement of its content. Citations may be occurring to highlight inaccurate, unusual or unfathomable coverage, and the sentiment behind sharing further shapes how others seeing an article in a social media user's feed may interpret this. Disruptions to power, to agendas and information flows are not restricted to sharing content from established sources, though. The creation of news and political content by social media users, and the co-production of news by journalists and their audience alike (Ekstrom et al., 2013), introduce different voices and dynamics into this environment. This includes sites encouraging new and expert voices to provide analysis and commentary, from the academic-instigated *The Conversation* to the long-form socially mediated writing on *Medium*, as well as the original reporting, listicles and GIF-augmented pieces on *BuzzFeed*.

The opportunities for social media users to contribute to new spaces for political commentary, and to consume a variety of topical sources, do not necessarily mean that traditional power relations are completely and irreversibly altered. As the historical evolution of digital and social media within political contexts has shown, mainstream media organizations respond to and make use of newer platforms, both institutionally and individually. Journalists start blogging, tweeting or adapting personal platforms for professional purposes, incorporating social media commentary and animated GIFs into their reporting, and the presentation of news follows approaches popularized on blogs. Power is instead negotiated, where newer and amateur voices obtain influence and reputation within political and media settings through their contributions and practices, their networks and interactions. This also means that related questions around reliability, authenticity and objectivity in a social media environment apply to traditional voices too.

The accuracy of social media coverage of news and politics, and whether it portrays truth, truthiness (Munger, 2008) or incorrect yet seemingly plausible information is an ongoing debate shaped by affordances of platforms. After all, the question of authenticity is central to the social mediation of everyday experiences, from presentation through profile pictures and statuses on Facebook to ideals of aesthetics and cultural logics on Instagram.[28] The use of artistic filters as provided by Instagram and other apps allows users the opportunity to refine and reframe their visual representations; when used for journalistic purposes, such as war reporting, the impact of filtered and constructed images on both reporting and on objectivity is disputed (Alper, 2014). Previous concerns around visual media content and its accuracy and authenticity, from fake images, to the influence of Photoshop and other editing software, and staged photographs, highlight that these current framings are part of an evolving concern predating social media (Burgess et al., 2012). They also demonstrate, though, that the means for these practices are increasingly prevalent and everyday, where popular apps are used for mundane and journalistic practices, as the political and personal are documented using ever-converging approaches.

This convergence also alters perceptions of social media and traditional media. It is important to remember just what the aims of social media and mainstream media alike are – and distinguishing between the aims of individual users and the social media platforms themselves, for that matter. The networks and contacts, resources and access available to mainstream sources mean that these will remain important components of media/politics, distinguishing journalism from other forms of commentary and reporting online. However, Facebook's push in early 2015 to host news content from major titles (Dredge, 2015), and changes to its algorithm impacting upon the visibility of links, highlight the continuing evolution of the mainstream/social dynamic, and the increasingly fuzzy distinction between the two parties. The overlap between the mainstream and the social, at the organizational level, at the content level, at the audience and abilities, is in a state of flux, not in terms of one replacing the other, but in constantly evolving relationships and technologies.

Narratives and counter-narratives

One impact of social media is the ability to establish narratives and counter-narratives in the coverage of political topics. Analysis from social media users can shed light on particular themes or issues, setting out a specific line of enquiry. In the process, dominant and traditional mainstream media agendas and framings of current political events can be challenged, rejected and ignored by social media users. Within the blogosphere, the promotion by the conservative Australian news media of the 'Utegate' scandal directed at then-Prime Minister Kevin Rudd was criticized by (primarily left-leaning) political bloggers as a distraction from more pertinent political issues, and the sensationalistic coverage of the scandal a reflection on contemporary journalistic standards and ethics (for full details, see Highfield, 2011).

As noted in chapter 2, humorous devices like parody and satire provide further means for social media to establish alternative framings and counter-narratives. Gilbert (2013) argues that the popularity of *Downfall* parodies 'enables a critical (re)vision of YouTube as a political medium, specifically one that through chicanery can foster a critical mass' (p. 421). I argue for the expansion of this idea to social media at large, as irreverent interpretations of politics and news utilize the cultures, affordances and vernaculars of different platforms. In January 2015, the US-based Fox News's ongoing coverage of the *Charlie Hebdo* attack featured a terrorism expert, Steve Emerson, discussing Muslim society within the UK. Part of this exposition included the remark that Birmingham – the second-largest city in England – was a Muslim-only community; by the time Emerson acknowledged the error, it had already inspired extensive responses on social media. The #FoxNewsFacts hashtag was used to present deliberately incorrect tweets with humorous intentions (Buchanan, 2015).[29] Fox News is a regular target of critique and ridicule for its right-leaning, conservative and exclusively pro-American stance in its coverage (and this is once more not a social media-only phenomenon), and the watchdog-like functions of social media document and spread Fox's errors and blinkered reporting, from screencaps and videos to irreverent hashtaggery.

There is a degree of holding media accountable in the #FoxNewsFacts humour, as a popular topic specifically aimed at highlighting the mistakes of a traditional media source. However, the hashtag is perhaps more reflective of established media cultures, both on social media and within the wider mediasphere: the attitudes of Fox News are not new, and criticism by local and international audiences is similarly long-standing. While the spread of #FoxNewsFacts brought the original gaffe to a wider audience and contributed to the eventual apology, there is a difference between highlighting a media organization's errors and actually instigating changes in attitudes and practices; commercial and corporate success means that Fox, just like other news organizations which attract particular attention on social media (including but not limited to other News Corporation titles), will require more dramatic and extreme circumstances to change than just a humorous hashtag – see, for instance, the changing attitudes and dedicated campaigning against the sexism and objectification apparent in the UK newspaper the *Sun*'s tradition of brazenly featuring topless women on page 3.

Conjecture about the power of digital and social media has also focused on the potential for marginalized individuals and groups to have a voice not otherwise afforded them. Dominant media situations may be challenged by enabling groups not traditionally featured in mainstream channels to share their content, opinions or comments. This can be personalized, as in rotation curation projects highlighting indigenous experiences. Counteracting oppressive governments or regimes and tightly controlled media systems is also possible – to a certain extent – through online platforms. Individually, blogs, Twitter, Facebook, Tumblr and other popular platforms might be co-opted for sharing updates and reports in the face of oppression; collectively, sites like *Global Voices* collate and curate international citizen reporting and campaign for tolerance, human rights and political freedoms.

While social media discussions and other online approaches challenge and critique problematic norms and practices, promoting alternative behaviours, these same abilities mean that the opposing voices can be subject to abuse, threats and worse in defence of the status quo. The opportunities provided by social media to promote what would be seen as positive and necessary changes in attitudes and practices are then also applicable to challenges to these changes: users variously confront and promulgate problematic social norms. The power and potential of social media are thus not always a positive or supportive change; their dynamics and relations, though, continue to evolve, with new platforms, practices, users and technologies shaped by wider political, social and cultural contexts.

Conclusion

This chapter has examined the impact of social media users and content on traditional media and political power and dynamics. From early alternative media and citizen journalism projects, to blogs and then Twitter, online platforms challenged and changed the coverage of news and politics by professional and amateur voices alike. Despite the fears or claims of blogging and its ilk seeking to replace journalism, what this chapter has demonstrated instead is a mediasphere where both the mainstream and the new are important influences – for audiences and for one another.

The mainstream media impact upon social media, and vice versa; within this dynamic, acceptance, co-option and resistance are taking place, and it becomes increasingly difficult to distinguish between the old and the new. Indeed, delineating between the mainstream and social as completely separate entities is reductive and simplistic. The former are represented on the latter, and embrace social media practices such as audience participation and shared experiences through hashtags and politically oriented live-tweeting. The ritual of such backchannels underlines the continued importance of mainstream media content and the adoption of social media as reactionary platforms: social media users are political media omnivores, consuming mainstream and alternative sources alike and engaging with different contexts on newer platforms.

This chapter has examined an augmented and ameliorated media ecology that offers public and centralized mechanisms for sharing, challenging and correcting if necessary as well as contributing new content, and the views towards relevant platforms by traditional actors in the political mediasphere. This has generally focused on patterns that have emerged over time, reflective of everyday uses and fairly routine topical contexts. In the next chapter, I look at the extraordinary, through the lens of breaking news, scandals and crises, to demonstrate how these patterns shape – and are confirmed and challenged – by uncertainty and rapidly unfolding events.

4

Breaking News, Scandals and Crises

I will not be lectured on sexism and misogyny by this man.

So declared the Australian Prime Minister Julia Gillard in the middle of a riposte to Leader of the Opposition Tony Abbott during Parliamentary Question Time, on 9 October 2012. For fifteen minutes, Gillard spoke passionately and angrily about Abbott's sexism and misogyny, about the treatment she had to endure as a female politician and as Prime Minister (for video of the speech, see ABC News, 2012; for the transcript, see Commonwealth of Australia, 2012).

This moment had been coming. Gillard, the first female Prime Minister in Australia's history, had been the subject of misogynistic commentary in parliament, the Australian news media and in general for an extended period, including remarks about her unmarried and childless status. Only a fortnight earlier, radio broadcaster Alan Jones had been widely condemned for suggesting in a speech at the Sydney University Liberal Club that Gillard's recently deceased father had 'died of shame' given Jones's view of Gillard's performance as politician. This sentiment was seemingly echoed in the motion moved that day against the embattled Speaker, Peter Slipper, who was at the time accused of sexual harassment and misusing taxpayer funds: Tony Abbott repeatedly used the word 'shame', and claimed that the government should have 'died of shame' following its appointment of Slipper as Speaker. Gillard's reply to this motion was then a very public and personal response to recent events as well as the long-standing elements of misogyny and sexism within Australian politics.

Reports of Gillard's speech spread quickly. Question Time was screened live on the ABC and streamed on its website, and live updates on blogs, Twitter, Facebook and news websites highlighted choice quotes as they happened. The ABC put the video of the speech on its website and on YouTube soon after Gillard concluded. Its spread was not limited to Australia; the speech attracted attention from commentators and audiences around the world.

The social media response to Gillard's unexpected diatribe demonstrates how breaking news is spread using online platforms, and how stories evolve from initial media events to diverse topical interpretations. In the case of the misogyny speech, tweets linking to the video spread across the Australian Twittersphere and beyond (for network analysis of this case, see Bruns and Sauter, 2014). As the video spread locally and internationally, the accompanying commentary extended its focus by positioning the speech within wider feminist critiques of contemporary politics and societal attitudes. These patterns are also apparent within other unfolding events documented online, such as crises, disasters and scandals. Such cases are examples of extraordinary politics rather than the everyday; however, they are flashpoints that can serve to highlight and amplify trends, practices and attitudes which have long been part of the background hum of everyday politics.

News and Politics as They Happen: Unfolding Events and Sense-Making on Social Media

The immediacy of publication and ease of disseminating information, as well as their ubiquity within everyday communication, make online platforms central to the coverage of breaking news. Reporting on events as they happen occurs through tweets and posts, accompanied by audio and visual documentation: news-gathering and production is socially mediated in the same manner as everyday life, presented first, in brief, on social media and followed by coverage in full on news websites and traditional media. Initial social media coverage helps to break a story, supplemented and revised by follow-up posts, tweets and analysis – although it can also distract from issues, and sensationalize and over-hype non-events.

Contributing to the dissemination of breaking news is the ability for information to be shared immediately, across networks, platforms and devices. The affordances of social media platforms, including functions of retweeting, sharing and reblogging, enable content to be circulated among a user's friends and followers without requiring additional contributions. Ease of publication and a diverse media diet also mean that social media users, in addition to journalists, are part of the information curation and sense-making processes taking place around unfolding events. Within crises and unrest, those sharing information from affected areas are often not professional reporters, but their messages are noticed and amplified as their first-hand coverage spreads through the mediasphere.

Live sense-making of breaking news and current events can be collaborative and curated online. Gathering together the various social media contributions, from professional and amateur sources alike, may involve further adaptations and affordances of existing platforms. The *Guardian*'s use of the live-blogging format has become a central part of its coverage of unfolding events, whether breaking news or Saturday afternoon sport (Thurman and Walters, 2013). Offering updates and analysis as they happen, the blogs – in scope if not in name – have evolved over time in response to corresponding technological developments and improvements. Where reverse-chronological live coverage in 2005 was predominantly text-only, the equivalent reporting in 2015 incorporates dynamic updates, embedded tweets, videos, photos, contributions from readers via email and social media and comments. The live blogs serve as a repository for journalists and their audience, collectively engaged in observing and making sense of an event. They are curated assemblages of relevant commentary from across the (social) mediasphere: highlighting tweets of interest denotes the awareness of additional coverage taking place on other platforms (and alternative ways of interacting with the writers running the blogs), while the longer-form freedom of the live blog allows for more extensive reflection than would be found in a tweet.

Social media information flows

The impact of online platforms on how information is sourced and shared has been the subject of research investigating, variously, news flows and coverage, including on Twitter (Kwak et al., 2010), Digg (Lerman and Ghosh, 2010) and social media overall (Nahon and Hemsley, 2013). The networked aspect of online communication, through the relationships between users supported by individual platforms, has afforded the opportunity for applying and updating theories of information-sharing to the new media context. Concepts like the two-step flow of information (Katz and Lazarsfeld, 1964), where in a mass media environment news went from the traditional media and political figures to individuals acting as 'opinion leaders' for others, filtering and framing information, can be reimagined for the contemporary mediasphere; adaptations of the two-step flow have responded to the increased abilities of individuals to source and interpret information online (for example, Bennett and Manheim, 2006).

The flow of information across and between social media platforms is an important consideration for the coverage of news and politics – and for everyday practices, since the mechanisms at play are applicable to the sharing of information outside of breaking news, scandals or crises. Building on the ideas raised in the previous chapter about the interplay between traditional and new media, this chapter explores the roles played by social media users in disseminating and framing news as it happens. This includes the dynamics apparent between mainstream media and social media and the presence of intermedia news flows, as information is shared, challenged, supplemented and updated as it moves between users and platforms.

Social Media Omnipresence

The mechanisms for sharing news as it happens, including image and video material in addition to text reports, are used in everyday contexts. The widespread dissemination of Julia Gillard's misogyny speech is an example of breaking news amid more mundane circumstances – it was an unprecedented condemnation, occurring without warning in an otherwise routine parliamentary sitting day. Sharing the Gillard speech online included several social media elements: tweeted coverage of the remarks and live quoting; links to the live stream or details of the ABC broadcast of Question Time; links to the video and story posted by the ABC; transcripts offered by various sources; and ongoing analysis and commentary in tweets, statuses and longer-form blog posts and news articles. These represent professional, journalistic content (on traditional and new media) and contributions by other social media users. Constructing the narrative of the Gillard speech and its aftermath, as with other breaking news contexts, involves a diversity of resources and media types, a reflection of omnivorous news tendencies enabled by social media.

These patterns around the consumption, presentation and sharing of news on social media highlight 'social infomediation', which is the result of the interactions between 'content, sharing platforms, and users' (Smyrnaios and Rieder, 2013, p. 361). The different affordances and architecture of social media platforms impact upon what is seen and shared – the algorithms determining visibility of trending topics or news feed items, for instance – and Smyrnaois and Rieder also note the influence of social media users' appetite for news and content-sharing on this process. Platforms like YouTube, Twitter and Facebook offer different mechanisms for publishing and sharing content. Together, these platforms are used every day as part of a multi-platform approach to communicating, interacting and informing.

The processes of social infomediation studied by Smyrnaois and Rieder were identified on Twitter, but similar patterns have been apparent on other platforms, pre-social media. Specific blogging types developed around fulfilling a news collation role, including filter and link blogs providing lists of articles of interest, around multiple topics and in response to current events. Other political bloggers would also draw upon diverse sources in their analysis and framing of issues. This was particularly apparent for bloggers whose coverage was specialized around their own interests, such as environmental concerns or economics, for they would use relevant, topic-specific resources in addition to mainstream news media, alternative media and popular online platforms.

The curated approach to covering political news extended to repositioning events around themes and frames more relevant to individual bloggers. For instance, as a major news and political event, the inauguration of Barack Obama for his first term as US President in January 2009 was discussed by political bloggers in Australia and France (and elsewhere) (this case is examined in full in Highfield, 2011). Although common themes emerged from the two networks, from commenting on the inauguration ceremony itself to the global financial crisis, military action in Afghanistan and Iraq and US foreign policy, French bloggers were more likely to frame the Obama inauguration within their own domestic political context. In particular, the ongoing coverage of Nicolas Sarkozy within the French political blogosphere meant that Obama was often mentioned as a secondary element or used as an impetus for more posts discussing Sarkozy.

French bloggers discussing the inauguration linked primarily to local mainstream media in their topical posts, but Australian bloggers used more international sources in their inauguration coverage. The focus on the international rather than the domestic also saw Australian bloggers discuss the inauguration without recontexualization: their posts did not extensively frame the inauguration within local political contexts, but rather raised topics like climate change or internet policy in opining on what the Obama presidency would, or should, do. The use of a mix of international and local, mainstream and alternative media in discussing the Obama inauguration highlights the capabilities and tendencies of social media users to choose from an extensive array of voices and analyses beyond the traditional, dominant sources.

This diversity within the coverage of current events is apparent on other platforms. The long-term tracking of links to Australian news sites on Twitter has identified the most popular sources (and fluctuations over time), and also the overlap between audiences. Twitter users cite a variety of mainstream and alternative, broadsheet and tabloid publications (Bruns et al., 2013). Of course, the intent behind the links may vary dramatically: a citation might be to highlight offensive commentary or questionable journalism, just as it might imply an article's quality or interest. However, there is an awareness and engagement with an extended range of media sources online, used together and discussed further on social media in the coverage of breaking news and everyday topics alike.

These discussions also foster the evolution of stories on social media, with different themes, styles and perspectives accompanying unfolding events. The changing scope of news commentary is seen in examples like the Twitter coverage of the doping scandal that dogged controversial American cyclist Lance Armstrong in 2012 and 2013 (Highfield, 2015b). Cheating allegations had followed Armstrong throughout his career, especially during his record seven Tour de France victories. The rumours intensified in mid-2012, amid suggestions that former team-mates had testified against Armstrong. Over the following months, the scandal continued to unfold, with its eventual denouement coming in January 2013 when Armstrong confessed to doping throughout his career in an interview with Oprah Winfrey. Having maintained his innocence throughout his career, Armstrong's fans responded to the initial rumours by defending the cyclist and attacking the anti-doping authority's apparent 'witch-hunt'. This was not a universal stance, though: Armstrong had not been the most affable of public figures during his career, including in his relationship with the cycling media and confronting journalists who alleged that he had doped.

By the time of the Oprah interviews, the scandal's coverage had changed tone, form and audience. Rather than a sudden, unprecedented story breaking and shared through mainstream channels first, Armstrong's confession unfolded through a broadcast that was seen by many people simultaneously (and where the content was expected). The live-tweeting of Armstrong's confession demonstrates ritualized practices within a breaking news context. Portmanteaunic hashtags, mixing snark and topicality, were used to frame tweets, including popular examples playing on Armstrong's Livestrong Foundation – #livewrong and #liestrong – as well as the interview-specific #doprah. These emergent hashtags came about during the interviews, and their spread is another element of information flows on social media: it is not just the news and opinion that are shared, but additional means of framing and denoting these topics. Snark and topical irreverence also combined news stories in commentary, using juxtaposition and incongruity as mechanisms for original interpretations of news. Comments published in August 2012 included tweets referencing both Lance and the recently deceased astronaut Neil Armstrong, while tweets during the interviews referenced the concurrent scandal involving American footballer Manti Te'o and the revelation that he had been hoaxed in an online relationship.

This breaking news context shows a diversity of unfocused social media practices, from reporting and sharing news to presenting topical humour as commentary or meta-commentary. The ritualized aspects of how a media event plays out on social media, including the styles of coverage such as backchannels and the importance of irreverence, snark and wordplay, are not unique to the Armstrong context. Some events, though, while still receiving a mix of serious and silly coverage, encourage more of the former than the latter, and different practices around information flows, tone and participation from social media users.

Crisis Communication

For many, disasters and crises are not everyday occurrences,[30] but they have significant influence on how online tools and platforms are used for communication. The need for information to be shared quickly and widely makes social media important resources, especially given the extensive user bases for popular platforms, distributed infrastructure and mobile access. While not the only channels used at these times, politicians, government departments and public authorities employ social media to push information, and attempt to control the messages being promoted by vouching for their veracity. Broadcasters and mainstream media are similarly active here as part of their emergency coverage.

The use of online platforms and tools for crisis communication, relief efforts and sense-making has been studied in response to numerous disasters and crises, including the Haitian earthquake in 2010 (Meier, 2012; Zook et al., 2010) and the terrorist attack in Oslo, Norway, the same year (Kaufmann, 2015). Crises and unforeseen events also influence how social media are used in general. Hashtags on Twitter initially emerged for crisis communications purposes through the use of keywords preceded by the # symbol as a marker for tweets about bushfires in California in 2007 (Halavais, 2013; Messina, 2007). This built on the use of the '#[keyword/channel name]' marker in earlier online communication spaces, including internet relay chat (IRC); but in its initial form the Twitter hashtag was an informal practice: only in 2009 did Twitter officially support hashtags, automatically turning them into links to searches for other tagged comments.

Within crises, hashtags are critical elements of online communication, acting to centralize important information.[31] A common marker allows social media users to find relevant details among the wider coverage of the unfolding events, the hashtag acting as an unstructured and automated aggregator of information (although at times swamped by personal responses from distant observers rather than critical updates). Hashtags are the result of negotiation and contestation: an unforeseen event might give rise to several rival hashtags about the same crisis before one becomes popularly used (and promoted as 'official'). This is seen through #eqnz, which gained visibility in response to earthquakes and aftershocks in Christchurch, New Zealand, in 2010 and 2011, and, having now been established as a crisis communications channel on Twitter, has since been employed following other seismic activity in New Zealand. Similarly, the #qldfloods marker was established during devastating flooding in Brisbane and other parts of southeast Queensland in January 2011, but in being temporally non-specific has been reused following floods in other parts of the state post-2011. These markers are specific to particular types of event, but general enough to be applicable to relevant examples distributed over time and geography: while #eqnz was initially associated with Christchurch, for instance, it has also been used in response to distinctly separate cases in other parts of the country.

The extensive analysis of the Twitter response to the 2011 Queensland floods provides a rich overview of social media and crisis communication, from organizational, sense-making and personal and affective perspectives (for full details, see Bruns et al., 2012; F. Shaw et al., 2013). It also highlights the Western – and predominantly Anglocentric – context of the social media platforms I have focused on in this book, since support for Twitter hashtags in non-Latin script was not immediate. Tweeting in Japanese in response to the 2011 tsunami and earthquake, for instance, required combining scripts as the hashtag functionality had not yet extended to the kanji and kana writing systems (see Johnson, 2014). In her analysis of the post-tsunami Twitter activity, Johnson notes how Twitter Japan provided explanatory material about hashtags using Latin script, including nominating markers to use. Rather than the ad hoc origins of other crisis (and mundane) hashtags, where users drive developments, Twitter Japan's approach suggests that the platform is getting involved in directing new activities and practices (at least at a time when efficiency is paramount).

Within these socially mediated responses to crises, key actors include government bodies and emergency services, humanitarian and charity organizations and media (both mainstream and social, as seen in Twitter's own involvement in Japan). During the 2011 Queensland floods, prominent accounts among the #qldfloods activity on Twitter – as determined by retweets received and @mentions and @replies directed at them – included major news media, political figures and emergency services (Bruns et al., 2012). Within such contexts as crises, social media information flows become more reliant on traditional actors – emergency services, government bodies, mainstream media – than may be seen in other, everyday settings. However, individuals still play a part in sharing information. As Bruns et al. (2012) note, successful crisis communication practices from traditional actors rely on their messages being 'able to "cut through" effectively: to reach [their] immediate audience as well as be passed along and thus amplified many times over, with the help of other Twitter users acting as further information disseminators especially at the height of the crisis' (p. 48). For emergency services and authorities, everyday social media strategies are important for times of crisis: understanding the messages being published, what kind of information is most important, how to frame it for the specific platforms being used, are critical during disasters, but regular engagement with social media outside of these periods develops skills in this area. Awareness of the conventions and affordances of social media within everyday contexts is a useful foundation for application within crisis communication.

Crises, disasters, terror and unrest encourage highly affective responses, documented in text and visual media which highlight the extreme personal experiences taking place – the 'intimate banalities' described by Hjorth and Burgess (2014). However, the application of social media for widely and immediately circulating content of interest is not always accompanied by similarly instantaneous verification processes. Fake images are shared to depict false accounts of unrest and disaster. Repurposed photos from other disasters and crises, as well as photoshopped images, have been found on social media alongside the authentic coverage of various incidents (without users necessarily realizing that they are fake), from the impact of Hurricane Sandy on New York City in 2012 to the unrest and protests in London in 2011 and Baltimore in 2015 (Burgess et al., 2012; Johnson, 2014; mac Suibhne, 2015; Vis et al., 2013). These images may be used to present false accounts of the extent of damage, and of the identities and strategies of protest (including rioting and looting), and this is an issue relevant to social media activity in other contexts. To this end, in response specifically to memes and viral scambaiting images which encourage and promulgate racist attitudes (see chapter 1), Nakamura (2014) argues for a 'social media image ethics', since 'as memetic pleasures figure ever more largely in our lives within digital media, the origins of these images matter even more' (p. 260).

Information-sharing, collaborative projects

Although fake images offer an unhelpful, misleading, and at times malicious representation of crises, other social media activity within these contexts reflects more compassionate and constructive aims. The response to crises and disasters includes relief efforts, sharing information, coordinating aid and fundraising. These take formal and informal forms, realized through dedicated crowdsourced and collaborative platforms and more ad hoc hashtagged reactions. The crisis mapping platform Ushahidi was first used to monitor disputes and violence in Kenya following the 2007 presidential election, but has since been employed for disaster relief in response to incidents like the Haitian earthquake in 2010 (Meier, 2012; Zook et al., 2010). Similar projects employing crowdsourcing and collaborative mapping to obtain and share information, supported by institutional backing and tools, have variously mapped fires, earthquake effects and recovery efforts in New Orleans following Hurricane Katrina in 2005 (Liu and Palen, 2010). These projects often rely on volunteered geographic information in charting disasters and relief efforts, complementing humanitarian and government responses.

Other responses to crises offer alternative information flows, by challenging or counteracting existing media situations and by promoting new narratives and counter-narratives. Monroy-Hernández et al. (2013) analyse the tweeting practices of 'civic media curators' contributing information and commentary within the context of the Mexican drug war. By collating reports and media, these users share content that is not necessarily featured within traditional media, positioned as being 'collectively engaged in resistance to both the flawed media ecosystem and the powerful role of the drug cartels' (p. 1450). As with other crisis contexts, though, the curation of social media posts in a highly volatile setting like the Mexican drug war is accompanied by the risk of misinformation and unverified rumours – as well as personal danger if curators' anonymous identities become compromised.

Collaborative and curatorial approaches to information-sharing are witnessed in other political contexts. Investigating collaborative and interactive mapping within protests, Rodríguez-Amat and Brantner (2014) link these processes to the construction of identity. There is a strong connection between activism and place, visible both through the use of locative media and representations of place, and through the symbolic applications of the online in standing in for physical locations (Croeser and Highfield, 2014; for locative media in detail, see Wilken and Goggin, 2015). This relationship between place and social media is also examined in Amy Johnson's (2014) study of 'changing choreographies of place' within the context of Twitter and the March 2011 tsunami and Fukushima nuclear disaster in Japan.

Collaborative disaster responses can also take more informal approaches. When riots broke out in London, and later in other parts of the UK in 2011, social media were used to share information about the unrest. This included documenting violence, providing live updates from the scene, and sharing commentary and opinions, images and videos (Procter et al., 2013; Vis, 2013). However, social media and mobile communication (in particular BlackBerry messages) were criticized for possibly enflaming the riots further, helping to spread the violence and used for provocation (discussed by Hands, 2014; McCosker and Johns, 2013). Once again, though, these same mechanisms were used for practices that would be viewed more positively; the #riotcleanup hashtag, and related undertakings on other social media platforms, show a grassroots mobilization to fix the damage caused by the riots (Glasgow and Fink, 2013). The political is the inspiration for, but not necessarily the subject of, the activity. Regardless of the view individuals might have of the causes promoted by those rioting, cleaning up afterwards is a social necessity – or a means of differentiating those cleaning from the 'criminal' rioters, creating what Hands (2014) describes as 'a manifestation of a truly bourgeois phenomenon, an *idiotic collective*, keeping the neighborhood spic and span and transforming it ever more into an enclosed and gated idiot space' (p. 245).[32] Social media in this context are used for organization (and other functions) for collective action purposes, discussed further in chapter 5. #riotcleanup might not be an explicit protest movement – and is certainly not immune to critique (Fuchs, 2012; Hands, 2014) – but its associated social media practices are demonstrative of ideas and rationales that can also be seen in, for example, social media use within the Occupy movement.

As with the other aspects of social media and politics I have discussed, though, it is crucial to remember that these platforms are not the sole means that are used for these purposes. Disaster relief projects incorporate various media and devices appropriate for their specific context (including what infrastructure is available following natural disasters). Crawford and Finn (2015) highlight how text messaging and email, along with social media contributions, are used for collaborative mapping and information-sharing. This raises immediate issues for research (and for the projects themselves), including analytical and ethical concerns regarding the inclusion of diverse data sources, of varying degrees of publicness and visibility, within studies of social media crisis communication, and about the publication of personal or private communication within public, collaborative responses to crises.

Social Media Omnishambles

The ever-present nature of social media, online tools and smartphones for sharing information and communal sense-making is not always a boon. Unfolding events also highlight the caveats concerning social media: that not all information that is circulated is accurate, and that corrections are not necessarily going to follow or reach the same audience. Misinformation occurs deliberately and less maliciously (but still sharing unverified and erroneous material). Fake images shared online during crises can present particular false illustrations of rioting and looting, placing blame on innocent people and promoting racist or intolerant agendas, or of the extent of damage from natural disasters. These contexts are also subject to trolling, both during disasters and after the fact, as fakery and hoaxing can promote different agendas. Whitney Phillips (2015) uses the creation of GIFs and photoshopping images of the 9/11 terrorist attacks in the US to demonstrate 'the complimentary relationship between trolling humor and mass – and in this case, digitally – mediated disaster coverage' (p. 117) (see also Frank, 2004). At other times, incorrect information shared widely is not deliberately misleading or serving trolling purposes, but it encourages further scrutiny alongside the potential benefits of social media at times of crisis.

reddit and the Boston Marathon bombing

On 15 March 2013, explosions at the Boston Marathon resulted in the deaths of three people, extensive injuries and a city-wide shutdown and police manhunt, vividly documented online from Bostonians and external observers. Embracing the information-sharing and collaborative abilities that had been witnessed in other crises and the aftermath of major crimes, internet users became detectives, seeking out details about the attack and possible suspects. This documentation took place across social media, with images shared across platforms and tweets providing live accounts of police movements. Attention to the manhunt and the grassroots investigation was focused on reddit, as it had in July 2012 when seeking information about the shooter in the Aurora Theater mass shooting in Colorado; however, the Boston Marathon is not an example of social media getting it right. As Hermida (2014) argues, 'While the Aurora shooting demonstrated the wisdom of the crowd, the marathon bombings exposed the madness of the mob' (p. 12).[33]

The convergence of platforms and audiences has led to multiple forms of online participation and response within crisis and disaster contexts. Unlike disasters like the 2004 tsunami or the 2005 London bombings, where a clearer delineation was possible between those directly affected, providing citizen journalism and similar content from the scene, and those following online, the 'as it happens' documentation of crises on Facebook, Twitter and other platforms features different levels of contributing bystander: Tapia et al.'s (2014) analysis of social media following the Boston bombing identifies immediate, original bystanders and those participating virtually, collating new information and investigations online.

Popular social media such as Twitter and Facebook were used for sharing information about the attack and the manhunt, but what also attracted attention was the detective work carried out on reddit and 4chan. While much focus on social media and crises has been on Twitter, this is not the only platform used for crisis communication and disaster responses. The more specialized user base of reddit and 4chan, though, means that their contributions were not always widely noticed. The Boston Marathon bombing, then, represents 'one of the first crises where both spaces were highly visible to those outside of their communities' (Potts and Harrison, 2013, p. 144).

In the aftermath of the bombing, the FBI publicly released information, asking for assistance from civilians in helping to identify suspects and deconstruct events. The investigations continued for several days before the authorities released photographs and details of the confirmed suspects, whose killing of a police officer led to a manhunt that left one suspect dead and the other captured on 19 March. During this period, though, the online detective work had clearly identified and shared details about several suspects – the problem being that these people were not connected to the attack.

When the FBI had appealed to the public for information and assistance, dedicated channels on social media platforms were established to analyse and investigate different aspects of the incident. These are explored in detail by Potts and Harrison (2013), in particular the think tank contributions of 4chan in working through visual records of possible suspects, and the subreddit /FindBostonBombers. What is underlined by these analyses is the importance of visual documentation – of individuals, the bombing and its aftermath (see also S. Allan, 2014; Mortensen, 2015) – and the personal digital traces and records available for grassroots investigations. The distributed resources available to these socially mediated detective efforts allowed research to be extensive and immediate, drawing on the volunteered time of contributors – which could also mean that plausible but unverified information was spread quickly before authentication, and more extensively than any follow-up corrections. While hosted on specific platforms like the subreddit, these investigations were also shared and discussed on other social media and in mainstream media coverage, amplifying their findings and leads, whether accurate or not (Tapia et al., 2014).

Misinformation – deliberate or unintentional – was a prominent part of the social media activity occurring during the manhunts after the attack (Maddock et al., 2015; Starbird et al., 2014). The contexts for misinformation vary.[34] It can come from commentary about an event or attempt to influence a particular interpretation (and can be quickly identified as fake based on elements including presentation style – see Potts and Harrison, 2013). It can also come from the speed of collaborative investigations online, based on unverified information. The material available for carrying out social media detective work makes following leads and sharing resources a valid option for users, crowdsourcing their enquiries and having participants across time zones and countries. The permanence of online content, though, means that rumours and wrongful accusations involving publishing individuals' personal details are not automatically undone by apologies and corrections. In their study of Twitter and misinformation and rumours following the Boston Marathon bombing, Starbird et al. (2014) found that the unverified reports were published more often than their subsequent corrections. While some examples of misinformation, like the incorrect explicit identification of a suspect found to be deceased, saw very definite corrections put an end to their circulation, other rumours continued to receive retweets after they had been debunked.

The publication of personal information about suspects later found to be unconnected to the bombing was not restricted to social media: mainstream media reported on the leads in the social media investigations, including noting the (innocent) suspects. In general, journalists have clear mechanisms and extensive resources for verifying material sourced online (Schifferes et al., 2014). The recirculation of incorrect information drawn from reddit, though, demonstrates this was not universally employed after the Boston bombing.

The habitual usage of social media as a means of documenting everyday life and sharing information was also an inconvenience for the police response to the Boston bombing, and in other crisis situations like the Sydney siege in December 2014. Social media users were reporting on police actions in their own vicinities and sharing details taken from police scanners – and indeed listening into these channels via online streams – but were subsequently asked not to share details of police movements since popular social media were also being monitored by the subjects of the police operations. While valuable mechanisms for widely disseminating information during crises, then, the advantages of social media were also perceived to have several less positive, if unintended, implications.

It should also be noted, though, that the failings of the /FindBostonBombers subreddit were not reflective of the community norms and rules set out on reddit, especially in revealing personal, identifiable information about individuals (Potts and Harrison, 2013). As the subreddit attracted more attention, it was made private and apologies were issued about its erroneous accusations. This response is part of the 'self-correcting crowd' (Starbird et al., 2014, p. 654) apparent in the social media coverage of the Boston bombing. Although the corrections to misinformation did not receive the same levels of activity as the original rumours they were debunking, there were still attempts made to counter inaccurate stories originating from social media sources (just as social media users will also attempt to hold mainstream sources accountable) (Maddock et al., 2015). The various rumours spread, including the report of a young spectator killed in the attack that turned into the tragic, but false, story of an eight-year-old girl killed running the marathon, also highlight a further, popular element of the socially mediated coverage of crises and breaking news: the affective framing of narratives and sub-narratives within these events.

Emergent, Affective Social Media

The omnipresence of social media within the coverage of breaking news, crises and scandals, and its positive and negative impacts, mean that numerous narratives and counter-narratives are at play within this activity. Crisis communication is not solely responding to one aspect of a natural disaster but features sub-themes around critical information, personal requests for help, reports from affected areas and thankful comments following aid and support (F. Shaw et al., 2013). As events develop, new narratives emerge in response to different issues and topics. These might remain peripheral to the main coverage of breaking news or crises, but in some cases new perspectives and framings might redirect discussions, presenting new and affective interpretations of current events.

#illridewithyou and evolving frames

On the morning of 15 December 2014, customers and employees at the Lindt cafe in central Sydney suddenly became part of a siege situation, taken hostage by a lone gunman, Man Haron Monis. The area around the cafe was shut down, with police establishing an exclusion zone as they attempted to negotiate with the gunman. Over the following sixteen hours, the siege was maintained, punctuated by occasional successful escapes on the part of hostages, until a police raid led to the end of the siege, leaving two hostages and Monis dead.

Monis was acting alone; while he claimed to be representing the Islamic State in his attack, local Muslim groups condemned the actions. Honis had also been previously convicted for harassment and was facing charges of sexual assault at the time of the siege. As the standoff between the gunman and the police continued, new information (verified and rumoured) circulated through the mediasphere, attempting to identify what was happening, who was involved and why. As with other breaking news contexts, this reporting and analysis involved traditional and social media alike, with journalists, the New South Wales government and emergency services sharing messages through multiple platforms.

The Sydney siege highlights further how everyday social media practices intersect with unfolding events, disasters and breaking news. Crises impact upon mundane experiences, making them more exceptional. As the siege continued, reports from the scene commented on – and criticized – people coming down to the exclusion zone opposite the Lindt cafe in order to take selfies (Dow, 2014; White and Di Stefano, 2014). The documentation of everyday experiences through selfies and smartphone photography extended to the siege – indeed, as an extraordinary occurrence it set it apart from an individual's regular routine and images – so the appeal of the siege selfie is perhaps understandable, even if a lack of awareness and empathy is also apparent. The flow-on effect of the siege on Sydney through the shutdown of central areas of the city, and thus its transport infrastructure, also had implications for actions reliant on social and mobile media. Sydney users of the crowdsourced taxi app Uber reported a major price hike as demand for the service surged due to the siege, although following extensive criticism and outrage – on social media and elsewhere – the company reversed this completely by making rides in the area free (Bel, 2014; Cresci, 2014).

However, perhaps the most pertinent – and unexpected – social media-led outcome following the siege was #illridewithyou. Again, the combination of political and personal, the exceptional and the everyday, came to the fore. Initial speculation (and misinformation) about the background and motivations of the hostage-taker had provoked fears about racist and anti-Islamic sentiment. This was especially pertinent given previous Australian history of racism (see, for example, Hartley and Green, 2006), and the various applications (and fears) of social media for combating and perpetuating racist stereotypes and fuelling hatespeech (McEnery et al., 2015). In response, as the workday finished and the siege continued, a new hashtag emerged: #illridewithyou (ABC News, 2014). This marker was intended for social media users to provide support and company (especially physical solidarity) for Muslims in

Sydney, and elsewhere, who felt threatened using public transport given sentiments provoked by the siege. The outpouring of support for this hashtag – on Twitter and across other platforms – was seen as a positive outcome, especially in demonstrating the prominence of tolerant views among Australian society.

This is not to say that there was no criticism; the campaign was also seen as simplistic and a further demonstration of white privilege, and encouraged practices that should already be commonplace for all public transport users, regardless of gender, race, ethnicity, age or religion. However, the intentions behind the hashtag showed a desire to change attitudes and to foster community spirit which had been absent, and which could be swamped by more xenophobic and racist attitudes. The coverage of the hashtag also prompted an additional angle in the siege coverage itself, through reporting on this ad hoc, community-led campaign and the prevailing public sentiment.

As an emotional and personal response to breaking news, #illridewithyou marks a transition in the social media coverage from news event to ambient, affective aftermath. While the siege and its reporting continued, the social media discussion brought forth an additional focus. What social media could contribute to the actual siege reporting is questionable, beyond circulating statements and confirmed details from sources involved in the police operation and negotiations. However, the #illridewithyou campaign – and its use of a separate hashtag to delineate the discussion and potentially avoid swamping hashtags used for sharing critical information – was an approach that social media users could participate in and contribute to. Its influence extended beyond the Sydney siege, too. In the aftermath of the *Charlie Hebdo* tragedy in Paris in January 2015, French social media users promoted their local version of #illridewithyou – #voyageavecmoi – in response to similar social, political, cultural and religious tensions and unease (Lexpress.fr, 2015). In tweeting and posting to Instagram or Facebook about taking public transport home, social media users are documenting the highly mundane; in the #illridewithyou context, though, the personal is also suddenly a very affective political expression.

Conclusion

Affective publics in the form of social media discussions emerging from major news and political events are not new, but they demonstrate the continued practices of engaging with and reshaping debates online. The connections with other contexts, such as protests and collective action, are also clear. Weeks prior to the Sydney siege, outrage in the US focused on Ferguson, Missouri, and Staten Island, New York, generated mass demonstrations across American cities and online (Bonilla and Rosa, 2015). Accompanying these protests was social media coverage, from live-streaming and updates from marches (as will be discussed further in the following chapter) to reflective, political and empathetic publics.

The #CrimingWhileWhite hashtag, for example, was a consideration of white privilege in the face of the targeted police oppression experienced by Black Americans. By documenting criminal and antisocial activities that individuals had done and got away with, white Americans acknowledged the racial divide present in US society and their own positions of (relative) power and safety. While these comments were intended to be displays of solidarity and support, the #CrimingWhileWhite was criticized for doing what it aimed to change: by turning the discussion back to white America, it was ignoring, overpowering or not giving attention to the voices that were being specifically discriminated against in the first place. In response, the #AliveWhileBlack hashtag documented Black Americans' experiences with the police, returning to the original context in an additional affective public (Galo, 2014).

While these publics were clear reactions to particular triggers, there are long-running hashtags with similar intentions to #CrimingWhileWhite and #AliveWhileBlack, documenting discrimination, prejudice and offensive behaviour directed at others, and which overlap and intersect. #everydaysexism, for example, highlights experiences from women that demonstrate the sheer pervasiveness of sexist and misogynist attitudes in society. In the following chapter, *Everyday Sexism* is featured alongside other examples of collective and connective action that respond to everyday political themes as well as protest and activist movements.

5

Collective and Connective Action

In February 2006, I was studying in Lille in northern France. What began as a bit of culture and climate shock (going from the heat of the Australian summer to an actual winter), became an extremely different educational experience when Dominique de Villepin, the French Prime Minister, proposed new legislation aimed at reducing youth unemployment. In the process, though, de Villepin's *contrat première embauche* (CPE) would also permit employers to terminate the contracts of first-time employees without warning – a decision that many noted would not reduce the sense of precarity for under-25s in France.

The reaction across the country was, as the stereotypical perception of the French would suggest, to go on strike; across the *hexagone*, universities were blockaded by student groups, occupied to prevent access to classes, exams or meetings, with support from university staff and unions. International media attention was drawn to the Sorbonne, the bastion of Parisian higher education, which was the site of demonstrations featuring riot police, tear gas and burning cars. Marches in other parts of the country were less violent, although there remained a whiff of pepper spray in the early spring air.

The university at which I was studying was one of the first in the country to go on strike, and the *blocage* of the campus continued for weeks. Back in 2006, sans smartphone or text message updates from university administration, my friends and I would rely on online updates about the strikes in order to find out what was going on, including whether it was actually worth walking thirty minutes in the cold only to find that the campus was still closed. The updates we sourced were not just from the university website; indeed, the more frequent and informative bulletins came from websites organized by student activists and by localized alternative media. Student groups set up blogs providing reports from meetings and details of marches, representing campuses from around France (and linking to other anti-CPE student groups in the region). *Indymedia*, too, was a regular source of information, carrying first-hand experiences of the protests. As the anti-CPE protests continued into March and April, the same approaches were used for opposition to the *blocage* tactic; blogs protesting the blockades were not supporting the CPE, but asking for a return to university and alternative ways of challenging the proposed law (Crouzillacq, 2006; Fansten, 2006).

The Conseil Constitutionnel passed the bill, but in the face of public opinion the President, Jacques Chirac, stepped in and announced that the CPE would be withdrawn; meanwhile, back in Lille, one vote open to the entire student body had been in favour of continuing the occupation, and it was only in early April, just before the Easter break, that the strike officially ended. This was not the end of my experience of the CPE strikes, though: the context of the protests and studying the use of blogs and alternative media for organization and information was, in a sense, my first step on the path which led to this book.

The anti-CPE protests – and the anti-*blocage* movement, too – made use of online technologies as part of their activities, from documentation of meetings and votes to reporting on marches, promoting their own aims and sharing messages of solidarity with other groups around the country. The adoption of social media for collective action – and thus a part of what W. Lance Bennett and Alexandra Segerberg (2013) describe as a 'logic of *connective* action' – has been an element of protests and activist groups around the world in recent years. Indeed, cases such as the Arab Spring and the Occupy movement, and their use of Twitter, Facebook and other social media platforms, have received extensive attention and debate around the extent to which social media were responsible for the movements and their success.

Connective action, as Bennett and Segerberg (2013) describe it, extends notions of collective action within protests and activism, as individuals form groups to campaign for change: within connective action, such political engagement is also personalized and digitally mediated, as social media and other digital technologies offer additional means for organization, information and mobilization (see also Earl and Kimport, 2011). Of course, social media's uses and functions within the collective/connective action context are not limited to just protest movements explicitly demonstrating against governments or regimes. These same logics and practices are apparent in initiatives responding to more everyday political themes, and in campaigns that attempt to make use of everyday social media behaviours. Blogs, Twitter, live-streaming, *Indymedia*, Facebook, email, streaming radio, forums and bulletin boards and other online technologies are employed for activism-related purposes as well as more generic approaches (see David, 2010 on the everyday practices of cameraphones and live-streaming). Digital media are used by activists in demonstrations, and by observers, supporters and opponents. They form part of different strategies in campaigns around the world, from Brazil to Korea (Bastos et al., 2014; Lee, 2015). Protest-specific platforms are not the norm here, although as will be noted later on, the use of popular but commercial platforms is not without its challenges or its concerns, and the rise of Facebook and Twitter has not meant that older forms like blogs or *Indymedia* have been abandoned.

I want to stress that I am not arguing that social media alone cause or sustain protests, demonstrations or revolutions. Similarly, I am not saying that social media are completely irrelevant and a distraction from studying the real movement (otherwise this could be a really short chapter). There are many factors at play here, of which social media, online and mobile communication and media use in general are just part (see Tufekci, 2013; Tufekci and Wilson, 2012), and socially mediated movements have their roots in other forms of activism, protest and campaigns for social justice. However, social media are a key component of social movements' activities, and for providing information about them, bringing visibility and organization.

Collective Action Online

The internet has long been part of the activist communication, organization and mobilization toolkit. From the Zapatistas in Mexico in the 1990s (Garrido and Halavais, 2003) to the World Trade Organization protests and the 'Battle of Seattle' in 1999 (Meikle, 2002), email, alternative media, citizen journalism, e-petitions and online chat platforms have been adopted, and co-opted, for activist purposes, followed later by social networking sites and social media (for a full examination, see Lievrouw, 2011). Technological developments have been quickly integrated for collective action: the rate of change with mobile and smartphones has provided new functionalities, particularly coupled with improved mobile data access and camera capabilities (see, for instance, mobile use by the Indignados in Spain: Monterde and Postill, 2014).

There has been extensive research into popular social media within specific social movements, covering individual platforms and extended social media activism alike (for the latter, for example, see Poell and Borra, 2012). Two prominent cases from 2010 and 2011, the Arab Spring uprisings in the Middle East and North Africa (MENA) and the Occupy Wall Street movement and its global offshoots, have been studied in-depth by scholars from different fields and international perspectives.[35] Comparative research has also enabled examinations of social media use within both activist cases (Gerbaudo, 2012; Papacharissi, 2015). However, as is noted in these studies, and as I will reiterate throughout this chapter, the high levels of social media use (especially the public visibility of tweeting) do not mean that Twitter or Facebook *were* the social movements. Criticisms of – and praise for – 'social media revolutions'[36] (Gladwell, 2010, 2011; Morozov, 2011, 2013; Shirky, 2011) are an overly reductive treatment of a complex situation in which social media variously and concurrently are helpful, banal and problematic (reflective too of the frictions within and between social movements in general, identified by Tsing, 2011).

Part of the criticisms directed at over-ascribing importance to social media within protests have focused on the fleeting engagement with these events by geographically distant online bystanders (to build on ideas raised by Tapia et al., 2014). Tweeting once using a campaign hashtag, signing an online petition or changing a user icon in solidarity can demonstrate engagement with an issue or movement, but not necessarily ongoing activism. Criticisms of this activity as 'slacktivism' (see H. S. Christensen, 2011) decry the brief and minimal political participation it can represent, especially the apparent disparity between occasional tweeting and physically attending a protest.

Activism in various forms does arise out of online communication and socially mediated movements. Hacktivism is a general descriptor for activists not just making use of online tools and media, but commandeering and altering them for their own purposes, from appropriating memes to leading attacks on internet infrastructure as acts of protest and threat (Houghton and Chang, 2011; Milner, 2013). Groups associated with hacktivist practices include Wikileaks, whose leaking of diplomatic cables and other sensitive communiqués have also linked it to online piracy groups (Heemsbergen, 2015; Lindgren and Lundström, 2011), and Anonymous, which emerged from 4chan's /b/ forum in promoting disruptive and antagonistic acts, carried out for 'lulz' (an extension of the humorous internet culture of lols, but with malicious intent). As its profile and actions have grown, though, publicly targeting groups like the Church of Scientology and the Westboro Baptist Church, a distinction is apparent between Anonymous as collective and Anonymous as dangerous political radicals (G. Coleman, 2015; Jarvis, 2014; W. Phillips, 2015; Woods, 2014).

As with the various overlapping discussions, tangential and emergent politics within everyday talk and seemingly non-political stimuli, collective action brings together myriad perspectives and issues around a common context. Croeser (2014) argues that:

> social movements are inherently multifaceted, fluid, and messy. Even those as well-established and extensively researched as the feminist movement or the environmentalist movement can be seen as a kaleidoscope of other movements, with participants flowing in and out of various overlapping movements. (p. 77)

Online, collective action involves a diverse cast of actors, platforms, tools and issues, using social media and their affordances as part of strategies of promotion, organization, resistance, subterfuge and surveillance. Advocacy groups from GetUp to MoveOn utilize social media and online communication as part of their campaigns. Approaches like protest and affective hashtags are a key element of gaining visibility and support for a campaign, despite the 'slacktivist' critique, and these spread across platforms and media formats – from Twitter to Tumblr to Instagram, mixing the textual and the visual, the personal and the political. Collective action on social media attempts to harness the advantages of these popular platforms – rather than relying on Twitter alone, campaigns invite participation from users across the social media ecology and beyond. As Portwood-Stacer and Berridge (2015) argue in their introduction to a series of commentaries and critiques around feminist hashtag campaigns,

> so-called 'hashtag activism' is not an insular practice but rather an attempt to mobilize feminist community across mediums, in a reflection of the transmedia ecology in which feminist issues, like all issues today, arise and travel. (p. 154)

Everyday Tactics and Responses

By adopting and adapting popular social media platforms, collective action campaigns invite the incorporation of everyday practices into their activism. There is an element of playing on and hooking into the informal and mundane, as seen in strategies that use memetic and viral logics in content generation and extended engagement. From the 'We are the 99%' tumblr to political campaigns and charity fundraising/awareness drives like the 'Ice Bucket Challenge' or #nomakeupselfie (Deller and Tilton, 2015), the sharing and networking aspects of social media encourage users to connect their friends to these issues, and to participate. The practice of hashtag campaigns, too, is a reflection of the attention given to trending topics, and of the logics around memes and social media rituals: the #YesAllWomen hashtag, described by Thrift (2015) as a 'feminist meme event', was also a response and counter-narrative to #NotAllMen and related threads around misogyny and sexism, also apparent within Gamergate commentary.

Everyday social media practices are used for collective action purposes through encouraging contributions from other users and sharing them to highlight social issues and problems. The *Everyday Sexism* project started by Laura Bates in 2011 is an example of collective and connective action of sorts, using social media as a tool for documenting and disseminating reports of experiences of sexism with an aim of changing societal attitudes and practices. The project makes use of Twitter to highlight volunteered contributions, using the #everydaysexism hashtag and retweeting accounts, with longer-form writing submitted through the project website (for more, see Bates, 2014). *Everyday Sexism* as a project shares elements with other pre-social media approaches to documenting experiences, underlined by Rentschler's (2014) description of socially mediated, feminist responses to rape culture as

> an affective and technological deployment of the testimonial tradition, in which girls and young women digitally record and transcribe personal stories based in their experiences of sexual violence and harassment, and in their roles as witnesses to others' harassment and experience of sexual violence. (p. 66)

Other projects work along similar lines to report and challenge everyday experiences, especially by women. The *Hollaback!* initiative, for example, collates volunteered reports of public harassment. There are multiple websites for the project, centred on particular locales – the project was launched in New York City in 2005, and has since grown in scope and format (Dimond et al., 2013; Lingel and Bishop, 2014). The political dimensions of *Everyday Sexism* and *Hollaback!* are social and cultural; they are responses to inequalities and abuses that reflect ingrained attitudes on the part of men especially. Addressing issues around misogyny, sexism, gender equality, diversity and physical, verbal and emotional harassment is political. As has been seen in previous chapters, these issues are found in many different contexts, appearing as additional themes within political commentary and events.

Such projects are also endorsements of some of the affordances of social media: the locative aspect of mobile and social media for the likes of *Hollaback!*, in order to map abuse and harassment; the shareability, spreadability and ease of contributing experiences in a supportive environment for *Everyday Sexism*. It is worth noting, of course, that these projects are not social media-specific, for they employ multiple channels, websites and formats which an individual Twitter feed could not do in isolation. Social media act as visible and centralizing streams, combining organizer and contributor reporting and extending the scope of and audience for the projects.

Campaigns like #PadsAgainstSexism and #freethenipple, too, are not purely socially mediated, but, as with many contemporary examples of collective action, the movement develops a hashtag which is employed as a common marker across different platforms. The attitudes challenged by these projects are also reflected in campaigns with notable physical manifestations. 'Slut walks' are a counter to conservative and sexist societal beliefs about female promiscuity and presentation, and to related practices of 'slut-shaming' and call-out culture (Darmon, 2014; Reger, 2014; Shah, 2015; Webb, 2015).[37] Similarly, campaigns responding to racism, prejudice and injustice, including #BlackLivesMatter and #ICantBreathe, further demonstrate the combining of the political and the personal in collective action (Bonilla and Rosa, 2015; Kang, 2015). Together, these examples of hashtagged activism and their related projects and manifestations demonstrate a collective realization of, and reaction against, social divisions and attitudes that are both commonplace and intolerant. From #everydaysexism and #BlackLivesMatter to #CrimingWhileWhite, #AliveWhileBlack and #illridewithyou, by drawing attention to pressing social issues, hashtag campaigns highlight developed norms that are problematic, and the need to change them.

Affective collective action

Within socially mediated collective action, the affective plays a prominent role, from individual reports of everyday sexism to personal statements as part of 'We are the 99%'. A hashtag like #illridewithyou clearly presents affect within a politically motivated setting, while the Canadian indigenous and First Peoples campaign #IdleNoMore uses a highly affective hashtag to centralize its communication (Dahlberg-Grundberg and Lindgren, 2014). Affective action and solidarity emerge from unfolding events. During Wendy Davis's filibuster in the Texas

Senate in June 2013, in opposition to a bill significantly decreasing access to abortions and related care, supporters adopted the #StandWithWendy hashtag to demonstrate their solidarity (Stevenson, 2014).[38] The international response in 2014 to militant Islamist group Boko Haram's kidnapping of hundreds of young Nigerian women and girls included the similarly affective hashtag #BringBackOurGirls. This coverage featured visual and textual support from prominent public figures, as well as extended comment and sharing on social media (not immune from critique in its framing of non-Western politics and backgrounds; see Loken, 2015).

These critiques can also be directed at other social media campaigns that respond to international events, issues and political figures. The Kony2012 campaign used strategies around affective and celebrity mobilization to achieve its aims (see, for example, Zuckerman, 2012): run by Invisible Children, the campaign intended to increase awareness and political action about Ugandan warlord Joseph Kony and his tactics (including forcing children to become soldiers). Invisible Children's tactics behind the Kony2012 campaign hooked into everyday practices and affordances of social media in order to spread awareness and to raise funds. In addition to producing an emotive video broadcast globally, Kony2012 made use of YouTube, Facebook and Twitter as part of its promotion and engagement processes (boyd, 2012b; Kligler-Vilenchik and Thorson, 2015). The campaign appealed to individual users to share content, but it also recognized the extensive audiences (in terms of fans and followers) of celebrities on social media.

Invisible Children targeted the accounts of celebrities and prominent political figures on social media for Kony2012. Visitors to the campaign website were encouraged to support the campaign, most notably by directing messages at particular public figures in order to get them to join up and promote the campaign. Users did not even have to craft their own messages; they could simply use a standard tweet available on the website. The sheer volume of messages, it was anticipated, would demonstrate the groundswell of public opinion supporting the campaign, and lead the celebrities to share this message further.[39] Unlike the solicited messages of projects like *Everyday Sexism*, Kony2012's social media strategy in part was more akin to spam, attempting to gain traction and responses by simply repeating its message and shouting at the same people until they acquiesced and supported the campaign.[40]

Practices of Collective Action on Social Media

Kony2012 and *Everyday Sexism* are movements and campaigns that could be seen as primarily socially mediated. Other contexts, though, use social media as part of a wider activist organization and mobilization strategy. In 2006, the use of blogs by anti-CPE, and later anti-*blocage*, protestors served to provide information about when demonstrations and general assemblies were being held. These sites also provided solidarity with other groups around the country, providing updates from campuses across France. Within the Occupy movement, Twitter was similarly employed across multiple protest sites (see, for example, Papacharissi, 2015). In addition to its social media origins – including the promotion of #occupywallstreet in Adbusters' initial campaign (2011) – the research that Sky Croeser and I carried out on Occupy Oakland (Croeser and Highfield, 2014) found findings and practices in common with observations from Occupy Wall Street (Gerbaudo, 2012) and Occupy Seattle (Agarwal et al., 2014a). These practices also clearly connect the online and the physical. Rather than perpetuating an online/offline divide (Dahlberg-Grundberg, 2014), there are intrinsic links between what happens on social media and in the physical marches and demonstrations of a movement.

The role of social media within contexts like the Arab Spring has been questioned by studies examining whether the likes of Twitter and Facebook were used by protestors in Cairo, for instance, or if the attention on these platforms was primarily from a global audience looking in (Harlow and Johnson, 2011). Social media were certainly active during the uprisings. In Egypt, the Mubarak regime moved to block access to the internet as the protests in Tahrir Square continued to grow; Twitter and Google responded by providing access via international voicemail to Egyptian users so that they could continue to post updates (York, 2011). The extent of Twitter or Facebook use in Egypt, Tunisia, Libya or other MENA countries in which uprisings occurred in late 2010 and early 2011 has been noted in analyses evaluating the significance of social media to the revolution, and Aouragh and Alexander (2011) explore in depth the online and physical organization that took place in Egypt. Less publicly visible yet, online and mobile communication was used for organizational purposes, including text messaging and private Facebook groups, but other functions were also apparent within the activity on popular social media.

In particular, tweeting about the uprisings served informative purposes, making events and experiences visible outside the region. Individuals with expert knowledge and familiarity with the contexts for the uprisings became critical sources for analysis and accuracy. The NPR staffer Andy Carvin, for example, was a focal bridge in the Twitter coverage of the Arab Spring, sourcing and collating reports from the region for a diverse, distributed audience (Hermida et al., 2014). Tweets from users in Egypt provided personal takes on the revolution, mixing information with individual experiences and sentiments in the production of 'affective news' and storytelling (Papacharissi, 2015; Papacharissi and de Fatima Oliveira, 2012).

The presentation of the personal as part of updates from revolutions and scenes of unrest – which might not have explicit political commentary but are still politically oriented because of their context – also highlights the diversity of topical coverage here. Twitter activity about #egypt, #syria, #londonriots, or #ows does not lead to cohesive, single-issue datasets. The use of hashtags highlights the numerous sub-topics within individual protests and the repeated interconnection between movements as they get invoked in tweets symbolically (or thematically) connecting activists in Tahrir Square, Gezi Park and Oscar Grant Plaza. This serves informational purposes – sharing resources and updates from different protests – as well as demonstrating solidarity.

In the case of Occupy Oakland (Croeser and Highfield, 2014), while the movement as a whole was denoted using the #oo hashtag,[41] other hashtags co-occuring within the #oo dataset represented themes and discussions around specific demonstrations, other Occupy sites and local events. Isolating different hashtags within the collected #oo activity highlighted that, rather than an activist public on Twitter contributing consistently to all topics and issues, the users tweeting about Occupy Oakland had their own interests and foci: while some prominent users did tweet with all of these various hashtags, there was also a separation between users present within the filtered datasets corresponding to #ftp (Fuck the Police marches), #ows (Occupy Wall Street), #ogp (Oscar Grant Plaza), or to events like general assemblies and public forums. This distribution reflects the different roles and intentions behind activists' contributions on social media. In addition to a core group (in terms of presence in multiple thematic areas if not in social cohesion), users might concentrate on tweeting and live-streaming from marches and assemblies or provide resources and links in response to police raids, arrests and events elsewhere in the Occupy movement. Similarly, users regularly tweeting with #oo and #ows, or other Occupy site-specific hashtags, might not be physically located in Oakland – or a part of Occupy Oakland – but connect different branches by broadcasting messages concurrently.

Information-sharing as part of collective action can serve to support and aid purposes, such as the tweeting of details to explain how to report incidents involving police, or legal contacts for those arrested at marches. It can also be a form of documentation and recording. Live-streaming and tweeting from meetings allow people geographically distant to be updated (and to contribute by proxy, if need be). These processes also provide evidence of what happened at these events, especially with regard to police actions at marches, although as will be seen later in this chapter live-streaming within protests has not been without its critics. Streaming is also used for audio, from activist radio stations to making police scanners available online. Central repositories also collate reports from protests around the world, such as *Protestify*, as well as reporting on sites like *Global Voices*.

While Twitter and Facebook have received extensive attention as social media of choice for collective and connective action, these information-sharing practices demonstrate that activists' use of social media involves a multi-platform approach that responds to the affordances – and limitations and concerns – of different platforms. Activists will share details of video streams and audio feeds through Twitter, but they are not necessarily hosted there. Twitter's release of Periscope, its own native video-streaming tool, might change this, although suspicions about, and risks of, relying on one single platform might also mean that a mix of commercial and independent platforms continue to be employed (see for instance the analysis of Greek activists' online communication strategies: Croeser and Highfield, 2015a).

Networks of solidarity

From live-streaming and photo-sharing to tweeting and collaborative mapping, online communication offers activists and protest groups a visible means of organization and coordination, and this can help to increase feelings of solidarity between those physically protesting and those only active online (Gerbaudo, 2012). The accessibility of the associated media also allows for connections between different movements and activists around the world (see also the serial activists studied by Bastos and Mercea, 2015). Social media are variously employed to show support, to share updates from different protests and for organizing actions in solidarity. The Occupy movement in itself is a clear example of this: the individual Occupy sites in New York City, Oakland, San Francisco, Portland, Seattle, Houston and other US (and international) cities had their own local concerns but were also part of a wider collective (Agarwal et al., 2014a). Marches would occur in solidarity with other branches of Occupy, resources would be shared, and reports of raids and arrests would be retweeted using multiple Occupy hashtags in order to spread the word further and reinforce the connections within the movement. These connections also transcended the Occupy context; Occupy Oakland tweets and marches, for instance, also promoted solidarity with protestors in Egypt, Turkey and Greece.

Activists' use of blogs and other online media prominently feature connections and support for different protest sites. French student blogs protesting the CPE in 2006 linked individual campuses with others around France, including the multiple campuses found in many larger French towns. Anti-fascist activists in Athens, too, connect their online presence to other related activist movements, both elsewhere in Greece and across Europe (Croeser and Highfield, 2015a). The solidarity aspect is also apparent for groups being protested against, of course. In the French political blogosphere, bloggers supporting the far-right Front National or expressing fascist or anti-Islamic views in particular formed a highly interlinked group (Highfield, 2011). These bloggers were not as strongly connected to the rest of the French political blogosphere; instead, they presented their sites as part of a community of extremist bloggers across Europe, using blogrolls and banners to demonstrate their support of groups opposing mosques in France and solidarity with nationalist parties like the British National Party (BNP). This partisan behaviour reflects slightly different contexts from a specific protest movement, but the rationale is similar: social media provide an opportunity to overcome geographic distance to demonstrate support for, and solidarity with, similarly minded groups in other cities, regions and countries.

Expressions of solidarity can be used as a means for garnering support in other ways, too. Social media disseminate appeals to supporters and fellow protestors for financial support, either for the movement as a whole or for individual activists seeking funding for protest purposes. Following the enforced shutdown of Athens *Indymedia* in April 2013, donations were sought to support RadioBubble, an independent activist web radio station that was a focal resource for updates about *Indymedia* as well as sharing reports from other demonstrations (Croeser and Highfield, 2015a). Kickstarter, Indiegogo and other crowdfunding sites have also been employed to raise funds for activists requiring financial aid for legal costs, for equipment and transport and for documenting protests as films as well as live streams.

Social Media Protest

Through practices like live-streaming and live-tweeting, social media can be seen as backchannels for protests – they are not the actual demonstrations themselves, but provide reports and responses to what is happening in marches, occupations and meetings. These platforms are also employed for explicit expressions of protest, either as an additional channel for activism – including as a 'holding space' standing in for physical demonstrations – or as the main display of collective action (Croeser and Highfield, 2014). Hashtag activism is a visible and commonplace approach to this, used in response to social injustice, problematic trends and crises, scandals and breaking news alike, for varying degrees of 'political' topics (Kang, 2015; Stache, 2015). The practices of hashtag activism incorporate elements of everyday social media behaviours highlighted in chapters 1 and 2. They also reflect elements of the disruptive spaces online described by Lindgren (2013), embodying 'more or less conscious attempts at obstructing or providing an alternative to prevailing discourses' (p. 143). However, hashtag campaigns – and the particular arguments and framings they use – are not without criticism or their limits, especially if they create as well as counter different divisions between users (Bonilla and Rosa, 2015; Loza, 2014).

Hashtag campaigns can reflect distinctly non-political contexts, including promotional drives (including contests or shopping promotions) and social appeals. The *BuzzFeed*-initiated #Tay4Hottest100, which encouraged Australians to vote for Taylor Swift's 'Shake It Off' for the 2014 edition of Triple J's Hottest 100 listener poll (essentially trolling the hipster-friendly poll, since Triple J – shamefully – had not previously played 'Shake It Off'), and the resultant social media support and inevitable backlash, is just one prominent example (ABC News, 2015b; Di Stefano, 2015a; triple j, 2015). These non-political hashtag campaigns are otherwise similar to political concerns, making use of trending visibility and amplification through prominent accounts and media in order to develop a groundswell of attention. Regardless of the inherent 'seriousness' of the issue behind the campaign, and its importance to the day-to-day lives of others, the supporting logics are similar.

Hashtag activism is not the only way for protests to occur on social media. Demonstrations, particularly around internet-related political topics, can bring in different elements of the personal in displaying solidarity and resistance. This incorporates the visual as well as text-based expressions of protest, involving user profiles as well as their comments and content. During protests in Iran in 2009, Twitter users displayed solidarity by colouring their user icons green and changing their location to Tehran (Alex Burns and Eltham, 2009). In the same way that users might display logos and slogans in their user icons and avatars during election campaigns, these visual displays provide a recurring, semi-permanent outlet for protest – appearing alongside each tweet and comment posted by the account – rather than a one-off hashtagged tweet or status. Of course, not all comments might be related to the protest, but activist imagery provides a reminder about issues and causes that further brings the political into personal, mundane communication on social media.

Blackouts

Social media, and the internet in general, are also at times the subject of protests as well as the venue for them; proposed legislation pertaining to digital rights, data retention and privacy and copyright law, which is seen to restrict or impinge upon digital liberties, is contested using the channels it aims to influence. The US government's SOPA/PIPA bills were protested through internet blackouts, where websites restricted access to their content, and where internet users turned their profile pictures and avatars black in solidarity (for more on the surrounding debate, see Benkler et al., 2015). Similar approaches have also been adopted in other countries, in reaction to local internet and digital rights-oriented legislation.[42]

In 2008, the French government proposed a new administrative body and legislation to counter digital piracy. Its 'Création et Internet' bill was, essentially, a 'three strikes' approach to piracy: a citizen caught pirating content would be subject to different levels of punishment for their first, second or third offence, with the third act of piracy warranting the citizen's internet access being cut off for a year. To police this and to protect artists' rights, the bill established HADOPI: the *Haute Authorité pour la diffusion des œuvres et la protection des droits sur internet* (High Authority for the Distribution of Works and the Protection of Rights on the Internet). This body became synonymous with the bill itself, and was the focal point of protests against the legislation, both as the authority responsible for protecting rights but also for suspicion of its potential abilities to undertake surveillance and internet filtering.

Led by advocacy group *la Quadrature du Net*, anti-HADOPI protests in early 2009 employed the internet blackout technique in order to demonstrate the extent of French sentiment against the bill. This was not the first example of this approach – in New Zealand, the Creative Freedom Foundation NZ had organized a similar blackout campaign against internet filtering legislation just prior to the anti-HADOPI campaign – but it was a key unifying tactic for French activists. By voluntarily changing icons and avatars to black images and blacking out websites, the campaign aimed to increase public awareness of the bill and to influence its progression through the French legislature (Breindl and Gustafsson, 2011). As with other campaigns, the internet focus of the anti-HADOPI protests did not mean that it was online-only. Physical demonstrations, from marches to flashmobs, were organized and promoted online, as further means of showing popular opposition. However, as the space directly threatened by the legislation, online channels from Twitter to YouTube and blogs were widely employed for HADOPI coverage and protests (for full details, see Highfield, 2011).

Ultimately, the anti-HADOPI campaign did not prevent the bill becoming law. Over the first half of 2009, the HADOPI bill required additional votes and amendments, especially in response to the Conseil Constitutionnel's verdict that internet access was a basic human right and that the proposed law was thus partially unconstitutional. The campaign did demonstrate, though, additional forms of online collective action, most notably through the blackout, and the types of information and organization associated with this. In preparation for HADOPI becoming law, French bloggers outlined ways of counteracting the legislation through anonymous browsing, using encryption and linking to tools that helped users to subvert surveillance through changing IP addresses. The law might change, but everyday practices need not – and protecting users' privacy and rights is an everyday concern that has not become less pertinent in the years since 2009.

Subverting censorship, sur- and sous-veillance

An alternative form of blackout[43] works against social media activism: the intervention by governments and regimes to block access to these technologies used for organization and information-sharing (Howard et al., 2011). These can be targeted at individual sites and servers, like the shutdown of Athens *Indymedia* in 2013, or at the extended infrastructure level, as seen in Egypt during the Arab Spring. In Turkey, social media have variously been blocked in response to anti-Ertogan sentiments and the Gezi Park protests (Harris, 2015; Varnali and Gorgulu, 2015; Yalkin et al., 2013), while permanent blocks are seen in China, where the 'Great Firewall' restricts access to Facebook and Twitter. While there are methods that individuals can use to circumvent these obstructions, including using virtual private networks (VPNs), these approaches are not used by – or are appealing for – all users. The blocks imposed by governments and regimes influence what people do online and what platforms they use instead, and the practices and affordances that develop in response. Practices on *weibo* in China, simultaneously comparable with and yet with marked differences from Twitter, offer insight into different cultures of microblogging and political influence in commentary, moderation and surveillance (Gleiss, 2015; Sullivan, 2012; Tong and Zuo, 2014).

Sharing information about how to subvert government surveillance, to go against new legislation or to access sites deemed problematic by authorities, is also a strategy used by protestors. The shutdown of Athens *Indymedia*, seen as being at the instigation of the Greek government, led activists to move towards alternative approaches to hosting and operating the site (Croeser and Highfield, 2015a). One strategy was to adopt the anonymity-focused network Tor, and its associated browser, to both run and access Athens *Indymedia*. However, although Tor offers increased user privacy from surveillance, through encryption and rerouting, its use is more specialized than browsers like Firefox, Chrome, Safari or Opera. Activist websites, blog posts and tweets then acted as how-to guides for activists (and other visitors) outlining the additional knowledge required to access Athens *Indymedia* via Tor.

Social media – in activist contexts and beyond – can be used for both sur- and sous-veillance (Carlsson, 2014), and this is an advantage and a disadvantage. Live-streaming of protests is a regular feature of demonstrations, from Occupy to the marches and 'die-ins' across the US in late 2014. As noted earlier in this chapter, providing a live, video account of the marches enables protestors geographically distant to be connected to the event and express solidarity. It also, though, allows for recording what transpires at marches, including documenting violence and arrests. This is not uncontested: in Occupy Oakland, live-streamers were variously treated with approval and suspicion (Croeser and Highfield, 2014). Live-streaming has been criticized at times by movement participants since it can provide law enforcement agencies with footage and evidence to use against activists. Conversely, live-streaming and videoing marches have also been endorsed as a means of recording the actions of police officers (Reilly, 2015; F. Shaw, 2013b). Having this documentary evidence means that it can also be reviewed and shared after the fact. Video footage of the arrest – and fatal suffocation – of Eric Garner in New York in 2014 was recirculated through social media following the decision not to indict the officer responsible, promoting #ICantBreathe as protest slogan and as hashtag. The review process works both ways, though, with authorities monitoring streams and feeds, giving rise to further fears and contestation about surveillance, censorship and privacy on social media.

Censorship, monitoring and platforms – critiques of connective action

Concerns about surveillance, and actions by authorities and governments to block access to internet infrastructure, have meant that the use of everyday social media platforms for activism has not been without criticism or tension. Activists are not universally comfortable with the use of popular social media such as Facebook and Twitter, whether in the US or Greece (Croeser and Highfield, 2014, 2015a). The suitability of the platforms for different purposes is questioned: while Twitter is useful for quickly disseminating information, its character limit for tweets makes debate and discussion less likely without confusion, misunderstandings, abuse or outright trolling.

Some activists also see the role of the platforms as cause for concern. Alleged censorship by Twitter in not promoting protest hashtags as trending topics – coupled with the unknown parameters of its algorithms, as noted in chapter 1 – raises questions about the openness of corporate-owned social media. With further concerns about data retention strategies, the monitoring of location and activity across different platforms and websites and the personal information provided on social media, highly political use of Facebook or Twitter is not necessarily seen as advantageous. While the public sharing of information is a necessity for social movements in attempting to disseminate details to as many people as possible, the accessibility of such communication means that other, unintended audiences can also view this. Activists suspect the monitoring of public communication by police and law enforcement agencies, while also flagging concerns about deals between social media companies and governments and authorities.

The popularity and accessibility of Twitter and Facebook also create a tension regarding their use and non-use: activists are not universally present online as well as at physical protests, partly in response to these fears of monitoring and surveillance. Activists' choices not to participate online means that their voices are not directly included in hashtagged discussions, and that other voices might obtain a prominence on social media that is not replicated on the streets. In Greece, activists make use of alternative and independent platforms where possible, but still employ popular social media for communication and information-sharing due to their audience and reach (Croeser and Highfield, 2015a). While there may be clear desire to use other online platforms for activist purposes, the lack of a critical mass means that the everyday, popular and proprietary social media remain key channels (see also Fuchs, 2014).

(It's Actually About) Ethics in Collective Action

Social movements represent a research subject with potential political risk for participants, and the social media components of protests and campaigns are not removed from this. While studies of the Arab Spring or Occupy and Twitter draw upon publicly accessible social media activity, there are still questions of research ethics in the presentation of data and results, in the coverage of sensitive and controversial topics and behaviours and in the role of researchers within collective action. As with other political and politicized contexts on social media, these questions are also applicable to the study of other forms of online activity. The following discussion acts as a brief reflection on ethics and social media research more generally, elements of which are covered in more detail in collaborations with Sky Croeser (Croeser and Highfield, 2015b) and Tama Leaver (Highfield and Leaver, 2015).

The ethical responsibilities of social media researchers are inconsistent between institutions, projects and platforms (Zimmer and Proferes, 2014). In general, research drawing on publicly available data, gathered while adhering to the terms of use for the platforms in question and presented without identifying information (such as purely quantitatively), has been classed by university ethnics boards as negligible or low risk. Yet not all public data are equal in terms of risk: discussions about different topics by different users, gathered in the same way from the same platform, may reflect very dissimilar political and personal implications.

Within social movement (and similar contexts) and social media studies, then, concerns over anonymity and risk, of decontextualizing information and inadvertent revelations, are critical ethical dilemmas (Monroy-Hernández et al., 2013; Tufekci and Wilson, 2012). This extends to researchers themselves: in studying controversial and sensitive topics on social media, researchers may become targets or unwitting participants in contested discussions (see Chess and Shaw, 2015). How visible a social media researcher may be within a social movement might vary dramatically. Collecting Twitter data can happen on another continent, far removed from protests or uprisings, and the participants on the streets and online may have no idea that they are being studied (or certainly not by any particular individual). This advantage of social media research, its mobility in terms of data capture and analysis, can have undesired impacts upon the resulting study, however, for the surrounding context for this activity might be lost (not just online, but the political, social and cultural factors causing and shaping the social media discussions).

In this book, I have tried to avoid any extended discussion of the benefits and perils alike of big data analysis of social media (or of any other single approach, really – there is no one perfect solution to every research question). The provocations raised by boyd and Crawford (2012) remain critical considerations for researchers about the strengths, gaps and limits of their research design and datasets (see also the multiple perspectives of big data mentioned by Crawford et al., 2014). Similarly, Tufekci's (2014) illustration of Twitter activities that subvert established practices but which might be missed without close reading and contextual awareness underlines how we cannot treat all online communication as having the same structural and affective intentions. The cases of erroneous crisis communication, of fake images and misinformation noted in previous chapters, further highlight the need for dedicated examination of practices and content as well as patterns. As Baym (2013) has noted, it is crucial to recognize the varying audiences and intentionality for social media activity – which are often very different from the perspectives brought by a researcher. In order to do justice to the subjects of our studies, we need to consider our responsibilities as researchers in a field where data are public – and may give away more information via locative meta-data, background imagery or subtexts than the contributing user might realize – but the personal idea of 'public' and the intent behind it is not a constant.

Conclusion

As with other elements of the everyday and the political, collective and connective action further underlines the importance of treating the online not as a separate and isolated setting, but as part of an extended, hybrid media and political system. While disruption can occur as online-only, Lindgren (2013) argues that 'in order for disruptive spaces to actually make a difference, and not just as sources of inspiration, identity, and mutual support in electronic isolation, they must be hybrid' (p. 150). The social mediation of protests and activism is just one part of social movements, which also incorporate physical demonstrations, collaborations, meetings, mobile telephony and private communication in-person and online. Tweets about the Arab Spring or Occupy are important sources for studying protest contexts on social media, but they are not representative of the whole movement or the individuals participating within it.

Talking about collective action may initially imply the extraordinary: occupiers in New York City, mass demonstrations in Tunis and Cairo, panic in the streets of London. The cases of *Everyday Sexism* and *Hollaback!*, among many others, indicate that collective action is also an everyday practice to provide support, change attitudes and counter prevalent societal norms. Collective and connective action as realized and reinforced by social media is seen in campaigns and hashtags, emergent responses and long-running discussions which make use of similar mechanisms and affordances. Through retweeting strategies, affective and impactful visual media, or employing platforms for the live and public recording of experiences, demonstrations and meetings, very different movements make use of social media for informational, organizational and solidarity purposes. The strategies employed here reflect approaches that are also used in mundane contexts by a variety of users. This extends to political actors themselves, too, and in the next chapter I examine social media use by politicians, as an outlet for partisan commentary, and, as an extension, for antagonistic, vitriolic and offensive communication.

6

Partisan Politics and Politicians on Social Media

Australia Day, 2015.[44] Having previously reintroduced the honours system, whereby the Australian government could bestow upon chosen individuals the title of Knight or Dame, Tony Abbott announced that receiving a knighthood in the Australia Day Honours was... Prince Philip, Duke of Edinburgh and husband of Queen Elizabeth II. As the consort to the Queen, Australia's head of state, the Duke had a long association with the country even if he was not Australian, had never lived in Australia and his work in general did not directly involve Australia. This, Abbott apparently decided, was a perfectly reasonable rationale for the Duke to receive the title of Knight of the Order of Australia, ahead of local individuals who might be seen as, perhaps, more deserving or appropriate choices.[45]

The day before, the award of Australian of the Year had been given to Rosie Batty, who had established a foundation and tirelessly campaigned against domestic violence following the murder of her son by his father, her ex-husband. The three other Australian of the Year awards – given by the national Australia Day Council, not the government – were also all received by women, for the first time.

Tony Abbott's decision to give a knighthood to Prince Philip was immediately criticized. The social media reaction was inevitably fierce, questioning the point of the award, the reasoning behind it, the mockery it made of Australia. The Australian of the Year awards had been seen as a step forwards; 'Sir Prince Philip' was several leaps backwards.

The criticism was not limited to social media, though: the mainstream media also questioned Abbott's decision, as indeed did politicians from other parties and from Abbott's own Liberal–National coalition. Abbott responded to this criticism by calling social media 'electronic graffiti' (Chan, 2015), something not worth paying attention to and a social blight. Besides denigrating the millions of Australians who use social media, this view also focuses in on only one particular practice on social media, most visibly on Twitter.[46] There is a diverse range of functions for which social media platforms are employed, which can be far more positive and beneficial than 'electronic graffiti' might suggest.

After all, among the people and groups using social media – either themselves or their staff in their name – are politicians and political parties, including Abbott himself. Despite the description of 'electronic graffiti', ignoring social media is not necessarily a strategy that will be successful, or appropriate in the long-term. Other politicians may have a far more positive view towards using the internet for political purposes. In this chapter, I examine social media within the context of politicians and partisan politics, where specific ideologies, parties and individual political figures heavily influence discussions. The final section of the chapter also transitions from heated, partisan commentary to extreme views, before a brief reflection on trolling and hatespeech.

Politicians and Social Media

For politicians, the adoption of internet communication has followed an uneven pattern, whether digital platforms are used for engaging with their electorate and with issues, or for simply broadcasting their press releases and speeches. A few early adopters of blogging, for instance, did not translate into universal take-up of these sites, although later platforms have seen wider adoption: whereas in 2004 the Howard Dean campaign for the Democratic nomination for that year's US Presidential election was a novelty in some regards for its internet strategy (Hindman, 2009; Meraz, 2007), politicians and candidates having a social media presence is now more expected and mundane. How politicians and their staff employ these platforms outside electioneering and other periods of heightened interest, though, remains more variable, as the everyday is brought back to the political.

The opportunity to use these platforms does not mean that any or all will be successful for the politicians or parties concerned, whether in attracting or retaining an audience or in making effective use of the platforms and their affordances. As with other users, politicians' approaches to social media may find that one platform is more appropriate for one type of content or communication than another. The user base of Facebook, and its capabilities for more extended comments than Twitter, may make it a better option for making politicians' contributions visible and encourage interactions and responses.

While this chapter focuses at first on individual politicians, and then on expressions of partisan politics, it is also important to note that government departments and official bodies also employ online platforms. Official government documents and archives are made available online, while different projects encourage participation and interaction between citizens, departments and bureaux in extending the scope and application of government work for its citizens; the Icelandic Constitutional Council, for example, encouraged social media participation, across multiple platforms, for a bill reviewing and rewriting the Constitution in 2011 (Valtysson, 2013). There are also various schemes introduced by government bodies about open government, sharing data and encouraging collaboration with citizens. These can involve open data initiatives and institutional support for social media, while different projects make use of publicly available sources, such as the Hansard archives used by *They Work For You* in the UK (theyworkforyou.com) and *Open Australia* (openaustralia.org.au). There are also events like GovHack where government datasets are made available for developers, designers and analysts who use them in intensive collaborations to create apps, visualizations and more (GovHack, 2015).

Socially mediated politicians

Analyses of politicians on Twitter, Facebook and other popular platforms have their foundations in previous studies of political websites, which have examined elements such as interactivity and information-sharing (Jackson and Lilleker, 2009; Lilleker and Malagon, 2010). Research into politicians' uses of social media, meanwhile, has covered different platforms, including video blogs (Yanoshevsky, 2009), Twitter and Facebook, as well as national contexts and practices from linking strategies to communication styles. Blogging politicians have been studied to identify typologies of blogs (Lehti, 2011), the place of blogs within political communication (S. Coleman and Moss, 2008) and networks of affiliation and discussion (Park and Jankowski, 2008; Soon and Cho, 2011).

Such studies have also examined interactions between politicians and citizens, and the coverage of topical discussions on these sites (Kushin and Kitchener, 2009). These approaches are apparent in the extended analysis of national political discussions on Twitter in Austria (Ausserhofer and Maireder, 2013), studying the contributions of politicians, journalists and citizen experts alike. The interactions apparent here show how politicians engage in socially mediated discussions, and if established and new actors are participating and connected in this coverage (or, for that point, whether or not established actors communicate among themselves). Similarly, Larsson and Kalsnes (2014) have studied the everyday use and non-use of Facebook and Twitter by Norwegian and Swedish politicians, while intersections between politicians and social media in New Zealand are examined by K. Ross et al. (2015).

How politicians actually use these platforms depends on a variety of factors, influenced by partisan and personal elements. Twitter can serve as a broadcast platform, disseminating links and updates without engaging in interactions with other users, and can facilitate dialogues between elected representatives and their constituents. While there are general national trends that are apparent – Australian politicians tend towards broadcasting (Grant et al., 2010), as do their British counterparts, while Dutch politicians favour dialogue (Broersma and Graham, 2012) – a wide variety of practices are still present. The status of the politician in question, their party affiliation (and thus partisan social media strategy) and contemporary factors can direct individuals towards broadcasting, interacting, or different approaches altogether.

There is also a perception that social media – and online communication in general – can represent unnecessary risks for politicians. In an environment where comments and actions are carefully controlled for desired impact and interpretation, social media are spaces where messages might be taken out of context or, more pertinently, where off-the-cuff, ill-advised or seemingly private remarks suddenly spread widely. For major parties, active social media use is perhaps less required: avoiding the risk of gaffes is more important than engaging with a small, unrepresentative population 'just because'.

For minor and extremist parties, however, social media offer platforms for posting messages from voices not always featured in traditional media (for various reasons) and for engaging in different ways, connecting with similar groups in other regions and countries (see also the use of Twitter by third-party candidates in the US, studied by C. Christensen, 2013b). Far-right voices in particular have made extensive use of blogs and other online platforms, taking to the internet as a means to promote messages that can be interpreted as controversial or offensive. Other parties and politicians make use of these channels though as part of their engagement with issues and policies related to the internet. While digital rights and related issues are only part of their purview, representatives of Green parties have been found to have notably active web presences and participate in social media discussions around data retention, piracy and privacy. Similarly, groups like the Piratpartiet in Sweden, and its related Pirate Party offshoots around the world, have clear interests in these issues. While their level of outline activity might make them appear more politically prominent than seen in their election results, Greens and Pirate Party politicians and members also have a responsibility to be active on social media in directing and discussing digital issues (Ausserhofer and Maireder, 2013; Larsson and Moe, 2012).

These practices are not limited to national politics: networks of affiliation and party presence extend to the regional and local levels. From blogs representing each French department, for parties including the centre-right UMP and the Greens, to Facebook pages for local members and candidates, social media cover multiple tiers of institutional politics. Different levels of visibility, audience scope, and activity are apparent here, of course. In Australia, the day-to-day coverage of #wapol or #qldpol (representing Western Australian- and Queensland-focused political themes, respectively) features far lower levels of tweeting than the national #auspol: during 2012, for example, the 10,000 #wapol tweets collected in the first six months of the year represented fewer than two days of average #auspol activity over the same period (Highfield, 2013). These lower-profile hashtags may also be less prone to spam and trolling; whereas the most prolific contributors on #auspol include highly partisan uses attacking their opponents, the state-level discussions are less inflammatory. Local politicians and journalists are among the most active participants in the likes of #wapol and #qldpol, tweeting regularly, but such participation from established political actors is less common for #auspol.

Different social media platforms offer their own benefits for political communication and strategies. Facebook may be a stronger option for engagement, and for monitoring this through centralized metrics around likes, shares and comments on a politician's or party page. Twitter, meanwhile, offers advantages of quick and concise commentary and sharing information. Furthermore, even if politicians are not actively using Twitter or engaging with other users, their account names will be mentioned in others' comments as a topical marker and as a shorthand for the politician – while not a universal practice, it is established to the point where politicians are regularly the most @mentioned accounts within Australian hashtagged political discussions. Other platforms may be used similarly extensively, or as one-off experiences, such as engaging in 'Ask Me Anything' sessions on reddit or hosting question and answer streams through YouTube.

As I have reiterated throughout this book, though, platforms are rarely used in isolation. Even if attention is primarily directed at Facebook or Twitter, a presence is often maintained on various popular platforms. Emergent practices present the personal element of a politician's social media activity, such as the stylistic norm of prominently signing off tweets *by* the politician (as opposed to their team) with names or initials: BO for tweets by Barack Obama rather than his staff, JG for Julia Gillard and so on. There is an acknowledgement here, by extension, that even though accounts may be in the name of individual politicians, they are also managed channels run by staffers. Such practices have continued to evolve, too, moving away from the individual or staff team running an account to completely managed presences (as noted with regard to @BarackObama by Bump, 2013).[47]

Politicians are people too: banal and everyday social media practices

Despite the fact that many politicians' web presences may be heavily managed, presenting only the essential information and not interacting with others except as needed, everyday strategies are still apparent within individual politicians' social media activity. Signing off a tweet as the politician in question highlights that they are like other users, using social media personally and for campaigning or electioneering. At times, the approaches employed can show off (or expose) a politician's personality, their quirks and individuality, in mixing everyday practices with their political image. Malcolm Turnbull, the former Leader of the Opposition, was not only one of the few Australian politicians in 2009 and 2010 with an explicit blog on his website, but also has a second blog dedicated to his dogs (malcolmturnbull.com.au/dog-blog). The posts here can mix the political and the banal, written from the perspective of his dogs while commenting on Turnbull's activity and recent (political) visitors. While far from a commonplace approach, Turnbull's dog blog demonstrates a particularly high-profile (in terms of his status within government) personal framing for politicians online.

A thorough embrace of social media can still be problematic for politicians – and viewed negatively by their electorate. During his first term as Australian Prime Minister, Kevin Rudd had seen his Twitter account become widely followed (unsurprising, given his position); while he, like most Australian politicians of the time, had not taken up blogging, his tweeting established his (and his staff's) familiarity with at least some social media. In 2013, though, as he made a successful challenge for the ALP leadership and then prepared for an election campaign, Rudd's social media strategy levelled up as he started to post selfies. This approach included a photograph of him post-shaving, having cut himself in the process. While the strategy here might have been to make Rudd seem more relatable and 'normal', given common perceptions of him as an awkward, micro-managing nerd (itself a new view compared to Rudd's early media-friendly image; see Wilson, 2014), it was seen as more baffling and ill-advised than engaging. Furthermore, Rudd's apparent lack of selfie control – posting multiple images in a short period of time – served to make him appear more desperate and trying to fit in with a social media audience than being social media literate in his own right (depicted in Manning and Phiddian, 2015).

Other politicians to have embraced – and been criticized for – selfie-taking include Indian Prime Minister Narendra Modi (Baishya, 2015). Furthermore, a selfie taken in 2013 and featuring Danish Prime Minister Helle Thorning-Schmidt, US President Barack Obama and UK Prime Minister David Cameron attracted intense media attention (dubbed 'Selfiegate') – because it was taken at the memorial service for former South African President Nelson Mandela (examined in depth by Miltner and Baym, 2015). As Miltner and Baym note, part of the tensions within the 'Selfiegate' scandal was in the solemn context – global leaders and a memorial service – and the extraordinary application of a mundane (but also somewhat decried) practice of selfie-taking, the carrying out of an emergent social media norm, with some degree of technological literacy, by three national leaders.

Politicians do not need to post this content themselves in order to participate and demonstrate their awareness or understanding of the form (or their willingness to publicly engage in activities, at least). During the G20 summit in Brisbane, Australia, in November 2014, German Chancellor Angela Merkel's evening stroll saw her pose outside bars for selfies with bystanders (Kent, 2014). The incorporation of politicians into memes and macros, such as 'Texts from Hillary', can warrant responses and even knowing references and adaptations of the forms by the subjects themselves in meta-commentary and meta-memeing (Anderson and Sheeler, 2014). Of course, if politicians do create their own memes, either from existing templates or new constructions, this does not mean that they will be successful as humorous or popular content. Nevertheless, politicians use of memes, selfies and emoji do at least show some acknowledgement of social media cultures and attempts to engage with this – however misguided in the eyes of social media users (see the response to the White House tweeting its own version of the *Straight*

Outta Compton meme in reference to Iran's nuclear capabilities in August 2015: Brown, 2015).

Political representatives and their staff are also affected by behaviours and practices that are not ostensibly political but more mundane parts of everyday social and digital media cultures. These include practices like sexting, as highly personal social and mobile mediated communication, and by extension the risks, scandals and debates around privacy and harassment raised in chapter 1; see, for example, the sudden public visibility of US Congressman Anthony Weiner's dickpics and sexts in 2011 (Oravec, 2012). Finally, politicians might not even be active on individual platforms, but their public activity is used as a framing device in the narratives presented for other users. Jill Walker Rettberg's (2009) examination of personal narratives and data-constructed self-portraits notes personalized reports from travel-sharing platform Dopplr that compared the individual user's travel in 2008 with that of Barack Obama. Here, Obama's well-known public narrative (in an election year) 'became a cultural template or a filter' for the personal accounts, where mundane elements of the political – the travel, not the politics – are reference points for the personal (p. 453).

The public visibility of politicians, especially leading figures, means that they can attract extensive followers and likes on social media. However, these figures can be inflated deliberately by purchasing followers, or by unwittingly attracting large numbers of fake and spam followers. Examining the Twitter follower accession history of prominent Australian politicians, including Tony Abbott, Bruns et al. (2014b) found noticeable influxes of fake followers. While Abbott's team denied purchasing followers, the presence of unsolicited fake and spam accounts occurs alongside practices of gamification and deliberate manipulation of metrics for prestige and attention on Twitter (Paßmann et al., 2013). These phenomena reiterate that spam, abandoned platforms and profiles, and noise in general are a recurring part of social media research: these elements might not be the intended or desired object of study, but they are still part of political – and everyday – activity (Li and Walejko, 2008; Yardi et al., 2010).

Partisan Politics

The opportunity for internet users to create sites and participate in political discussions online was variously treated as potentially democratizing, offering voices to many, and possibly divisive and self-isolating. This latter view is witnessed in arguments about cyberbalkanization and echo chambers among political bloggers (Sunstein, 2008): while the blogosphere might contain individuals presenting a diverse range of views and ideologies, users might not actively seek out opposing and alternative views. Instead, they might coalesce in like-minded groups that share the same views and reinforce pre-existing attitudes, not bridging any partisan divide. This fear was not entirely realized: while partisan clusters did form on the blogosphere, they also overlapped with different topics and themes of interest, rather than forming completely isolated groups. Studies of different international political blogospheres have found connections between different partisan groups, too, showing that bloggers are aware of what other people with opposing views are posting and link to this content, if only to point out its errors (Adamic and Glance, 2005).

Networks of affiliation and/or partisan divides

While recurring questions of the blogosphere or Twitter have tended towards asking if these spaces are left- or right-leaning (A. Shaw and Benkler, 2012), these are relatively moderate positions. Extremist parties and their supporters from the far-right of politics make extensive use of online platforms, creating an international network of groups promoting nationalism and opposing immigration, multiculturalism and, especially, Islam. Perhaps due to their minority and ostracized status within their own national contexts, these parties form connections with their similarly minded counterparts in other countries, taking advantage of the comparative freedom provided by the internet to share their beliefs and messages. Within the French political blogosphere, bloggers affiliated with the extreme-right Front National party had distinctive linking patterns in their blogrolls. Rather than connecting their blogs to other bloggers from different sides of French politics, FN bloggers formed a close-knit group mostly separate from the French political blogosphere at large, as seen in figure 3. Instead, the extreme-right bloggers featured extended links to nationalistic groups and anti-mosque, anti-Muslim and anti-immigration campaigns in France and elsewhere in Europe.

A network visualization like figure 3 provides only a partial picture of the connections between individual users online, though. Blogrolls, the source of the links used to construct this particular visualization, are just one type of link present on blogs, which represent particular intentions and norms (Schmidt, 2007). As a semi-permanent element of a blog, appearing on most (if not all) pages of the site, and a separate entity from an individual post, a blogroll enables bloggers to list links to sites of interest, friends, associates, related groups and affiliations, and any other sites they choose. In contrast, links made in posts are

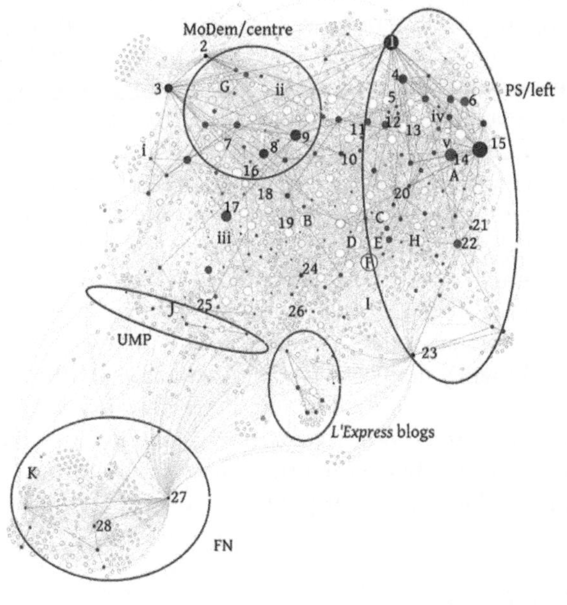

1. Partageons Mon Avis
2. Ataraxosphere
3. L'Hérétique
4. Kamizole
5. Trublyonne voit la vie en rouge
6. Pire Racaille
7. Hashtable
8. Toreader
9. Les jeunes libres...
10. Café Croissant
11. Ma vie en narcisse
12. Olympe et la plafond de Verre
13. Crises dans les médias
14. Intox2007
15. Sarkofrance
16. Journal d'un avocat
17. Koztoujours
18. Authueil
19. Coulisses de Bruxelles
20. Torapamavoa
21. Le mammouth...
22. Sarkostique
23. SarkozyNews
24. Nuesblog
25. Extreme Centre
26. I love politics
27. VoxFN Redekker
28. Yanndarc

A. Betapolitique
B. Agoravox
C. Mediapart
D. Bakchich
E. Arrêt sur images
F. Rue89
G. MoDEM
H. Parti Socialiste
I. Les verts
J. UMP
K. Front National

ideological groups are rough guides only

i. Réseau LHC
ii. Kiwisphere
iii. Les freemen
iv. Les vigilents
v. Leftblogs

Figure 3: French political blogosphere (selection) (from Highfield, 2011).

often more likely to be to sites and articles relevant to the featured topics, providing a more focused selection of resources (Halavais, 2008). Similar distinctions can be made between connections on Twitter, from @mentions and @replies to retweets and follower/following relationships (Halavais, 2013).

The connections that we create on social media represent different social – and political – intentions. We might choose to follow Twitter accounts or like Facebook pages which correspond with particular partisan views, just as political bloggers might prefer to feature like-minded blogs in their blogrolls. This does not mean, though, that the structural divides these imply are realized in everyday online communication. Instead, there is an awareness of what opposing views are voicing, especially prominent figures on social media, which can be seen through links and tweets highlighting (and critiquing or mocking) alternative commentary. There are less traceable ways of encountering different views, too: tweets quoting or reposting other comments may be seen in feeds without warranting a response – and thus not creating a tangible connection in the form of a link or mention – while lurking – reading without engaging or participating – is also present here. Furthermore, although politics can be a primary topic for individual social media users, it is rarely their only interest. The accounts they follow may represent various themes and issues, and these provide further potential for overlap and inadvertent exposure to different views: for instance, the follower/following network of the Australian Twittersphere positions Twitter users who tweet about (and follow other users connected to) left- and right-leaning politics respectively in close proximity – they are still distinct groups but with strong interlinking through common patterns of following prominent political accounts (Bruns et al., 2014a).

Partisan framing

The structural divisions suggested by blogrolls, like networks and follower/following connections, do not take into account the topical variations seen in the coverage of different issues and events: while users might be found within political clusters in a network, this does not mean that they will post about all political topics, or about any non-political themes. Focusing on a left/right or liberal/conservative divide can also overlook other forms of partisan schisms and antagonism, which might be short-lived but are very much vested in party politics. In April 2015, the Australian Greens posted an image celebrating their contribution to defeating a proposed toll road in Victoria. Feeling that the Greens were inaccurately taking credit, Labor supporters created a series of memes mocking the 'we did it!' stance by attributing various achievements to the Greens. The resulting 'Greens Taking Credit for Things' images reflected rituals and irreverent practices highlighted in chapter 2, including the use of intertexts and pop culture references (such as the Greens successfully 'making "fetch" happen', from the 2004 film *Mean Girls*) (Watson, 2015). Here, mockery and irreverence were devices for commentary, taking a different form to the outright antagonism and vitriol found in polarized political spaces like #auspol but still clearly fuelled by partisan support and beliefs.

Partisan views influence specific practices and approaches to discussing politics on social media. The creation of the French blog collective *les vigilants* was a response to Nicolas Sarkozy's victory in the 2007 presidential election: in addition to blogs acting as Sarkozy-specific watchdogs, the partisan views of the collective (predominantly leaning towards the left-wing Parti Socialiste) shaped their day-to-day framing of their posts. Blogs, and other social media accounts, can also be dedicated watchdogs for other prominent political and media actors, such as responding to and highlighting the work of journalists with opposing, controversial or inflammatory views.

It is important to stress that not all political talk on social media is explicitly partisan – while offering opinions and beliefs in their comments, users might not be advocating for a specific party's position, and indeed may well be criticizing all major parties. Similarly, everyday political discussions can occur without being on pages set up for this purpose, and without using established and obvious political markers. Larsson's (2014a) study of Twitter users engaged in political discussions in Norway and Sweden explored the stated political views and affiliations of prominent accounts, finding that 'a significant amount of activity is undertaken by established political actors as well as niche political groups' (p. 72). Such patterns demonstrate the prominence of traditional figures, including journalists (but not necessarily politicians), and marginalized or extreme views not otherwise afforded a public platform on social media. However, in focusing on major hashtags as data source, Larsson also notes the limits this puts on the analysis: other users not part of either of these groups might be actively discussing politics without using the hashtag.

Beyond the Partisan: Extreme Political Activity Online

The presence of extremist views within popular political hashtags, though, also reflects a strategy of hooking into these established markers to bring alternative views into a public forum. Extreme politics can extend beyond the partisan and take forms identified in chapter 1, through trolling and hatespeech perpetuating racism, sexism, homophobia, transphobia and other forms of intolerance. Mechanisms for promoting, documenting and challenging these attitudes reflect everyday social media practices – after all, these are everyday experiences – used for political and unrelated contexts.

Documenting, commenting and subverting

One reason for connections between different partisan clusters of bloggers or Twitter users is the highlighting of comments that might be offensive or inappropriate, from public figures and other users perpetuating problematic attitudes. Attention can be drawn to these remarks using clear linking approaches, such as retweeting them (accompanied by an explanatory note as required): such practices underline the standard disclaimer that 'retweets are not endorsements'. There are further practices that use social media to document comments without making a structural connection to another user (as a retweet does). Subtweeting and screencapping are processes that invoke another person's comments, indirectly or directly, yet without necessarily providing a link (and notification) for this individual. Tufekci (2014) goes into these practices in more detail, highlighting how such subversive and atypical uses of text and image can also be overlooked by automated and standardized analytical processes.

Screencapping and screenshots, too, also serve as means of recording comments that might soon be deleted or hidden behind changed privacy settings, allowing individuals to catalogue problematic, ill-advised or offensive remarks and hold their authors accountable. Documenting abuse in this way can allow affected users to counter hostility with solidarity (J. Allan, 2014), and becomes a particularly important consideration for collecting evidence of criminal activity or views relevant to investigations (Rentschler, 2014). It is also a pertinent practice for research into contentious subjects, recording material that can also be made available for later studies (Consalvo, 2012). Furthermore, the simple act of deleting a tweet does not mean it is completely erased: projects like *Politwoops* catalogue deleted political tweets – highlighting that even if a post is deleted after publication, whether because of a typo or publicly condemned remarks, it is not gone forever.

Documentation of problematic comments is predicated on the adoption of social media for sharing prevalent social attitudes and intolerance: rather than being purely partisan, antagonistic and offensive remarks also include trolling and confrontation carried out for lulz, and outright hatespeech. Prominent political hashtags get taken over by highly active users flaming and trolling other users, attacking others and attempting to get reactions out of them; although #auspol originally started out as a marker for general discussion of Australian politics, its evolution into polarized and hostile comments has led to descriptions where:

> Viewing and participating in 'discussions' on the Twitter stream of #auspol is to immerse yourself in a political cesspit. It is the dark alley in Twitter you walk down when you wonder if you have told anyone where you were going that night. (Jericho, 2012, p. 276)

Trolling's emergence as an everyday behaviour, extending beyond its origins on platforms like 4chan's /b/ forum (taking in different users and practices), is a reflection of its validation by mainstream attention. Whitney Phillips's (2015) study of trolling as subcultural practice argues that media stories about Anonymous and /b/ 'helped legitimize the development of a discrete, deliberate, and highly recognizable trolling identity' (p. 61). While the trolling that she studies is only one practice among others also dubbed 'trolling' (like cyberbullying), Phillips notes both the banality of these actions – using everyday practices, including appropriating existing texts and intertexts (see also Milner, 2013) – and how trolling behaviours 'complicate (or even outright defy) traditional notions of political action' (2015, p. 7).

Trolling is a disruptive form of political action online, fitting Lindgren (2013)'s description of disruption by actively challenging and subverting narratives and practices. It can also be personal – in its targets, rather than being framed around the individuals making the posts – and in its various forms can become an additional instance of online harassment and abuse (Jane, 2014; F. Shaw, 2013a). While not limited to 4chan and /b/, trolling demonstrates elements of these communities' chaotic culture in its practices, from anonymous attacks to the use of visual media (including very graphic images) and misogynistic and racist attitudes (Bernstein et al., 2011; Knuttila, 2011; Manivannan, 2013). Higgin (2013) argues that 'anons who engage in racist, sexist, and homophobic trolling are also representative of a larger effort to preserve the internet as a space free of politics and thus free of challenge to white masculine heterosexual hegemony' (p. 138). This is also apparent in Whitney Phillips's (2015) comment that racist trolling and racial humour suggest that 'participating trolls are either consciously or subconsciously *performing* whiteness' (p. 54).

Racist, sexist and other forms of hatespeech are prevalent in response to breaking news, media events and popular culture developments (Cisneros and Nakayama, 2015). They fester in channels noted for their hostile and unmoderated (or not well-policed) remarks, including in comments threads on news websites (Hughey and Daniels, 2013), and are found within trending topics and hashtags explicitly directed at social groups (Chaudhry, 2015). As noted in chapter 1, the approaches for users and platforms to address these practices are evolving but inconsistent, including policies around harassment (Matias et al., 2015). However, there has been an increased visibility of social media activity directly attacking individuals and perpetuating everyday sexism and racism, and a groundswell of counter-activity challenging these views through movements and campaigns like #BlackLivesMatter (Kang, 2015) and #YesAllWomen (Thrift, 2015) – if not without their own problems of inclusivity (Loza, 2014). Such trends underline the prevalence of hatespeech and the desire and necessity to fix this and its prevailing social and political causes. Social media enable the hugely problematic as well as the potentially positive through common mechanisms, affordances, practices and platforms, and these are not online-only issues: how they are realized on social media, though, provides new and changing challenges in response to physical and online stimuli alike.

Conclusion

Activity around politicians and partisan politics on social media incorporates the everyday and mundane into additional settings. Politicians post selfies and memes and write blog posts about their dogs in addition to tweeting links to their latest press releases, mixing the personal with the professional. Their activities are noted by supporters and opponents, with prominent politicians represented among the focal accounts bridging partisan groups of Twitter users. Indeed, while social media users will tend to follow others with similar views, promoting like-minded sites and commentators, interactions that are variously hostile, mocking, critical and sarcastic take place between supporters of different parties or groups reflecting various ideological alignments.

Hostility can extend to outright trolling and hatespeech, as the potential for debate, discussion, or conversation is instead replaced by a situation more akin to shouting and abusing others, en masse and without respite. The everyday nature of these experiences, for instigators and targets, demonstrates how social media are employed for purposes that are political, personal and harmful. The fact that these occur in the same ways as 'nice' or positive political discussions and themes shows the efficacy of the platforms in enabling communication and participation, and the challenges of combating the problematic while maintaining the 'decent'. While dealing with these behaviours on social media is necessary, there is also the wider context shaping this activity to address.

I will comment further on some of these ideas in the conclusion. In the final chapter, though, I return in part to the institutional context by examining social media within election contexts. Elections, through campaigns and the votes themselves, bring forth the various practices and settings studied throughout this book: not only do these periods bring forth heightened coverage of political topics, but they also showcase the everyday and the mundane within what is both a rather extraordinary and a ritualized setting.

7

The Everyday of Elections

On 31 January 2015, I voted in my fourth election (in which I was required to vote) in less than twenty-three months. Each time had been at a different polling place, with a different ballot paper – no one election had been for the exact same group of candidates. Because everything is a possible research topic, I also studied aspects of each of these elections, from candidates' use of social media to photographs of sausages.

I have covered parts of these events – the 2013 Western Australian state election, the 2013 Australian federal election, the 2014 special re-run of the Senate vote for Western Australia alone and the 2015 Queensland state election – as well as earlier campaigns, in previous publications and presentations. To avoid redundancy, in this chapter I am less interested in the minutiae of election campaigns, for there is a wealth of research into Twitter and elections from around the world already, but rather in how everyday practices and politics are realized in the election context.

After all, when it comes to politics and social media, elections are perhaps the best-researched topic, encompassing multiple platforms and campaigns; their regularity and defined lifespan make them appealing objects of study. They are guaranteed topics of interest and attention, instigating activity and commentary from candidates, political parties, traditional media, alternative media and voters alike. However, elections are, in a sense, artificial examples of political talk, since they provide heightened activity and interest beyond the levels of day-to-day, banal political discussions.

I have included elections as the focus for this final chapter because they act as a microcosm of the various practices and trends outlined in the previous chapters. While political interest and activity might increase during campaigns and on election days, these periods also demonstrate the further mixing of approaches to the coverage of politics on social media. From the personal experiences of voting and individual framing of election issues, to associated rituals and campaigning, social media platforms are employed for many different functions and purposes in elections which have their roots and analogues in everyday practices.

Campaigns

In some contexts, of course, it could be argued that electoral politics, and especially campaigns, are everyday examples. The US setting, for instance, and its state of 'permanent campaign' with regard to presidential nominations, fundraising and campaigning, sees speculation and reporting about elections occurring years before the relevant vote; see, for example, the April 2015 launch of Hillary Clinton's campaign for the Democratic nomination for the 2016 US presidential election…in April 2015.

Elmer et al. (2012) argue though that the concept of the 'permanent campaign' is not restricted to electoral contexts and their own heightened levels of political activity, but is adaptable to socially mediated coverage of crises and activism, and the use of these platforms for fundraising and commentary (p. 130). Instead of discriminating between 'politics as usual' and election campaigns, Elmer et al. examine how practices and relationships between political actors and social media platforms are articulated within the setting of permanent campaigns. In this book I have endeavoured to carry out a similar appraisal of political activity on social media, analysing recurring practices and their applications and alterations for different contexts.

Partisan politics during campaigns

The partisan patterns identified in chapter 6 are amplified in the election context, where a focused period of intense promotion, support and challenging is apparent. Numerous social media-related strategies are focused on garnering and spreading support for candidates and parties, some of which have been more successful than others. Barack Obama's successful US presidential campaign in 2008 featured prominent applications of social networking as a grassroots means of obtaining support (Fraser and Dutta, 2008). This harnessed elements of Howard Dean's prominent, yet ultimately unsuccessful, campaign for the Democratic nomination in 2004, when blogs had been a key part of his online fundraising strategy (Hindman, 2009; Meraz, 2007).

In other nations where election campaigns are shorter, and fundraising a less prominent part of campaign advertising, there are still appeals to internet users and social media for support. The 2007 French presidential election saw the Parti Socialiste candidate Ségolène Royal's campaign encourage supporters to create blogs, or connect their existing blogs, to a 'Ségosphère' of like-minded sites (Fouetillou, 2006). Meanwhile, the Australian federal election later in 2007 featured the ALP positioning its campaign strategy around its leader, Kevin Rudd, rather than the party. Branded 'Kevin07', the successful campaign had links to popular social networking sites in its presentation (particularly MySpace) (Flew, 2008; Penney, 2011; Wilson, 2014). In keeping with collective action strategies, supporters of particular parties and candidates will also change their user icons and publish statuses and imagery during election campaigns to demonstrate their affiliations.

With the adoption of Facebook and Twitter as popular social media for political and everyday purposes, the incorporation of these platforms into campaigns becomes more prominent (both are studied from a Scandinavian perspective by Larsson, 2014b; Larsson and Moe, 2012). As more politicians and candidates are represented with their own accounts, the management of social media within campaigning becomes increasingly important. While social media alone are highly unlikely to win an election or individual electoral contest for a candidate, avoiding gaffes and scandal from tweets or Facebook statuses, as well as elsewhere, is critical. This is one reason why social media use is not universal for candidates and parties in elections: during the 2013 Western Australian state election, for instance, the Liberal Party's considerable advantage in opinion polling and projected victory meant that they could avoid any risks of new candidates campaigning on social media.

When politicians and candidates are active on social media during campaigns, strategies feature a mix of promotion and topical engagement, variously following broadcasting and conversational strategies. The comparative research by Broersma and Graham (2012), studying Dutch and British politicians on Twitter during their respective campaigns, found differences in styles of tweeting between the two nations. Dutch politicians were more likely to engage with other users, replying to messages, while British politicians chose a more one-way, broadcast-like approach (see also Graham et al., 2013). Campaigns are also tailored to the platforms employed: during Barack Obama's 2012 presidential campaign, Tumblr was used as a repository for GIFs, memes and commentary under the official Obama banner – including the President's own version of 'McKayla is Not Impressed' with Olympic gymnast McKayla Maroney, as mentioned in chapter 2 (Garber, 2012).

There are differences too in how politicians and candidates engage with other social media users in general, and their fellow candidates specifically. During the 2013 Australian federal election, the @mentions between candidate accounts demonstrated not just clustering in part along party lines, but also concerted promotion of leading figures by other candidates from the same parties. This is not to say that there was no cross-party linking; indeed, prominent opponents from the major parties were often mentioned in the same tweets, such as the respective leaders of the ALP and the Liberal Party, Kevin Rudd and Tony Abbott. Similarly, politicians directly connected through their parliamentary positions (such as the Treasurer, Wayne Swan, and Shadow Treasurer Joe Hockey) were also repeatedly linked in comments. Further connections were also apparent at the level of individual electorates, with close contests accompanied by the relevant candidates tweeting at each other (whether in debate or in critique).

Strategies of @mentioning are just one element of communication on Twitter, let alone an election campaign on social media, though: in comparison, retweeting is far more partisan, with candidates primarily choosing to rebroadcast only messages from their own side. It is also important to note that the level of social media activity is not necessarily an indicator of electoral fortunes: some parties, like the Pirate Party in Australia, may be extremely active on social media during elections, but their actual results do not reflect this. While monitoring social media buzz and commentary is used to predict election results (discussed by Murthy, 2015), then, taking into account who is and is not participating in discussions on Twitter or Facebook is a necessary consideration.

Election strategies include promoting particular slogans and messages, both in general and tailored specifically for social media. Hashtag campaigns, though, run the risk of going awry as opponents notice and hijack the discussion. The research by Gainous and Wagner (2014) into the 2012 US presidential election noted the Republican-originated hashtag #AreYouBetterOff, which was intended to highlight how Barack Obama's first term as President had not benefited Americans; this intention was not fully realized, however, as the hashtag was co-opted by Twitter users remarking that actually they were doing alright (p. 155). As with general campaign slogans, this type of partisan attempt at affective commentary and support is ripe for hijacking, and this is also experienced within corporate social media campaigns (as seen in chapter 2 with #freshinourmemories).

Hashtag hijacking can lead to unintended sincere commentary – Democrat supporters genuinely responding to the Republican question of #AreYouBetterOff – but can also foster more irreverent takes. During intense speculation about a Liberal Party leadership spill in Australia in February 2015, the #ImStickingWithTony hashtag spread on social media. Intended to demonstrate support for Prime Minister Tony Abbott, it was immediately hijacked by Twitter users instead offering obvious mockery of Abbott's previous views on women, global warming, asylum seekers and immigration, and his public appearances (Ryall, 2015). As with other politically themed practices on social media, the hijacking of hashtags is applicable within election contexts and everyday coverage of politics: as a partisan strategy and as an extension of irreverence and topical humour, it further demonstrates social media users' familiarity with, and appropriation of, the affordances of their chosen platforms as well as their engagement with political themes.

Campaign media politics

Rituals and established social media practices are also reflected within the wider media coverage of election campaigns. The adoption of social media as second screen, and its relationship with the mainstream media as stimuli and content provider inspiring tweeting, are apparent in patterns of activity during campaigns. The amount of relevant content posted per day, including but not limited to election-specific hashtags, increases over the course of the campaign, building just before election day itself, but outliers are found through spikes in response to televised debates and other major broadcasts (such as campaign launches).

The live-tweeting of election debates is given significance by parties and broadcasters as well as providing a common context for social media users discussing the campaign (Carlson and Ben-Porath, 2012; Elmer, 2013). For the television networks presenting debates, social media coverage offers an opportunity to monitor the audience, to gauge interest and encourage interaction, including through featured comments on-screen; when multiple broadcasters are showing the debate, a specific hashtag for a network rather than a generic debate marker enables a clearer picture of audiences, their distribution and their engagement with candidates and issues. Monitoring social media for electoral sentiment, tracking whether tweeting is trending towards particular candidates and measuring positive and negative views during the debate, is an extension of audience research in election contexts. Broadcasters' on-screen worms – graphics depicting the fluctuating audience sentiment towards candidates participating in the debate – draw on social media activity as a proxy for the electorate at large (but with the usual caveats about the representativeness of social media users).

Other practices applicable to 'social tv' at large are realized within the coverage of election debates, and other political broadcasts, on social media. The unusual and the weird, the unintentionally comedic and ill-advised phrasing will be widely and immediately documented by the social media audience, turned into memes while the debate continues. The US presidential election debates in 2012 provided notable examples of this: Mitt Romney's 'binders full of women', Barack Obama's retort about the US military having 'fewer horses and bayonets' than in 1917 and Romney's love of the *Sesame Street* character Big Bird (but not of funding the Public Broadcasting Service) all inspired humorous and sarcastic activity on social media (Driscoll et al., 2013; Freelon and Karpf, 2015).

Gaffes and campaign tangents

Social media can be unforgiving; a gaffe can become the defining element of a candidate's campaign or image – especially since the social media coverage as a whole may run a punchline into the ground long after it has stopped being vaguely humorous. Minor candidates who 'enjoy' a brief moment in the spotlight due to their remarks or mistakes[48] are relentlessly dogged by references to these comments, while prominent political actors see their every appearance subject to increased scrutiny.

This tendency occurs during highly mediatized contexts, as with Mitt Romney's 'binders full of women', and as lower-profile events spread after the fact across social media and beyond. The final week of the 2015 UK general election campaign, for instance, saw Labour leader Ed Miliband's ploy of unveiling a large stone tablet inscribed with his election promises roundly mocked on social media. The response to Miliband's strategy featured new variations on ritualized practices, including re-imagining the promises by photoshopping them with song lyrics and other intertextual references, and the irreverent hashtaggery of #edstone (Alexandra, 2015; Ashton, 2015).

Further elements of campaigns bring out the irreverent and tangential practices outlined in chapters 1 and 2 but move beyond an electoral context. The defining image of Barack Obama's 2008 presidential campaign, for example, was the 'HOPE' poster designed by Shepard Fairey

(Cartwright and Mandiberg, 2009). The visual impact and public appeal of this image saw it adopted for further contexts: automated image generators provided the means for internet users to transform their own images into the 'HOPE' form, including adding alternative slogans. These new productions could be politically themed or completely unrelated (beyond the reimagined inspiration), and the longevity of the original poster's impact is seen in its influence on visual social media content in other electoral contexts years later.

Hooking into the visual, critiquing and appropriating styles, did not originate with the Obama campaign, and predates social media and online political activity in general. These spaces, though, as I have argued throughout this book, offer immediate and shared means for realizing and expanding practices. Later elections have similarly featured popular and user-generated responses to campaign material. The immediate aftermath to the launch of Hillary Clinton's campaign for the Democratic nomination in April 2015 saw a dissection of the typographic style of her campaign material, including its imagery and symbolism. It also saw the mock-up, and later release, of an unofficial typeface based on the 'H' styling in her campaign logo, with inevitable social media portmanteaugraphy dubbing it '#Hillvetica' – although the quickly released typeface by designer Rick Wolff had already been named 'Hillary Bold' (Wolff, 2015). #Hillvetica reflects social media practices which have their roots and inspiration in the political, but which then become tangential to the 'political' context: the content cannot be entirely divorced from its political origins, even if it is later adopted for unrelated topics. The political is an impetus for new instances of everyday practices – the campaign context is almost an irrelevance beyond providing the source material. These developments are not limited to campaigns. On election days, such practices are part of the intense but topically diverse activity responding to and documenting the vote.

Election Day Practices

And so we come to election day itself, where multiple practices collide within this specific political context. In my research into various Australian elections at the federal and state levels, I have examined different ways that social media users discuss these events, especially in the immediate vicinity and aftermath of voting. There is a consistent pattern of election day tweeting, which encompasses three key stages with different presentations and practices. These phases are suggested through hourly posting rates for election hashtags, as seen in figure 4, which charts the tweets per hour for three Australian election days: on the left vertical

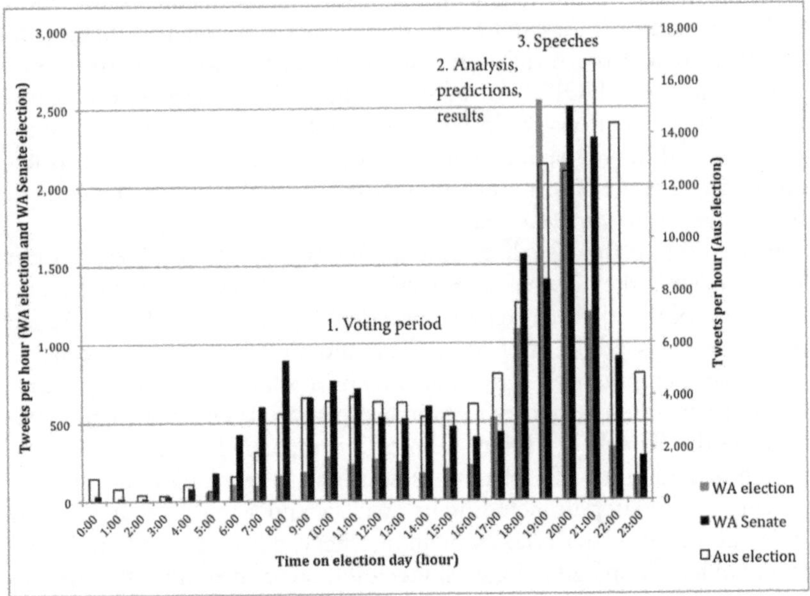

Figure 4: Hashtagged tweets per hour on election day for three Australian elections.

axis, the Western Australian state election (#wavotes tweets) on 9 March 2013 and the WA Senate re-run election (#wavotes) on 5 April 2014; and on the right vertical axis, the Australian federal election (#ausvotes) on 7 September 2013. The patterns identified are supported through close reading of the relevant tweets. Election days are, as would be expected, also the days which attract the highest levels of social media activity during campaigns; the different practices identified here, though, demonstrate that these patterns are due to a range of ways that citizens engage with the election, in addition to the relative political importance of the day.

The three phases of election day tweeting highlighted in figure 4 are: (1) posts during the voting period (8 a.m.–6 p.m.), representing the personal and individual experience of the election; (2) posts after the polls close and initial results come in, providing an analytical approach to tweeting; and (3) posts responding to the overall results and, especially, the live coverage of victory and concession speeches. These phases highlight a trajectory in the scope of tweeting, which starts at the micro level of the election and transitions to a mass context.

1. The individual

The first phase of election day activity on social media represents the most personal commentary, the descriptions of individuals' voting experiences. Tweeting still mentions candidates, parties and prominent figures in the election, but there is a strong personal angle to the posting here. Tweets about the election made while the polls are open are more uniquely individual in their content, as one person's voting experience will not be exactly the same as another's. Relevant posts might simply state that an individual has indeed voted – or complained about the obligation to do so (even if they decide to not vote). Other comments might provide more of an account of the scene at their chosen polling place, building on several rituals around social media and politics.

I began this book by talking about polling place selfies as a contentious practice in Europe in 2014. Taking photographs, including selfies, of the election day experience exemplifies the social mediation of everyday life, in which any event is potentially worth documenting and sharing. The political context is not necessarily required beyond providing a catalyst for this activity: the resulting images might have no obvious political content, in terms of promoting candidates or parties, or displaying completed ballot papers. Nevertheless, these visual recordings of election days remain political artefacts, combining everyday social media practices with politics, however fleetingly.

Socially mediated election day rituals: the partaking of #democracysausage

Polling place selfies underline that election day practices are not always explicitly political. In Australia, the compulsory nature of voting in federal and state elections has given rise to rituals around the experience of election days, predating social media and other means of online communication (Meikle et al., 2008). Ritualized to the point of stereotype, the shared experiences of voting at a school, church or community centre on a Saturday, accompanied by fundraising barbecues and cake stalls have become further mediated online over the course of several elections. Drawing on the collective intelligence of Australian voters who are obliged to report to a polling place and fill in their ballot papers, numerous projects have crowdsourced accounts of election day experiences. *Booth Reviews* (boothrev.net), for instance, solicits user-generated contributions about polling places; voters are asked to select their polling place and report on what they thought of their voting experience in a tweet-length comment (which is automatically posted to the project's Twitter account). The purpose here is accountability and documenting the nationwide experience of voting, providing a resource for future elections, similar to projects in other nations, such as the Twitter-specific *TweetVoteReport* during the 2008 US presidential election (Keim and Clark, 2009).

Other projects focus on some of the less substantial, but still highly ritualized, aspects of the election day experience. *Democracy Sausage* is an example of a further, informal approach that became more centralized and widely promoted over the course of several elections. The day before the 2013 Western Australian state election, an individual brainwave of using the #democracysausage hashtag to tweet whether or not a polling place had a sausage sizzle became adopted by followers and spread across networks of other WA voters on Twitter. As reports came in of the presence or absence of #democracysausage, other observers created custom Google maps of the dataset, providing a central resource for people still to vote to make their decision about polling places based on the availability of sausages. The success of the initial #democracysausage hashtag led to an 'official' *Democracy Sausage* Twitter account (@DemSausage) and website (democracysausage.org) for documenting future elections. During the 2013 Australian federal election, held six months later, and subsequent elections, the website hosted a new custom Google map of the Australian electorate, using geolocation data for polling places drawn from the Australian Electoral Commission and adding user-generated contributions, sourced from Twitter and other channels, about the availability of #democracysausage and #democracycake.[49]

Although Twitter is used as a primary means for documenting and sharing polling place experiences, these markers are also used on other social media, such as Instagram, as shown in figure 5. There is a mediation of the experience – and the use of a hashtag like #democracysausage – that might not contain any information relevant to the projects themselves beyond an image of an election day sausage sizzle. #democracysausage has, like many other hashtags before it, transformed from being a specific signifier to a de facto punchline used beyond its original purpose.

The success of these projects comes through election day rituals and social media rituals. Buying a sausage in a bun or a cake as a 'reward' for completing an individual's democratic duty has been a long-established part of Australian elections; social media, especially through hashtags and projects like *Democracy Sausage*, amplify these rituals, highlighting how they are shared experiences that connect voters around the country. The projects build on familiarity and repetition, and on social media-encouraged irreverence. *Democracy Sausage* arose out of

Figure 5: The author's #democracysausage photo, as posted to Instagram on 31 January 2015.

political engagement, but also from a playful take on election day rituals (although personal politics can still emerge here – critiques about discriminating against vegetarian, vegan and gluten-intolerant voters, and about meat farming practices, appear within #democracysausage tweets).

These socially mediated discussions do not overly mock or denigrate the voting experience. Rather, they use social media to enhance and share common experiences and provide resources that support and recognize the act that many Australians will perform that day (Zappavigna, 2014). They also represent highly specialized instances of collaborative, crowd-sourced projects around political and civic engagement (see chapters 4 and 5). While the motivations for participating in the likes of *Democracy Sausage* differ from the reasons and experiences shared with *Hollaback!* or Ushahidi crisis maps, they are further examples of the use of volunteered geographic information within political contexts. They are also intrinsically linked to the voting experience of election day. *Democracy Sausage* and its ilk represent practices that coincide with the personal, individual participation in an election, before the votes are counted, results are announced and social media activity turns to common contexts.

2. *The analytical*

Once the polls close (and even in the anticipation of the transition around this), there is a shift in coverage from the uniquely personal to a more shared context for commentary. This is positioned around – and responds to – broadcasts of results and analysis, predictions and conjecture. On social media, comments mix the personal with the analytical; the local context can still be important, especially for electorates with close contests, but they are reframed as part of the wider election narrative rather than the individual experience.

Networks and information sources

The importance of traditional media to social media coverage is reiterated in this second phase of election day activity. Mainstream sources broadcast results and analysis, making them key resources for getting updated information, and this is reflected in changing information flows online. Whereas the first phase of election day tweeting is generally unfocused and individual – to the extent that @replies and retweets are not widespread within tweets containing election hashtags[50] – the election night activity becomes more of a backchannel, with established political actors invoked in tweets. In particular, journalists, analysts and candidates featured in the rolling election broadcasts are prominent subjects of @mentions, following practices of using Twitter handles as shorthand for public figures even if not seeking a response.

During this second phase of election day tweeting, there is a clearer flow of information. While the personal framing of the first phase makes for a more disjointed selection, this subsequent phase sees established media and political actors become central – both through their comments being shared, and through their on-screen appearances being accompanied by audiences @mentioning them. Such patterns are further enhanced by broadcasters using common hashtags rather than their own, and by organizational networks of retweeting across their many accounts. On election nights in Australia, for example, the live coverage of the results by the ABC is accompanied by sequential retweeting: comments and posts from its analysts and national accounts are recirculated by state-based, regional and local accounts, and by individual journalists. These bridge different media represented on social media, flowing via the

Twitter accounts for state news teams and for local radio stations. Not all tweets from the parent organization are necessarily retweeted by regional accounts, though: filtering for the locally relevant is apparent here. This approach also demonstrates how, in the transition from the individual experiences of election day, local results and candidates do remain important, but they are also incorporated into the overall narrative of the election results. The second phase of election day activity on social media then acts as a tradition between the the personal model of election day and the mass, common context of the official results tally on election night.

3. *The reactive*

If the second phase of election day activity used traditional media as a catalyst for commentary, the third phase is strongly dependent on live broadcasts and a shared context en masse. As the overall results become known, and the leaders of the major parties make their respective victory and concession speeches, social media activity becomes even more a reaction to what is occurring, providing immediate responses to these developments. This represents a further narrowing of the scope of social media activity; whereas the first phase described various, diverse experiences of election day, this final phase sees myriad responses to a single, common factor. The shared focus from a mass audience makes the context for their comments universal in that moment; as users live-tweet quotes and interpret the speeches of the leaders, the setting for these comments is known without needing to provide extensive establishing information.

The subsuming of the individual experience angle to election day coverage by the shared responses to common topics and media broadcasts demonstrates a gradual shift in scope from the personal to the popular on social media. Like other examples of social media backchannels for televised content (Harrington, 2013), the common context of the final stages of the election day positions the audience as a step removed from the event: rather than documenting their own participation and interaction, social media users are responding to what they see on screen (accompanied by their analysis and commentary). Personal framings, though, are still apparent in this final phase of election coverage. Affective commentary, including hope and despair, relief and resignation, shapes individual responses to the victory and concession speeches and the overall results.

This final phase of election day coverage further illustrates how everyday practices and social media rituals remain popular means for engaging with politics online. The use of humour and memes, through irreverent hashtags and snarky commentary, enables social media users to share their views and reactions in different ways, incorporating textual and visual media to make their point. Retweeting others with similar sentiments, especially expressed with wit or sarcasm, is part of the sense-making of the election results. In the aftermath of the 2013 federal election in Australia, the ten most-retweeted comments in the collected #ausvotes data included five comments which explicitly responded to the results ironically or humorously: these tweets included remarks about the swing to the Liberals (Australia leaning so far to the right that it had collided with New Zealand), the Murdoch press support for Tony Abbott and general disbelief about the electorate voting for a conservative government led by a figure as unpopular (among non-conservative voters) as Abbott. On Facebook and Twitter, memes, especially about Abbott, circulated widely, shared across platforms as part of the shared electoral response.

The final phases of election day, then, demonstrate the changing foci of social media activity, from the individual experience to the shared, mass context responding to broadcast coverage. Traditional political and media actors remain important figures within this setting, both as participants and as symbols: they are referred to by social media users, and their comments are repeated, endorsed or critiqued on platforms like Twitter and Facebook. Even if politicians and journalists are not actively contributing to social media on election day, they are still reference points for other users, @mentioned and cited in passing.

The heightened political interest represented by elections also demonstrates the convergence of everyday social media users and practices with political subjects. Especially during the count, analysis and results phases of election day, there is a considerably greater level of social media activity than during the voting period, or indeed during the day-to-day coverage of many other political themes. Elections and their outcomes are common interests for social media users, in that they are affected by the results in terms of who forms government, their policies and views on current issues. This may lead to an audience participating in election day commentary that is more extensive than for other politically relevant topics, bringing their own everyday social media practices to their contributions. The diversity of experiences is also shown in the different phases of election day activity, as social media users employ various practices in engaging with the vote. Even within an explicitly political setting like an election, 'political' commentary and analysis are not the only approaches featured in social media activity. From irreverent remarks and memes to backchannelling, via collaborative information-sharing about polling places (and sausages), the everyday, the affective and personal experiences continue to play key roles in how politics is covered online.

Conclusion

In this chapter, I have provided a brief overview of how everyday social media practices are apparent within an extraordinary political context like elections. While they are examples of heightened activity and interest, elections also act as a microcosm for the practices examined in the previous chapters in this book. Across campaigns and voting periods, the coverage of elections on social media offers further insight into information flows online, as the work of traditional and new media sources alike circulate through networks and publics. Practices with irreverent and humorous foundations may be mixed with the partisan, offering sarcastic hijacking of campaign hashtags and memes mocking specific parties and candidates. Social media are also used to source and coordinate information about voting experiences, creating a record of features and facilities of different polling places.

What the election context also underlines is that, for the coverage of politics and for everyday social media practices, the mainstream and the social, alternative and corporate-owned platforms are all interlinked. The diversity of practices and experiences within the mediasphere fosters flows and activities that are shaped by the actions of other users and other media. Social media activity is at times highly indebted to the mainstream media, even if it is a reaction to what is not being shown or said. At other points, though, social media discussions are self-organized, using popular platforms to generate debate among users and taking advantage of the various affordances of these sites, which are then picked up on and amplified by mainstream media.

Conclusion: The Changing Face of Everyday Social Media and Everyday Politics

On 26 June 2015, the US Supreme Court voted that marriage equality was a constitutional right, simultaneously legalizing same-sex marriage across the fifty states, at the height of Pride festivities. The sudden acknowledgement of widespread social and cultural attitudes was met with an outpouring of support and congratulations on social media (as well as dissent, of course), recognized and reported in different ways by platforms, institutions and individual users: Twitter promoted the hashtag #LoveWins by appending a rainbow heart to mentions of the tag in tweets, while Facebook users took advantage of a platform-provided rainbow filter on their profile pictures, creating a sea of rainbows (that also spread to user icons on other platforms).[51] Coverage of the landmark decision also took advantage of technological capabilities and the norms of online commentary and discussions, adopted by institutions and mainstream media as well as individual users: in addition to putting its user icons in rainbows (and lighting up the physical building the same way), the White House's official Twitter account used an animated GIF to illustrate the recognition of marriage equality over time by individual states before the SCOTUS vote (@WhiteHouse, 2015). GIFs, Vine loops and other short visual media were similarly used by mainstream media and other sources to report on the latest developments and celebrations across the US – and in solidarity elsewhere.

These different responses further demonstrate the intersection of the personal and the political, both in terms of personal implications (such as being able to legally marry a same-sex partner) but also in the framing through individual elements like profile pictures. Everyday social media formats such as GIFs are incorporated into the coverage of unfolding events and used as part of contributing to social media commentary and analysis. These trends also highlight how the consumption and presentation of news, politics, sport, popular culture and more take a multi-platform form, with a desired diversity of interpretations. There is an omnivorous tendency where multiple analyses and discussions are sought out, covering text, video, images and audio, from professional and amateur perspectives, friends, followers and strangers alike.

As I set out in the Introduction, 'social media' is a fluid descriptor, encompassing many different platforms, apps, practices, audiences and contexts. The 'social media' I write about in 2014 and 2015 is different to that which I wrote about in 2010, and will also be different from what I cover in 2016 and beyond. The platforms used for everyday political purposes, and the practices involved, will continue to change, just as blogs, MySpace, Facebook, YouTube, Google+ and Twitter have all experienced fluctuating popularity. Online platforms for writing about news and politics continue to evolve, with some lasting and others being abandoned as rivals reach critical mass.

Regardless of which social media platforms and apps become popular in the future, which ones remain widely used and which ones are deserted, the political will remain a topic of interest. I have argued in this book that the political is featured in far more contexts and practices than just blatant and explicit 'politics', taking advantage of the social and cultural affordances and functions of social media. From niche networks to generic, multi-purpose spaces, promoting communication variously and concurrently through images, texts, videos or emoji or the continued instant sharing of everyday experiences, social media offer myriad ways for discussing and participating in political contexts. These extend beyond platforms alone, too, as new technologies from wearables to 3-D printing, via crypto-currencies and drones become used for personal, commercial, surveillance, military or social purposes, expand on existing logics and cultures of social media and raise new legal questions. The political and the everyday cannot be separated: from attempting to document and overcome prevalent sexist or racist societal attitudes, to the political sub-themes within popular culture contexts, our lives are politicized in many ways. Similarly, we actively and inadvertently, socially and privately, present our experiences on social media and in other personal contexts. Our motivations for using social media vary, as do our interpretations of content that we see online. We do not all use the same platforms for the same purposes – but in general we also do not use one single platform as the entirety of our 'social media' experience. Understanding our online activity and behaviours as a whole, rather than on platforms studied in isolation, is critical for social media research, whether focused on the political, cultural or other elements of platforms new and old.

Limits

In this book, I have endeavoured to incorporate research into multiple platforms into my discussion, drawing on my own empirical work as well as the published literature into social media and politics. Of course, this is filtered through my own research interests and background, and by what is available to researchers from different platforms. Most egregiously, Facebook is under-represented in my own research: the fuzziness around public/semi-private/private content, data access and archiving permissions, and the general implausibility of doing everything are all partly responsible here. Developing methods for studying social media in different ways is a known necessity for internet research – and digital methods, mixing qualitative and quantitative analyses, from digital ethnography to automated data-mining and sentiment-oriented processing of social media content, will continue to need to evolve with new platforms, practices and permissions.

Furthermore, it is important to acknowledge the biases and limits of my research, including the tools and methods used as well as the platforms studied. The data I study here represents visible, defined social media activity. However, political actions, comments, and contexts are seen, but less able to be traced, in many other ways, from filtering, blocking and reporting offensive users to responding to (or ignoring, or trying not to engage with) the political opinions shared by family and friends in Facebook statuses. Similarly, the users active on social media are not representative of their local populations – the Australian Twittersphere is not representative of the Australian population, for instance – and there are extensive differences apparent online that demonstrate global and local practices, or individual variations in social media use. I have not claimed to be providing a comprehensive and universal overview of everything that takes place online. Instead, this book has highlighted several practices of note which recur, and which fulfil and depict the intersection of the everyday and the political on social media.

What this book has underlined, though, is that, just as platforms are not used in isolation, the social media context is not separate from an individual's own experiences and background, or from environmental factors impacting upon access to, and uses of, the internet. Social media use occurs in response to, and in order to shape, external factors and events. We socially mediate our lives, and social media are part of our everyday experiences – the online and the offline are not disconnected, and ubiquitous access to the internet and the influence of associated practices mean that an already problematic dichotomy (just like online/ 'real life') becomes even more irrelevant. What we say and do on social media has repercussions, as is the case with what we say and do with any group of people, and responses to our actions happen in different forms and venues.

The ubiquity of access to the internet, to mobile data, to mechanisms for capturing, posting, sharing and responding to content instantly and everywhere (in a Western context, at least) means that everyday practices around social media are always-on and always-here. The social side of social media – tagging friends, taking selfies and group selfies, presenting a particular persona on specific platforms, for specific audiences – is important to note, especially for how it influences the coverage of and participation in everyday politics. Practices around visual and mixed-content media, including the appropriation of media from other sources and contexts and applying them to unrelated topics, are evolving and requiring further study. Internet Studies is currently at the confluence of big data and small media, across social media platforms, where content is instantaneous, spreadable and immediate. Together, these contribute to the extensive range of practices apparent on social media, reflecting highly individual and wildly different intentions, motivations and meanings. There are overlapping topics and themes, shared contexts and content on Twitter and Facebook, Instagram and Tumblr, but each user brings their own experiences and aims that are not obviously presented in a single tweet or meme, and for which different methods and research questions will provide different insights. In short, analysing social media practices, in political contexts and in general, is messy and confusing, where data can be easy to obtain but their significance can be unclear – and that is not a bad thing.

A recurring contradiction concerning social media and everyday politics has featured throughout this book. The advantages of social media – accessibility, ability to post and share quickly and instantly, challenging dominant frames and providing an outlet for voices in response to oppression or attacks – can also be disadvantages. Open registration, comment visibility and the ability to direct messages at other users means that mobilization of users can happen for trolling and abusive purposes, just as it can be used for campaigns around social justice and equality. The everyday practices I have discussed here are employed for various, seemingly contradictory purposes. I do not argue that social media use is all positive or a benefit for society or politics, because it is not: arguably, it *could be*, but I do not want to overlook the fact that individuals and groups who do try to challenge social norms through social media are subjected to unsolicited harassment, abuse and threats from strangers using the same channels. These are still everyday practices, and reflective of everyday politics – the freedom of expression on social media (within reason) is a contributing factor in the popularity of platforms. I do not want to ascribe a simple correct/wrong dichotomy here with regard to political views, to imply that social media users are representative of society at large or to claim that any groups in opposition are of equal size. The visibility or volume (in size and in messages) of a group (especially of affronted, technologically literate white men) does not mean that they represent all people of that demographic, or that they are in the right just because they seem to have the loudest voices.

Conclusion: Changing Everyday Politics and/with/through Social Media

We use social media to discuss politics, framed around our personal experiences, interests and beliefs. Our contributions, and our participation in politically themed activity, are also filtered and shaped through our social media practices. Everyday politics is framed by everyday social media. Our uses of memes, silly and punning hashtags, reaction GIFs, selfies, mash-ups and appropriated cultural media are integrated into how we feature political topics on social media. Using Twitter as a backchannel for engaging with television broadcasts as fans, commentators or hate-watchers extends to the political context. Choosing a specific hashtag to denote an event, group or topic is a feature of political topics as well as other social media activity. Social media-specific framing, from hashtag activism to political memes and parody accounts, can be criticized for being a simplistic, frivolous or fleeting acknowledgement of a topic warranting extended engagement and action. Yet social media alone are rarely the sole means for everyday political involvement and comment; they are merely a particularly publicly visible and active component.

The widespread use of social media as platforms for visible politically relevant comment, including dissent and shock, has been clearly demonstrated in various international examples, particularly in attempting to challenge dominant social norms and attitudes and to address injustices and intolerances. From misogyny and sexism, to homophobia and transphobia, via xenophobia and racism, these issues are experienced every day by populations around the world. Social media offer a means for vocalizing opposition to intolerance and support for marginalized groups, demonstrating – particularly alongside physical protests and other displays of solidarity – how there is a common desire and pressing need to change views, norms and legislation, to overcome prejudice and injustice.

These actions were especially apparent in response to decisions in November and December 2014 not to indict two US police officers in relation to the deaths of two Black Americans, Michael Brown and Eric Garner, in separate incidents in Ferguson, Missouri, and Staten Island, New York. Thousands took to the streets to protest, in Ferguson and New York City, and then in solidarity around the US. As with other protests around the world, social media coverage accompanied the demonstrations, providing updates and supporting material – especially through live-streaming. But what the accompanying discussions on Twitter and other channels also showed was an analytical, emotional and reflective frame in addition to sharing outrage, shock and support. Hashtags like #BlackLivesMatter, #ICantBreathe and #CrimingWhileWhite were not irreverent markers intended for humorous purposes; they variously displayed solidarity and open awareness, promoted protests while underlining the injustice of the Eric Garner case (Garner was killed in a choke-hold – a use of force and restraint banned under police policy), recognized and checked the privilege of white American experiences; but, in the latter case, they also took attention away from the prejudices and injustices being protested, and which was returned to in the counter-narrative of #AliveWhileBlack, where Black American encounters with the police were shared (Galo, 2014).

This is not to say that all social media commentary was supportive, and racist and hateful comments continued on Twitter, Facebook and in everyday conversation, including hooking into these same hashtags, using the same mechanisms for intolerant, offensive and bigoted remarks. Similarly, I am not saying that social media alone will or can change these situations. What these examples show is that social media can make these responses not just more visible, but additionally tangible: they add support, they provide additional avenues for analysing and describing injustice, intolerance and abuse, and more than anything, they highlight how commonplace, how ingrained and everyday these experiences have become – and why this is wrong.

A single tweet might not change policy; spread widely, as part of a growing groundswell of protest and dissent on social media and on the ground, though, and in combination, these factors might bring about change – and the visibility of positive, transformative views and attitudes, endorsed through social media platforms themselves, may help to combat attacks and trolling (Zimmerman, 2015). Change might not come – and maybe not in the ways that it is most desired – but to try and bring about change at the policy level and at the level of societal attitudes, actively challenging perceptions and practices can at least spread awareness and support. 'Awareness' is not a minor, irrelevant benefit of social media; if more people are aware and conscious of these problems, then a greater drive to do something about them might result.

Social media are not the only answer: they are one component of the means for participating in, discussing and challenging everyday political experiences. The social mediation of everyday life through Facebook, Twitter, Tumblr, Instagram, YouTube and more is not just for documenting irreverence and play through cats and coffee, meals and memes – and, as this book has shown, such mundane content can take political dimensions. When the personal and the political are so heavily intertwined, why shouldn't highly personalized and individual media be collectively and collaboratively used to report and to change this?

Notes

Introduction: Everyday Politics and Social Media

1 A quick note on platform nomenclature: in this book, I have not italicized platform names (like Twitter or Facebook), but occasionally do put non-English terms for types of platform in italics, such as *weibo* as a general descriptor of Chinese microblogs – this is as opposed to particular microblogging platforms in China like Sina Weibo. In general, platform names are capitalized, except for cases like reddit where the name is usually presented in lower-case. I capitalize Tumblr for the platform itself, while tumblr and tumblrs refer to blogs set up using this service. While I generally present hashtags in lower case in my own posts, I have attempted to use the established capitalization for individual hashtags where appropriate. Finally, my personal preference is not to capitalize 'internet', and apart from within quotes and citations this is the approach used in this book. I apologize for any errors and confusion here …

1 Personal/Political

2 In this introduction I am discussing content posted publicly either by the subject or author themselves, or with consent – I will come to practices which go against consent (if it was even obtained to begin with) later in this chapter.

3 In the following discussion, a noticeable gap in my research is around disability and social media, which has been studied in detail by Katie Ellis and colleagues (Ellis and Goggin, 2014; Ellis et al., 2015).

4 This discourse, and the activism represented by #BlackLivesMatter, also has its roots in historical movements, including the Civil Rights Movement; it is not a new development because of social media, but has socially mediated elements. #BlackLivesMatter later extended beyond the US context, adopted to document and counter racist attitudes in other countries, such as Australia and the treatment of – and views towards – indigenous Australians.

5 'LGBTQ' is used here while acknowledging the numerous sexual, asexual, intersex, genderqueer, nonconforming and variant identities that are not explicitly included in the acronym but whose (social media) practices and experiences should not be overlooked or discounted (see also Barker et al., 2009).

6 See also the ongoing debate around 'real name' policies online, including the 'nymwars' in response to Google's push to force 'real name' use when registering for its services and practices of anonymity and pseudonymity (van der Nagel and Frith, 2015), and the exploitation of Facebook's policy by trolls (Karppi, 2013).

7 This is not to ignore the overlaps between these communities or shared practices around hashtags or visual media.

8 See also the variously anonymous and identifiable nude and semi-nude content published on the /r/Gonewild subreddit (van der Nagel, 2013; van der Nagel and Frith, 2015).

9 For more discussion on sexting, including ethics, consent, trust, identity and legal and social repercussions, see: Albury (2015), Albury and Byron (2014), Albury and Crawford (2012), Chalfen (2009), Gabriel (2014), Hasinoff (2012).

10 See also the 'human flesh search engine' approach to sourcing information and fact-checking – especially about individuals, seen as a form of vigilantism – popularized in China (Gao and Stanyer, 2014).

11 Such as Georgia's intended entry in 2009 (titled 'We Don't Wanna Put In'), which was seen as negatively referencing Vladimir Putin.

12 Instagram's banned list of hashtags, for instance, still allows users to add these tags to their captions and comments, but searches for them will not return any results. Such tags include explicitly sexual terms, tags glorifying fascism and self-harm, and, with the April 2015 addition of emoji hashtags, the eggplant or aubergine emoji (#[emoji: http://emojipedia.org/aubergine/], used as a penis stand-in) (Griffin, 2015). Hiding hashtags from search results does not mean that explicit, obscene or offensive images are not posted to the platform, of course.

2 Political Rituals of Social Media

13 See also cultural phenomena such as 'Weird Twitter' (Herrman and Notopoulos, 2013).

14 Whereas in Soviet Russia, meme bans state?

15 Further debate about 'appropriate' ways to acknowledge ANZAC Day concerning social media arose the following week when a soccer journalist from the multicultural broadcaster SBS was sacked after refusing to delete tweets which expressed an opinion about wartime atrocities committed by Australians and their allies (Bacon, 2015).

16 Memetic rituals also raise questions about copyright, authorship and attribution that are part of a much larger debate around online material, piracy, access and ownership (Bannerman, 2013; Leaver, 2008; Meese, 2014, 2015). These concerns continue to evolve in response to new practices, platforms and content, and intersect with other elements of social media cultures and rituals. At the time of writing, these include questions about the potential for live-streaming apps Periscope and Meerkat to illegally share broadcast programming, and the singer Katy Perry's push to trademark 'Left Shark', the cult meme arising from her 2015 Super Bowl performance, following an enterprising fan's attempt to sell 3-D printed versions of Left Shark (Gardner, 2015).

17 McKayla being unimpressed later took on a political dimension itself when Maroney recreated the pose with President Obama while visiting the White House (Lavender, 2012).

3 Media Politics

18 An obvious callback to the Hillary Clinton memes mentioned in chapter 2 (see Anderson and Sheeler, 2014), and the Photoshop-heavy meme styles noted by Leaver (2013) and Bayerl and Stoynov (2014).

19 The episodes in question: *The West Wing*: season 1, episode 9 ('The Short List'); season 7, episode 15 ('Welcome to Wherever You Are'); *Parks and Recreation*: season 7, especially episode 5 ('Gryzzlbox'); *Veep*: season 2, episode 4 ('The Vic Allen Dinner'); season 3, episodes 1, 2 and 4 ('Some New Beginnings'; 'The Choice'; 'Clovis'); *House of Cards*: season 1, episode 6 ('Chapter 6'); season 2, episode 2 ('Chapter 15'); *The Thick of It*: season 3, episode 3.

20 *The West Wing*, season 3, episode 16 ('The U.S. Poet Laureate' – 2002).

21 For the diversity of blogging beyond the news and politics context studied here, see Walker Rettberg (2008) for blogging overall, and for specific subgenres and practices, including those emerging from political spaces, see, among many others, the edited collections by Bruns and Jacobs (2006) and Tremayne (2007). See also the diversity apparent among blogging platforms, from LiveJournal to Blogger, approaches from photoblogging to videoblogging or vlogging (Burgess and Green, 2009; Cohen, 2005), and international blogging spaces and platforms offering blog functions (Russell and Echchaibi, 2009).

22 Several sites in this visualization are thus no longer active or accessible (bar through tools like the Internet Archive's *Wayback Machine*).

23 See Highfield (2011) for extended analysis of these blogospheres, including comparisons of networks formed between blogroll links vs those formed through citations in blog posts.

24 Although writing in English should not mean an assumption of bridge-blogging intentions; see de Vries (2009).

25 As with later social media platforms, of course, political blogs could also be used for personal rants and unsupported arguments, which like considered political analyses could be widely read or attract no responses.

26 The seemingly obligatory presence of social media tickers inviting audience participation through their own programme- and broadcaster-specific hashtags is also the subject of mockery in satirical programmes such as *The Hamster Wheel* (from the team behind *The Chaser's War on Everything*; see Harrington, 2010; Higgie, 2015). Showcasing fake tweets from politicians and public figures responding to the show reflects the high degree of interlinking between the political, media and social media contexts (the show's own hashtag, #hamster, was used as an aggregational marker for audience responses but not featured on-screen).

27 Similarly, Australian mainstream media content offered inspiration for popular viral visual media when a 2007 newspaper page featuring a series of photos of John Howard was doctored to make it look like the Prime Minster was a DJ, complete with the scrawled caption 'Howard DJs like a mad cunt' (Di Stefano, 2015b).

28 Hashbrown nofilter.

29 #FoxNewsFacts also illustrates how different hashtags overlap and intersect in the creation of political commentary and humour. The affective hashtag #illridewithyou, emerging as a supportive marker in the wake of the Sydney siege (see chapter 4), was adapted as a punchline in #FoxNewsFacts tweets in offering support for non-Muslims travelling to Birmingham. This overlap further demonstrates the awareness, engagement and literacy of the social media audience: they are not just politically literate, but also active participants within social media and internet cultures.

4 Breaking News, Scandals and Crises

30 Although, as Monroy-Hernández et al. (2012) note in their study of Twitter use within the context of the Mexican drug war, 'in localities afflicted with armed conflicts, crises are part of everyday life, turning otherwise extraordinary events into ordinary ones' (p. 515).

31 Although Twitter's changing algorithms and approaches to choosing and displaying search results, and the potential impact of this on crisis communication especially, should be noted.

32 Hands (2014) uses the terms 'idiot' and 'idiotic' not for the general pejorative functions for which they are commonly used, but to convey 'a private, dislocated, self-serving subject' (p. 243).

33 While this section focuses on reddit and the specific context of the Boston Marathon bombing, see Adrienne Massanari's (2015) richly detailed research on reddit more broadly.

34 This is in addition to other forms of misinformation that may appear in these and other contexts, including misleading and partisan promotions like astroturfing and propaganda, posting fake images and other falsified media and trolling practices where deception may reflect ostensibly humorous, self-congratulatory and other manipulative motivations.

5 Collective and Connective Action

35 For the Arab Spring, see, among others: Barrons (2012), Harlow and Johnson (2011), Lotan et al. (2011), Markham (2014), Poell and Darmoni (2012). For Occupy: Agarwal et al. (2014a, 2014b), Costanza-Chock (2012), DeLuca et al. (2012), Gaby and Caren (2012), Juris (2012), Thorson et al. (2013).

36 'Social media', 'Facebook', 'Twitter' and 'internet revolutions' are also terms used to describe other cases, such as unrest and uprisings in 2009 in Iran and Moldova (Alex Burns and Eltham, 2009; Splichal, 2009).

37 Conversely, see Iranian women's experiences of social movements and photography, using the digital for freedoms not safely possible as physical manifestations: women participating in the #MyStealthyFreedom campaign used social media to post photos without their hijabs, and risks diminished as increased attention for the movement offered more informal protection for participants (Novak and Khazraee, 2015).

38 In keeping with other practices identified throughout this book around political discussions on social media, Stevenson (2014) notes that opponents adopted rival hashtags (including #SitDownWendy) to counter this coverage. The #StandWith[x]/#IStandWith[x] and #JeSuis[x] structures have become ritualized over time, following examples like the Davis filibuster and the *Charlie Hebdo* attack in 2015.

39 Twitter's architecture has changed since 2012, such that verified accounts can ignore tweets mentioning them from accounts that they do not follow, making such targeted campaigns unlikely to succeed now. This is also a means of ignoring constant requests from fans for 'follow backs' and spam (Twitter, n.d.).

40 This is not to say that 'Kony'-oriented activity was all of this nature: co-occurring hashtags included further reflections of the campaign's aims (#konysurrender, #makekonyfamous, #makehimvisible), responses to Kony's actions (#theresaspecialplaceinhell) and, a few days after peak Kony tweeting, commentary on the fleeting interest of social media users regarding the campaign (#internetadhd).

41 #occupyoakland was also used, but, as with #ows for Occupy Wall Street, the #oo acronym had the advantage of using fewer characters.

42 Blackout protests have also responded to decisions made by the platforms themselves, as users demonstrate their opposition to changes and policies

by deliberately not using the platforms, such as Tumblr (Orsini, 2011), for a given period.

43 The term 'blackout' was also used for an unrelated approach in 2015, when an individual campaign to promote 'the beauty of Blackness' (Color The Future, 2015) was adopted on Tumblr (and other social media) as 'BlackOutDay'.

6 Partisan Politics and Politicians on Social Media

44 Not to overlook the resistant framing of 26 January as Invasion Day and Survival Day, by and in recognition of indigenous Australians.

45 The other recipient of a knighthood in the 2015 Australia Day honours was Angus Houston, a former officer from the Royal Australian Air Force who had served as both Chief of Air Force and Chief of the Defence Force. No title of Dame was awarded.

46 Irreverent hashtaggery and portmanteaugraphy were again at play in the social media response, of which the punning #knightmare was perhaps the most successful combination.

47 In May 2015, Obama started tweeting through the newly launched and verified @POTUS account.

7 The Everyday of Elections

48 These might not even be made during the campaign, but uncovered while trawling through a candidate's past social media activity or comments archived online. This also applies outside the election context, of course. In Australia in August 2015, the Speaker Bronwyn Bishop resigned following controversy over her use of a helicopter to attend events, paid for by taxpayer funds. In the aftermath, a tweet posted by Tony Abbott in 2011 (when he was Leader of the Opposition) that had described the previous government as being 'in chaos' following the sudden resignation of Speaker Harry Jenkins, was widely shared by Abbott's opponents as an act of political schadenfreude (Koziol, 2015).

49 Other projects tracking Australian election day foodstuffs include *Election Day Sausage Sizzles* (#snagvotes) and *The Hungry Voter*; there is overlap and collaboration between these different projects, too, as in various campaigns they have pooled data and resources to extend their coverage of polling place options. My thanks to Keith Moss and Helen Ensikat for providing additional information about *Democracy Sausage* and its operations.

50 Acknowledging the limits of this interpretation – @replies might not incorporate the hashtags in question.

Conclusion: The Changing Face of Everyday Social Media and Everyday Politics

51 This filter was not created in response to the SCOTUS decision, but had been created in solidarity with Pride – its widespread take-up came on and after 26 June, though, as more and more users showed their support of marriage equality (see also Matias, 2015).

References

/r/serialpodcast (2014) 'A place to discuss Serial: The Podcast'. Retrieved from http://www.reddit.com/r/serialpodcast/

@WhiteHouse (2015, 26 June) '#LoveWins'. [Tweet]. Retrieved from https://twitter.com/WhiteHouse/status/614438061817114624

ABC News (2012, 9 October) 'Gillard labels Abbott a misogynist'. *ABC News (Australian Broadcasting Corporation)*. Retrieved from http://www.abc.net.au/news/2012-10-09/julia-gillard-attacks-abbott-of-hypocrisy/4303634

ABC News (2014, 15 December) '#illridewithyou: Support for Muslim Australians takes off following Sydney siege'. *ABC News (Australian Broadcasting Corporation)*. Retrieved from http://www.abc.net.au/news/2014-12-15/illridewithyou-hashtag-takes-off-following-siege/5969102

ABC News (2015a, 8 January) '#JeSuisCharlie: Social media reacts to the Charlie Hebdo shooting in Paris'. *ABC News (Australian Broadcasting Corporation)*. Retrieved from http://www.abc.net.au/news/2015-01-08/jesuis-charlie-social-media-reacts-to-charlie-hebdo-shooting/6005672

ABC News (2015b, 26 January) '#Tay4Hottest100: Triple j says Taylor Swift banned from Hottest 100 music poll'. *ABC News (Australian Broadcasting Corporation)*. Retrieved from http://www.abc.net.au/news/2015-01-26/taylor-swift-banned-from-2015-hottest-100/6046156

ABC News (2015c, 14 March) 'Prime Minister Tony Abbott eats an onion, skin and all, while touring an onion farm in Tasmania'. [Vine]. Retrieved from https://vine.co/v/O9deFBO6HZW

ABC News (2015d, 15 April) 'Woolworths "Fresh in our Memories" campaign inappropriate, Veteran Affairs Minister Michael Ronaldson says'. *ABC News (Australian Broadcasting Corporation)*. Retrieved from http://www.abc.net.au/news/2015-04-15/rsl-responds-to-woolworths-fresh-in-our-memories-campaign/6393498

Abidin, C. (2014) '#In$tagLam: Instagram as a repository of taste, a burgeoning marketplace, a war of eyeballs'. In: Berry, M. and Schleser, M. (eds.) *Mobile Media Making in an Age of Smartphones*. Palgrave Macmillan, New York, pp. 119–28.

Abidin, C. (2015a, 9 January) '#JeSuisAhmed speaks back to #JeSuisCharlie on Instagram'. *Wishcrys*. Retrieved from http://wishcrys.com/2015/01/09/jesuisahmed-speaks-back-to-jesuischarlie-on-instagram/

Abidin, C. (2015b, 9 January) 'Memetic tropes on #CharlieHedbo on Instagram'. *Wishcrys*. Retrieved from http://wishcrys.com/2015/01/09/memetic-tropes-on-charliehedbo-on-instagram/

Adamic, L. A. and Glance, N. (2005) 'The political blogosphere and the 2004 U.S. election: Divided they blog'. Paper presented at *2nd Annual Workshop on the Weblogging Ecosystem: Aggregation, analysis and dynamics*, 10 May 2005, Chiba. Retrieved from http://www.blogpulse.com/papers/2005/AdamicGlanceBlogWWW.pdf

Adbusters (2011, 13 July) '#OCCUPYWALLSTREET: A shift in revolutionary tactics'. *Adbusters*. Retrieved from https://www.adbusters.org/blogs/adbusters-blog/occupywallstreet.html

Agarwal, S. D., Barthel, M. L., Rost, C., Borning, A., Bennett, W. L. and Johnson, C. N. (2014a) 'Grassroots organizing in the digital age: Considering values and technology in Tea Party and Occupy Wall Street'. *Information, Communication & Society*, 17(3): 326–41.

Agarwal, S. D., Bennett, W. L., Johnson, C. N. and Walker, S. (2014b) 'A model of crowd-enabled organization: Theory and methods for understanding the role of Twitter in the Occupy protests'. *International Journal of Communication*, 8: 646–72.

Albury, K. (2015) 'Selfies, sexts, and sneaky hats: Young people's understandings of gendered practices of self-representation'. *International Journal of Communication*, 9: 1734–45.

Albury, K. and Byron, P. (2014) 'Queering sexting and sexualisation'. *Media International Australia*, 153: 138–47.

Albury, K. and Crawford, K. (2012) 'Sexting, consent and young people's ethics: Beyond Megan's Story'. *Continuum: Journal of Media & Cultural Studies*, 26(3): 463–73.

Alexandra, K. (2015, 3 May) 'Election 2015: #edstone'. *BBC News*. Retrieved from http://www.bbc.com/news/election-2015-32573812

Alexanyan, K. and Koltsova, O. (2009) 'Blogging in Russia is not Russian blogging'. In: Russell, A. and Echchaibi, N. (eds.) *International Blogging: Identity, politics, and networked publics*. Peter Lang, New York, pp. 65–84.

Allan, J. (2014) 'Privilege, marginalization, and solidarity: Women's voices online in Western Sahara's struggle for independence'. *Feminist Media Studies*, 14(4): 704–8.

Allan, S. (2014) 'Witnessing in crisis: Photo-reportage of terror attacks in Boston and London'. *Media, War & Conflict*, 7(2): 133–51.

Allard, L. and Blondeau, O. (2006) 'Racaille digit@le: Les émeutes de banlieues n'ont pas eu lieu'. *Contemporary French Civilization*, 31(1): 197–217.

Allen, M. (2012) 'Gaining a past, losing a future: Web 2.0 and internet historicity'. *Media International Australia*, 143: 99–109.

Alper, M. (2014) 'War on Instagram: Framing conflict photojournalism with mobile photography apps'. *New Media & Society*, 16(8): 1233–48.

Anderson, K. V. and Sheeler, K. H. (2014) 'Texts (and tweets) from Hillary: Meta-meming and postfeminist political culture'. *Presidential Studies Quarterly*, 44(2): 224–43.

Anstead, N. and O'Loughlin, B. (2011) 'The emerging viewertariat and BBC Question Time: Television debate and real-time commenting online'. *The International Journal of Press/Politics*, 16(4): 440–62.

Aouragh, M. and Alexander, A. (2011) 'The Egyptian experience: Sense and nonsense of the Internet revolution'. *International Journal of Communication*, 5: 1344–58.

Ashton, E. (2015, 3 May) 'The internet is flipping out over Ed Miliband carving his pledges in stone'. *BuzzFeed*. Retrieved from http://www.buzzfeed.com/emilyashton/between-a-rock-and-a-hard-place

Ausserhofer, J. and Maireder, A. (2013) 'National politics on Twitter: Structures and topics of a networked public sphere'. *Information, Communication & Society*, 16(3): 291–314.

Bacon, W. (2015, 6 May) 'Getting Scott McIntyre: Lest we forget the role of pundits, politicians and a social media mob'. *New Matilda*. Retrieved from https://newmatilda.com/2015/05/06/getting-scott-mcintyre-lest-we-forget-role-pundits-politicians-and-social-media-mob

Baishya, A. K. (2015) '#NaMo: The political work of the selfie in the 2014 Indian general elections'. *International Journal of Communication*, 9: 1686–700.

Bajekal, N. (2015, 8 January) 'French Twitter users says #jesuischarlie isn't for everyone'. *Time*. Retrieved from http://time.com/3659534/charlie-hebdo-social-media-hashtag-je-suis-charlie/

Bannerman, S. (2013) 'Fan fiction and copyright: Outsider works and intellectual property protection'. *New Media & Society*, 15(5): 803–5.

Barker, M., Richards, C. and Bowes-Catton, H. (2009) '"All the world is queer save thee and ME...": Defining queer and bi at a critical sexology seminar'. *Journal of Bisexuality*, 9(3–4): 363–79.

Barrons, G. (2012) '"Suleiman: Mubarak decided to step down #egypt #jan25 OH MY GOD": Examining the use of social media in the 2011 Egyptian revolution'. *Contemporary Arab Affairs*, 5(1): 54–67.

Bassily, N. (2015, 18 March) 'Young feminist uses menstrual pads to spread feminist messages'. *Young Feminist Wire*. Retrieved from http://yfa.awid.org/2015/03/young-feminist-uses-menstrual-pads-to-spread-feminist-messages/

Bastos, M. T. and Mercea, D. (2015) 'Serial activists: Political Twitter beyond influentials and the twittertariat'. *New Media & Society* (online first).

Bastos, M. T., Recuero, R. and Zago, G. (2014) 'Taking tweets to the streets: A spatial analysis of the Vinegar Protests in Brazil'. *First Monday*, 19(3). Retrieved from http://firstmonday.org/ojs/index.php/fm/article/view/5227/3843

Bates, L. (2014) *Everyday Sexism*. Simon & Schuster, London.

Bayerl, P. S. and Stoynov, L. (2014) 'Revenge by Photoshop: Memefying police acts in the public dialogue about injustice'. *New Media & Society* (online first).

Baym, N. K. (2010) *Personal Connections in the Digital Age*. Polity, Malden, MA.

Baym, N. K. (2013) 'Data not seen: The uses and shortcomings of social media metrics'. *First Monday*, 18(10). Retrieved from http://firstmonday.org/ojs/index.php/fm/article/view/4873/3752

Bel (2014, 14 December) 'Uber free rides during the Sydney Siege'. *Uber Blog*. Retrieved from http://blog.uber.com/sydneysiege

Benkler, Y. (2006) *The Wealth of Networks: How social production transforms markets and freedom*. Yale University Press, New Haven, CT.

Benkler, Y., Roberts, H., Faris, R., Solow-Niederman, A. and Etling, B. (2015) 'Social mobilization and the networked public sphere: Mapping the SOPA-PIPA debate'. *Political Communication*, 32(4): 594–624.

Bennett, W. L. and Manheim, J. B. (2006) 'The one-step flow of communication'. *The Annals of the American Academy of Political and Social Science*, 608(1): 213–32.

Bennett, W. L. and Segerberg, A. (2013) *The Logic of Connective Action: Digital media and the personalization of contentious politics*. Cambridge University Press, New York.

Berkowitz, D. and Eko, L. (2007) 'Blasphemy as sacred rite/right'. *Journalism Studies*, 8(5): 779–97.

Berkowitz, D. and Schwartz, D. A. (2015) 'Miley, CNN and *The Onion*: When fake news becomes realer than real'. *Journalism Practice* (online first).

Bernstein, M., Monroy-Hernández, A., Harry, D., André, P., Panovich, K. and Vargas, G. (2011) '4chan and /b/: An analysis of anonymity and ephemerality in a large online community'. *Proceedings of the Fifth International AAAI Conference on Weblogs and Social Media*, pp. 50–7.

Blood, R. (2002) 'Weblogs: A history and perspective'. In: Rodzvilla, J. (ed.) *We've Got Blog: How weblogs are changing our culture*. Perseus Publishing, Cambridge, pp. 7–16.

Bonilla, Y. and Rosa, J. (2015) '#Ferguson: Digital protest, hashtag ethnography, and the racial politics of social media in the United States'. *American Ethnologist*, 42(1): 4–17.

Boon, S. and Pentney, B. (2015) 'Virtual lactivism: Breastfeeding selfies and the performance of motherhood'. *International Journal of Communication*, 9: 1759–72.

Booth, P. (2010) *Digital Fandom: New media studies*. Peter Lang, New York.

Booth, P. (2014) 'Slash and porn: Media subversion, hyper-articulation, and parody'. *Continuum Journal of Media & Cultural Studies*, 28(3): 396–409.

boyd, d. (2011) 'Social network sites as networked publics: Affordances, dynamics, and implications'. In: Papacharissi, Z. (ed.) *A Networked Self: Identity, community, and culture on social network sites*. Routledge, New York, pp. 39–58.

boyd, d. (2012a) 'White flight in networked publics? How race and class shaped American teen engagement with MySpace and Facebook'. In: Nakamura, L. and Chow-White, P. A. (eds.) *Race After the Internet*. Routledge, New York, pp. 203–22.

boyd, d. (2012b, 14 March) 'The power of youth: How Invisible Children orchestrated Kony 2012'. *The Huffington Post*. Retrieved from http://www.huffingtonpost.com/danah-boyd/post_3126_b_1345782.html

boyd, d. (2014) *It's Complicated: The social lives of networked teens*. Yale University Press, New Haven, CT.

boyd, d. and Crawford, K. (2012) 'Critical questions for big data'. *Information, Communication & Society*, 15(5): 662–79.

boyd, d. and Ellison, N. B. (2008) 'Social network sites: Definition, history, and scholarship'. *Journal of Computer-Mediated Communication*, 13(1): 210–30.

Boyte, H. (2005) *Everyday Politics: Reconnecting citizens and public life*. University of Pennsylvania Press, Philadelphia.

Brabham, D. C. (2015) 'Studying normal, everyday social media'. *Social Media + Society* (online first), 1(1).

Breindl, Y. and Gustafsson, N. (2011) 'Leetocracy: Networked political activism or the continuation of elitism in competitive democracy'. In: Araya, D., Breindl, Y. and Houghton, T. J. (eds.) *Nexus: New intersections in internet research*. Peter Lang, New York, pp. 193–211.

Brock, A. (2009) 'Life on the wire: Deconstructing race on the Internet'. *Information, Communication & Society*, 12(3): 344–63.

Brock, A. (2012) 'From the blackhand side: Twitter as a cultural conversation'. *Journal of Broadcasting & Electronic Media*, 56(4): 529–49.

Brock, A., Kvasny, L. and Hales, K. (2010) 'Cultural appropriations of technical capital: Black women, weblogs, and the digital divide'. *Information, Communication & Society*, 13(7): 1040–59.

Brodsky, A. (2015, 27 March) 'Instagram bans photo for showing menstruation'. *Feministing*. Retrieved from http://feministing.com/2015/03/27/instagram-bans-photos-for-showing-menstruation/

Broersma, M. and Graham, T. (2012) 'Social media as beat: Tweets as a news source during the 2010 British and Dutch elections'. *Journalism Practice*, 16(3): 403–19.

Brown, H. (2015, 14 August) 'The White House just completely ruined the "Straight Outta Compton" meme'. *BuzzFeed*. Retrieved from http://www.buzzfeed.com/hayesbrown/are-bad-memes-an-impeachable-offense-just-asking#.axzPp5XwM

Bruns, A. (2005) *Gatewatching: Collaborative online news production*. Peter Lang, New York.

Bruns, A. and Burgess, J. (2011a) 'The use of Twitter hashtags in the formation of ad hoc publics'. Paper presented at *6th European Consortium for Political Research General Conference*, 25–27 August 2011, Reykjavik. Retrieved from http://eprints.qut.edu.au/46515/

Bruns, A. and Burgess, J. (2011b, 22 June) 'Gawk scripts for Twitter processing'. *Mapping Online Publics*. Retrieved from http://mappingonlinepublics.net/resources/

Bruns, A. and Burgess, J. (2015) 'Twitter hashtags from ad hoc to calculated publics'. In: Rambukkana, N. (ed.) *Hashtag Publics: The power and politics of discursive Networks*. Peter Lang, New York, pp. 13–27.

Bruns, A. and Highfield, T. (2012) 'Blogs, Twitter, and breaking news: The produsage of citizen journalism'. In: Lind, R. A. (ed.) *Produsing Theory in a Digital World: The intersection of audiences and production in contemporary theory*. Peter Lang, New York, pp. 15–32.

Bruns, A. and Jacobs, J. (eds.) (2006) *Uses of Blogs*. Peter Lang, New York.

Bruns, A. and Sauter, T. (2014) 'The emergence of trending topics: The dissemination of breaking stories on Twitter'. Paper presented at *Social Media and the Transformation of Public Space* conference, 18–20 June 2014, Amsterdam. Retrieved from http://snurb.info/node/1957

Bruns, A., Burgess, J., Crawford, K. and Shaw, F. (2012) '#qldfloods and @QPSMedia: Crisis communication on Twitter in the 2011 South East Queensland floods'. ARC Centre of Excellence for Creative Industries and Innovation, Brisbane. Retrieved from http://cci.edu.au/floodsreport.pdf

Bruns, A., Highfield, T. and Harrington, S. (2013) 'Sharing the news: Dissemination of links to Australian news sites on Twitter'. In: Gordon, J., Rowinski, P. and Stewart, G. (eds.) *Br(e)aking the News*. Peter Lang, New York, pp. 181–210.

Bruns, A., Burgess, J. and Highfield, T. (2014a) 'A "big data" approach to mapping the Australian Twittersphere'. In: Arthur, P. L. and Bode, K. (eds.) *Advancing Digital Humanities: Research, methods, theories*. Palgrave Macmillan, Basingstoke, pp. 113–29.

Bruns, A., Woodford, D. and Sadkowsky, T. (2014b) 'Towards a methodology for examining Twitter follower accession'. *First Monday*, 19(4). Retrieved from http://firstmonday.org/ojs/index.php/fm/article/view/5211/3864

Buchanan, R. T. (2015, 12 January) '#FoxNewsFacts: Twitter users react with aplomb to news that Birmingham is a "no-go zone" for "non-Muslims"'. *Independent*. Retrieved from http://www.independent.co.uk/news/uk/foxnewsfacts-twitter-users-react-with-aplomb-to-news-that-birmingham-is-a-nogo-zone-for-nonmuslims-9971829.html

Bucher, T. (2012a) 'A technicity of attention: How software "makes sense"'. *Culture Machine*, 13. Retrieved from http://www.culturemachine.net/index.php/cm/article/view/470/489

Bucher, T. (2012b) 'Want to be on the top? Algorithmic power and the threat of invisibility on Facebook'. *New Media & Society*, 14(7): 1164–80.

Bump, P. (2013, 8 April) 'You're not really following @BarackObama on Twitter'. *The Atlantic Wire*. Retrieved from http://www.theatlanticwire.com/politics/2013/04/youre-not-following-barackobama-twitter/63930/

Burchell, K. (2015) 'Infiltrating the space, hijacking the platform: Pussy Riot, Sochi protests, and media events'. *Participations*, 12(1): 659–76.

Burgess, J. (2008) '"All your Chocolate Rain are belong to us"? Viral video, YouTube and the dynamics of participatory culture'. In: Lovink, G. and

Niederer, S. (eds.) *Video Vortex Reader: Responses to YouTube.* Institute of Network Cultures, Amsterdam, pp. 101–9.

Burgess, J. and Green, J. (2009) *YouTube: Online video and participatory culture.* Polity, Cambridge.

Burgess, J., Vis, F. and Bruns, A. (2012, 6 November) 'How many fake Sandy pictures were really shared on social media?' *Guardian (Datablog).* Retrieved from http://www.theguardian.com/news/datablog/2012/nov/06/fake-sandy-pictures-social-media

Burgess, J., Galloway, A. and Sauter, T. (2015) 'Hashtag as hybrid forum: The case of #agchatoz'. In: Rambukkana, N. (ed.) *Hashtag Publics.* Peter Lang, New York, pp. 61–76.

Burns, Alex and Eltham, B. (2009) 'Twitter free Iran: An evaluation of Twitter's role in public diplomacy and information operations in Iran's 2009 election crisis'. *Record of the Communications Policy & Research Forum 2009*, pp. 298–310. Retrieved from http://networkinsight.org/verve/_resources/CPRF_2009_papers.pdf

Burns, Anne (2015) 'In full view: Involuntary porn and the postfeminist rhetoric of choice'. In: Nally, C. and Smith, A. (eds.) *Twenty-First Century Feminism.* Palgrave Macmillan, Basingstoke, pp. 93–118.

Burroughs, B. (2013) 'Obama trolling: Memes, salutes, and an agonistic politics in the 2012 presidential election'. *Fibreculture*, 22: 258–77.

Callimachi, R. (2015, 27 June) 'ISIS and the lonely young American'. *New York Times.* Retrieved from http://www.nytimes.com/2015/06/28/world/americas/isis-online-recruiting-american.html?_r=0

Campbell, J. (2015, 22 March) 'IKEA rainbow Putin pillow is a fake'. *Independent.* Retrieved from http://www.independent.co.uk/news/world/europe/ikea-rainbow-putin-pillow-is-a-fake-10126012.html

Campus, D. (2010) 'Mediatization and personalization of politics in Italy and France: The cases of Berlusconi and Sarkozy'. *International Journal of Press/Politics*, 15(2): 219–35.

Carlson, M. (2007) 'Blogs and journalistic authority: The role of blogs in US Election Day 2004 coverage'. *Journalism Studies*, 8(2): 264–79.

Carlson, M. and Ben-Porath, E. (2012) ' "The people's debate": The CNN/YouTube debates and the demotic voice in political journalism'. *Journalism Practice*, 6(3): 302–16.

Carlsson, E. (2014) 'Visibility and surveillance in a hybrid media culture'. In: Lindgren, S. (ed.) *Hybrid Media Culture: Sensing place in a world of flows.* Routledge, New York, pp. 34–50.

Cartwright, L. and Mandiberg, S. (2009) 'Obama and Shepard Fairey: The copy and political iconography in the age of the demake'. *Journal of Visual Culture*, 8(2): 172–6.

Cassidy, E. (2015) 'Social networking sites and participatory reluctance: A case study of Gaydar, user resistance and interface rejection'. *New Media & Society* (online first).

Castells, M. (2007) 'Communication, power and counter-power in the network society'. *International Journal of Communication*, 1: 238–66.

Castells, M. (2011) 'A network theory of power'. *International Journal of Communication*, 5: 773–87.

Chadha, M., Avila, A. and Gil de Zúñiga, H. (2012) 'Listening in: Building a profile of podcast users and analyzing their political participation'. *Journal of Information Technology & Politics*, 9(4): 388–401.

Chadwick, A. (2013) *The Hybrid Media System: Politics and power*. Oxford University Press, New York.

Chalfen, R. (2009) ' "It's only a picture": Sexting, "smutty" snapshots and felony charges'. *Visual Studies*, 24(3): 258–68.

Chan, G. (2015, 26 January) 'Abbott acknowledges internal critics but likens social media to "electronic graffiti" '. *Guardian*. Retrieved from http://www.theguardian.com/australia-news/2015/jan/26/tony-abbott-acknowledges-internal-critics-but-dismisses-electronic

Chaudhry, I. (2015) '#Hashtagging hate: Using Twitter to track racism online'. *First Monday*, 20(2). Retrieved from http://firstmonday.org/ojs/index.php/fm/article/view/5450/4207

Chess, S. and Shaw, A. (2015) 'A conspiracy of fishes, or, How we learned to stop worrying about #GamerGate and embrace hegemonic masculinity'. *Journal of Broadcasting & Electronic Media*, 59(1): 208–20.

Cho, A. (2015) 'Queer reverb: Tumblr, affect, time'. In: Hillis, K., Paasonen, S. and Petit, M. (eds.) *Networked Affect*. The MIT Press, Cambridge, MA, pp. 43–58.

Christensen, C. (2013a) '@Sweden: Curating a nation on Twitter'. *Popular Communication*, 11(1): 30–46.

Christensen, C. (2013b) 'Wave-riding and hashtag-jumping: Twitter, minority "third parties" and the 2012 US elections'. *Information, Communication & Society*, 16(5): 646–66.

Christensen, H. S. (2011) 'Political activities on the Internet: Slacktivism or political participation by other means?' *First Monday*, 16(2). Retrieved from http://firstmonday.org/ojs/index.php/fm/article/view/3336/2767

Cisneros, J. D. and Nakayama, T. K. (2015) 'New media, old racisms: Twitter, Miss America, and cultural logics of race'. *Journal of International and Intercultural Communication*, 8(2): 108–27.

Citron, D. K. (2014) *Hate Crimes in Cyberspace*. Harvard University Press, Cambridge, MA.

Cohen, K. R. (2005) 'What does the photoblog want?' *Media, Culture & Society*, 27(6): 883–901.

Coleman, G. (2015) *Hacker, Hoaxer, Whistleblower, Spy: The many faces of Anonymous*. Verso, London.

Coleman, S. (2006) 'How the other half votes: *Big Brother* viewers and the 2005 general election'. *International Journal of Cultural Studies*, 9(4): 457–79.

Coleman, S. (2008) 'Why is the Eurovision Song Contest ridiculous? Exploring a spectacle of embarrassment, irony and identity'. *Popular Communication*, 6(3): 127–40.

Coleman, S. and Moss, G. (2008) 'Governing at a distance – politicians in the blogosphere'. *Information Polity: International Journal of Government & Democracy in the Information Age*, 13(1–2): 7–20.

Color The Future (2015) 'T'von (expect-the-greatest), creator of BlackOutDay, speaks his piece'. *Color The Future*. Retrieved from http://colorthefuture.org/post/112564471328/tvon-expect-the-greatest-creator-of

Commonwealth of Australia (2012, 9 October) 'Motions – Speaker'. *House of Representatives Hansard*, pp. 11581–5. Canberra.

Consalvo, M. (2012) 'Confronting toxic gamer culture: A challenge for feminist Game Studies scholars'. *Ada: A Journal of Gender, New Media, and Technology*, 1. Retrieved from http://adanewmedia.org/2012/11/issue1-consalvo/

Cormack, L. (2015, 8 January) 'Paris terrorist attack: *Charlie Hebdo* shooting video provokes social media backlash'. *Sydney Morning Herald*. Retrieved from http://www.smh.com.au/world/paris-terrorist-attack-charlie-hebdo-shooting-video-provokes-social-media-backlash-20150107-12jvhf.html

Costanza-Chock, S. (2012) 'Mic check! Media cultures and the Occupy movement'. *Social Movement Studies: Journal of Social, Cultural and Political Protest*, 11(3–4): 375–85.

Couldry, N. (2003) *Media Rituals: A critical approach*. Routledge, New York.

Couldry, N. (2012) *Media, Society, World: Social theory and digital media practice*. Polity, Cambridge.

Crawford, K. and Finn, M. (2015) 'The limits of crisis data: Analytical and ethical challenges of using social and mobile data to understand disasters'. *GeoJournal*, 80(4): 491–502.

Crawford, K. and Gillespie, T. (2014) 'What is a flag for? Social media reporting tools and the vocabulary of complaint'. *New Media & Society* (online first).

Crawford, K., Miltner, K. and Gray, M. L. (2014) 'Critiquing big data: Politics, ethics, epistemology'. *International Journal of Communication*, 8: 1663–72.

Crawford, K., Lingel, J. and Karppi, T. (2015) 'Our metrics, ourselves: A hundred years of self-tracking from the weight scale to the wrist wearable device'. *European Journal of Cultural Studies*, 18(4–5): 479–96.

Crerar, S. (2014, 24 April) 'Newspaper has an absolute shocker'. *BuzzFeed*. Retrieved from http://www.buzzfeed.com/simoncrerar/newspaper-prints-world-is-fukt-on-front-page

Cresci, E. (2014, 15 December) 'Uber offers free rides after backlash over surge pricing during Sydney siege'. *Guardian*. Retrieved from http://www.theguardian.com/technology/2014/dec/15/uber-offers-free-rides-after-backlash-over-surge-pricing-during-sydney-siege

Croeser, S. (2012) 'Contested technologies: The emergence of the digital liberties movement'. *First Monday*, 17(8). Retrieved from http://firstmonday.org/ojs/index.php/fm/article/view/4162/3282

Croeser, S. (2014) *Global Justice and the Politics of Information: The struggle over knowledge*. Routledge, Hoboken, NJ.

Croeser, S. and Highfield, T. (2014) 'Occupy Oakland and #oo: Uses of Twitter within the Occupy movement'. *First Monday*, 19(3).

Croeser, S. and Highfield, T. (2015a) 'Harbouring dissent: Greek independent and social media and the antifascist movement'. *Fibreculture*, in press.

Croeser, S. and Highfield, T. (2015b) 'Mapping movements – social movement research and big data: Critiques and alternatives'. In: Langlois, G., Redden, J. and Elmer, G. (eds.) *Compromised Data: From social media to big data*. Bloomsbury, New York, pp. 173–201.

Crouzillacq, P. (2006, 30 March) 'Les pro et les anti-CPE secouent la Toile'. *01.net*. Retrieved from http://www.01net.com/article/310579.html

Dahlberg-Grundberg, M. (2014) 'Hybrid political activism and the online/offline divide'. In: Lindgren, S. (ed.) *Hybrid Media Culture: Sensing place in a world of flows*. Routledge, New York, pp. 67–89.

Dahlberg-Grundberg, M. and Lindgren, S. (2014) 'Translocal frame extensions in a networked protest: Situating the #IdleNoMore hashtag'. *IC – Revista Científica de Información y Comunicación*, 11: 49–77. Retrieved from http://www.icjournal-ojs.org/index.php/IC-Journal/article/view/295

Dahlgren, P. (2009) *Media and Political Engagement: Citizens, communication, and democracy*. Cambridge University Press, New York.

Daniels, J. (2009) 'Cloaked websites: Propaganda, cyber-racism and epistemology in the digital era'. *New Media & Society*, 11(5): 659–83.

Daniels, J. (2012) 'Race and racism in Internet Studies: A review and critique'. *New Media & Society*, 15(5): 695–719.

Darmon, K. (2014) 'Framing SlutWalk London: How does the privilege of feminist activism in social media travel into the mass media?' *Feminist Media Studies*, 14(4): 700–4.

David, G. (2010) 'Camera phone images, videos and live streaming: A contemporary visual trend'. *Visual Studies*, 25(1): 89–98.

de Vries, K. (2009) 'Bridges or breaches? Thoughts on how people use blogs in China'. In: Russell, A. and Echchaibi, N. (eds.) *International Blogging: Identity, politics, and networked publics*. Peter Lang, New York, pp. 47–64.

Dearden, L. (2015, 12 January) '*Charlie Hebdo*: Man regrets "stupid" decision to put police officer's death online'. *Independent*. Retrieved from http://www.independent.co.uk/news/world/europe/charlie-hebdo-man-regrets-stupid-decision-to-put-video-of-police-officers-death-online-9971750.html

Deller, R. (2011) 'Twittering on: Audience research and participation using Twitter'. *Participations*, 8(1). Retrieved from http://www.participations.org/Volume 8/Issue 1/deller.htm

Deller, R. (2015) 'Simblr famous and SimSecret infamous: Performance, community norms, and shaming among fans of The Sims'. *Transformative Works and Cultures*, 18. Retrieved from http://journal.transformativeworks.org/index.php/twc/article/view/615/503

Deller, R. and Tilton, S. (2015) 'Selfies as charitable meme: Charity and national identity in the #nomakeupselfie and #thumbsupforstephen campaigns'. *International Journal of Communication*, 9: 1788–805.

DeLuca, K., Lawson, S. and Sun, Y. (2012) 'Occupy Wall Street on the public screens of social media: The many framings of the birth of a protest movement'. *Communication, Culture & Critique*, 5(4): 483–509.

Di Stefano, M. (2015a, 13 January) 'Why isn't everyone voting for "Shake It Off" in the Hottest 100?' *BuzzFeed*. Retrieved from http://www.buzzfeed.com/markdistefano/tay-4-hottest100

Di Stefano, M. (2015b, 6 August) 'We found the guy behind Australia's greatest ever meme'. *BuzzFeed*. Retrieved from http://www.buzzfeed.com/markdistefano/seriously-john-howard-djs-like-a-mad-cunt#.cjBJbmk6Y

Dimond, J. P., Dye, M., Larose, D. and Bruckman, A. S. (2013) 'Hollaback!: The role of collective storytelling online in a social movement organization'.

Proceedings of the ACM Conference on Computer Supported Cooperative Work, CSCW, pp. 477–89.

Dow, A. (2014, 16 December) 'Martin Place siege: People share selfies and jokes on Twitter'. *Sydney Morning Herald*. Retrieved from http://www.smh.com.au/nsw/martin-place-siege-people-share-selfies-and-jokes-on-twitter-20141215-127mn4.html

Down Under Feminists' Carnival (n.d.) 'About'. Retrieved from http://downunderfeministscarnival.wordpress.com/about/

Doyle, S. (2011, 2 March) 'What Aaron Sorkin, Jon Stewart, and Tina Fey learned from their internet critics'. *Atlantic*. Retrieved from http://www.theatlantic.com/entertainment/archive/2011/03/what-aaron-sorkin-jon-stewart-and-tina-fey-learned-from-their-internet-critics/71842/

Doyle, W. (2012) 'No strings attached? *Les Guignols de l'info* and French television'. *Popular Communication*, 10(1–2): 40–51.

Dredge, S. (2015, 24 March) 'Facebook set to host content for news publishers'. *Guardian*. Retrieved from http://www.theguardian.com/technology/2015/mar/24/facebook-host-content-new-york-times-buzzfeed

Drezner, D. W. and Farrell, H. (2008) 'The power and politics of blogs'. *Public Choice*, 134(1–2): 15–30.

Driscoll, K., Ananny, M., Bar, F., Guth, K., Kazemzadeh, A., Leavitt, A. and Thorson, K. (2013) 'Big Bird, binders, and bayonets: Humor and live-tweeting during the 2012 US Presidential debates'. Paper presented at *IR14: Resistance + Appropriation*, 24–26 October 2013, Denver.

Duguay, S. (2014) '"He has a way gayer Facebook than I do": Investigating sexual identity disclosure and context collapse on a social networking site'. *New Media & Society* (online first).

Dutton, W. H. (2009) 'The Fifth Estate emerging through the network of networks'. *Prometheus*, 27(1): 1–15.

Duvall, S.-S. (2014) 'Not "simply the breast": Media discourse, breastfeeding, and normalcy'. *Feminist Media Studies*, 15(2): 324–40.

Eakin, M. (2014, 14 November) 'Introducing *The Serial Serial*, *The A.V. Club*'s new podcast about *Serial*'. *The A.V. Club*. Retrieved from http://www.avclub.com/article/introducing-serial-serial-v-clubs-new-podcast-abou-211881

Earl, J. and Kimport, K. (2011) *Digitally Enabled Social Change*. The MIT Press, Cambridge, MA.

Ekstrom, M., Eriksson, G. and Kroon Lundell, Å. (2013) 'Live co-produced news: Emerging forms of news production and presentation on the web'. *Media, Culture & Society*, 35(5): 620–39.

Ellis, K. and Goggin, G. (2014) 'Disability and social media'. In: Hunsinger, J. and Senft, T. M. (eds.) *Routledge Handbook of Social Media*. Routledge, New York, pp. 126–43.

Ellis, K., Goggin, G. and Kent, M. (2015) 'Disability's digital frictions: Activism, technology, and politics'. *Fibreculture*, in press.

Elmer, G. (2013) 'Live research: Twittering an election debate'. *New Media & Society*, 15(1): 18–30.

Elmer, G., Langlois, G. and McKelvey, F. (2012) *The Permanent Campaign: New media, new politics*. Peter Lang, New York.

Esco, L. (2014, 7 January) 'Facebook wages war on the nipple'. *The Huffington Post*. Retrieved from http://www.huffingtonpost.com/lina-esco/facebook-war-on-nipples_b_4548832.html

Esteves, V. and Meikle, G. (2015) '"LOOK @ THIS FUKKEN DOGE": Internet memes and remix cultures'. In: Atton, C. (ed.) *The Routledge Companion to Alternative and Community Media*. Routledge, New York, pp. 561–70.

Etling, B., Kelly, J., Faris, R. and Palfrey, J. (2010) 'Mapping the Arabic blogosphere: Politics and dissent online'. *New Media & Society*, 12(8): 1225–43.

Everett, A. (2015) 'Scandalicious: *Scandal*, social media, and Shonda Rhimes' auteurist juggernaut'. *Black Scholar: Journal of Black Studies and Research*, 45(1): 34–43.

Fansten, E. (2006, 4 April) 'Internet, le nouvel outil des mobilisations étudiantes'. *Le Monde*. Retrieved from http://www.lemonde.fr/societe/article/2006/04/04/internet-le-nouvel-outil-des-mobilisations-etudiantes_757776_3224.html

Fenn, D., Suleman, O., Efstathiou, J. and Johnson, N. F. (2006) 'How does Europe make its mind up? Connections, cliques, and compatibility between countries in the Eurovision Song Contest'. *Physica A: Statistical Mechanics and its Applications*, 360(2): 576–98.

Fink, M. and Miller, Q. (2014) 'Trans media moments: Tumblr, 2011–2013'. *Television & New Media*, 15(7): 611–26.

Flew, T. (2008) 'Not yet the internet election: Online media, political commentary and the 2007 Australian federal election'. *Media International Australia*, 126: 5–13.

Florini, S. (2014) 'Tweets, tweeps, and signifyin': Communication and cultural performance on "Black Twitter"'. *Television & New Media*, 15(3): 223–37.

Fouetillou, G. (2006) 'Ecologie de la Ségosphère'. *Observatoire Présidentielle 2007*. Retrieved from http://www.observatoire-presidentielle.fr/?pageid=12

Frank, R. (2004) 'When the going gets tough, the tough go photoshopping: September 11 and the newslore of vengeance and victimization'. *New Media & Society*, 6(5): 633–58.

Fraser, M. and Dutta, S. (2008, 7 November) 'Obama's win means future elections must be fought online'. *Guardian*. Retrieved from http://www.guardian.co.uk/technology/2008/nov/07/barackobama-uselections2008

Freelon, D. and Karpf, D. (2015) 'Of Big Birds and bayonets: Hybrid Twitter interactivity in the 2012 presidential debates'. *Information, Communication & Society*, 18(4): 390–406.

Fuchs, C. (2012) 'Social media, riots, and revolutions'. *Capital & Class*, 36(3): 383–91.

Fuchs, C. (2014) *OccupyMedia! The Occupy movement and social media in crisis capitalism*. Zero Books, Winchester.

Gabriel, F. (2014) 'Sexting, selfies and self-harm: Young people, social media and the performance of self-development'. *Media International Australia*, 151: 104–12.

Gaby, S. and Caren, N. (2012) 'Occupy Online: How cute old men and Malcolm X recruited 400,000 US users to OWS on Facebook'. *Social Movement Studies: Journal of Social, Cultural and Political Protest*, 11(3–4): 367–74.

Gainous, J. and Wagner, K. M. (2014) *Tweeting to Power: The social media revolution in American politics*. Oxford University Press, New York.

Gal, N., Shifman, L. and Kampf, Z. (2015) '"It Gets Better": Internet memes and the construction of collective identity. *New Media & Society* (online first).

Galo, S. (2014, 4 December) '#CrimingWhileWhite vs. #AliveWhileBlack: Twitter weighs in on Garner decision'. *Guardian*. Retrieved from http://www.theguardian.com/us-news/2014/dec/04/eric-garner-twitter

Gao, L. and Stanyer, J. (2014) 'Hunting corrupt officials online: The human flesh search engine and the search for justice in China'. *Information, Communication & Society*, 17(7): 814–29.

Garber, M. (2012, 28 November) 'The campaign tumblr is dead! (Long live the campaign tumblr!)'. *The Atlantic*. Retrieved from http://www.theatlantic.com/technology/archive/2012/11/the-campaign-tumblr-is-dead-long-live-the-campaign-tumblr/265688/

Garden, M. (2010) 'Newspaper blogs: The genuine article or poor counterfeits?' *Media International Australia*, 135: 19–31.

Garden, M. (2014) 'Australian journalist-blogs: A shift in audience relationships or mere window dressing?' *Journalism* (online first).

Gardner, E. (2015, 21 April) 'Katy Perry's "Left Shark" design rejected by trademark examiner'. *The Hollywood Reporter*. Retrieved from http://www.hollywoodreporter.com/thr-esq/katy-perrys-left-shark-design-790542

Garrido, M. and Halavais, A. (2003) 'Mapping networks of support for the Zapatista movement: Applying social-networks analysis to study contemporary social movements'. In: McCaughey, M. and Ayers, M. D. (eds.) *Cyberactivism: Online activism in theory and practice*. Routledge, New York, pp. 165–84.

Gehl, R. W. (2014) *Reverse Engineering Social Media: Software, culture, and political economy in new media capitalism*. Temple University Press, Philadelphia.

Georgiou, M. (2008) '"In the end, Germany will always resort to hot pants": Watching Europe singing, constructing the stereotype'. *Popular Communication*, 6(3): 141–54.

Gerbaudo, P. (2012) *Tweets and the Streets: Social media and contemporary activism*. Pluto Press, London.

Gibbs, M., Meese, J., Arnold, M., Nansen, B. and Carter, M. (2015) '#Funeral and Instagram: Death, social media, and platform vernacular'. *Information, Communication & Society*, 18(3): 255–68.

Giglietto, F. and Selva, D. (2014) 'Second screen and participation: A content analysis on a full season dataset of tweets'. *Journal of Communication*, 64(2): 260–77.

Gilbert, C. J. (2013) 'Playing with Hitler: *Downfall* and its ludic uptake'. *Critical Studies in Media Communication*, 30(5): 407–24.

Gillespie, T. (2010) 'The politics of "platforms"'. *New Media & Society*, 12(3): 347–64.

Gillespie, T. (2013, 26 July) 'Tumblr, NSFW porn blogging, and the challenge of checkpoints'. *Culture Digitally*. Retrieved from http://culturedigitally.org/2013/07/tumblr-nsfw-porn-blogging-and-the-challenge-of-checkpoints/

Gillespie, T. (2014) 'The relevance of algorithms'. In: Gillespie, T., Boczkowski, P. J. and Foot, K. A. (eds.) *Media Technologies: Essays on communication, materiality, and society*. The MIT Press, Cambridge, MA, pp. 167–94.

Gillmor, D. (2006) *We the Media: Grassroots journalism by the people, for the people*. O'Reilly, Sebastopol, CA.

Ginsburgh, V. and Noury, A. G. (2008) 'The Eurovision Song Contest: Is voting political or cultural?' *European Journal of Political Economy*, 24(1): 41–52.

Given, J. and Radywyl, N. (2013) 'Questions & answers & tweets'. *Communication, Politics & Culture*, 46: 1–21.

Gladwell, M. (2010, 4 October) 'Small Change – Why the revolution will not be tweeted'. *The New Yorker*. Retrieved from http://www.newyorker.com/reporting/2010/10/04/101004fa_fact_gladwell

Gladwell, M. (2011, 2 February) 'Does Egypt need Twitter?' *The New Yorker: News Desk (blog)*. Retrieved from http://www.newyorker.com/online/blogs/newsdesk/2011/02/does-egypt-need-twitter.html

Glasgow, K. and Fink, C. (2013) 'From push brooms to prayer books: Social media and social networks during the London riots'. *iConference 2013*, pp. 155–69.

Gleiss, M. S. (2015) 'Speaking up for the suffering (br)other: Weibo activism, discursive struggles, and minimal politics in China'. *Media, Culture & Society*, 37(4): 513–29.

González-Bailón, S., Wang, N., Rivero, A., Borge-Holthoefer, J. and Moreno, Y. (2014) 'Assessing the bias in samples of large online networks'. *Social Networks*, 38: 16–27.

Goodman, J. D. (2011, 14 December) 'Times of London cancels comedy podcast that mocked Murdoch'. *Media Decoder (blog)*. Retrieved from http://mediadecoder.blogs.nytimes.com/2011/12/14/times-of-london-cancels-comedy-podcast-that-mocked-murdoch/

GovHack (2015) 'About us'. Retrieved from http://www.govhack.org/about-us/

Graham, T. and Wright, S. (2015) 'A tale of two stories from "below the line": Comment fields at *The Guardian*'. *International Journal of Press/Politics*, 20(3): 317–38.

Graham, T., Broersma, M., Hazelhoff, K. and van't Haar, G. (2013) 'Between broadcasting political messages and interacting with voters: The use of Twitter during the 2010 UK general election campaign'. *Information, Communication & Society*, 16(5): 692–716.

Grant, W. J., Moon, B. and Busby Grant, J. (2010) 'Digital dialogue? Australian politicians' use of the social network tool Twitter'. *Australian Journal of Political Science*, 45(4): 579–604.

Gray, J. (2003) 'New audiences, new textualities: Anti-fans and non-fans'. *International Journal of Cultural Studies*, 6(1): 64–81.

Gray, J., Jones, J. and Thompson, E. (eds.) (2009) *Satire TV: Politics and comedy in the post-network era*. New York University Press, New York.

Gray, M. L. (2009) *Out in the Country: Youth, media, and queer visibility in rural America*. New York University Press, New York.

Griffin, A. (2015, 28 April) 'Instagram adds emoji to hashtags, bans aubergine emoji and adds new filters'. *Independent*. Retrieved from http://www.independent.co.uk/life-style/gadgets-and-tech/news/instagram-adds-emoji-to-hashtags-bans-aubergine-emoji-and-adds-new-filters-10208793.html

Habermas, J. (1989) *The Structural Transformation of the Public Sphere: An inquiry into a category of bourgeois society*. Polity, Cambridge.

Haig, F. (2014) 'Guilty pleasures: Twilight, snark and critical fandom'. In: Clayton, W. and Harman, S. (eds.) *Screening Twilight: Critical approaches to a cinematic phenomenon*. I.B. Tauris, New York, pp. 11–25.

Halavais, A. (2008) 'The hyperlink as organizing principle'. In: Turow, J. and Tsui, L. (eds.) *The Hyperlinked Society: Questioning connections in the digital age*. University of Michigan Press and University of Michigan Library, Ann Arbor, pp. 39–55.

Halavais, A. (2013) 'Structure of Twitter: Social and technical'. In: Weller, K., Bruns, A., Burgess, J., Mahrt, M. and Puschmann, C. (eds.) *Twitter and Society*. Peter Lang, New York, pp. 29–41.

Hands, J. (2014) 'General intellect or collective idiocy? Digital mobs and social media mobilization'. *Popular Communication*, 12(4): 237–50.

Hardman, I. (2014, 29 November) 'The menace of memes: How pictures can paint a thousand lies'. *Coffee House (The Spectator Blogs)*. Retrieved from http://blogs.spectator.co.uk/coffeehouse/2014/11/the-menace-of-memes-how-pictures-can-paint-a-thousand-lies/

Harlow, S. and Johnson, T. J. (2011) 'Overthrowing the protest paradigm? How *The New York Times*, *Global Voices* and Twitter covered the Egyptian revolution'. *International Journal of Communication*, 5: 1359–74.

Harman, S. and Jones, B. (2013) 'Fifty shades of ghey: Snark fandom and the figure of the anti-fan'. *Sexualities*, 16(8): 951–68.

Harrington, S. (2010) 'Chasing reporters: Intertextuality, entertainment and public knowledge'. *Media International Australia*, 134: 121–30.

Harrington, S. (2012) 'From the "Little Aussie Bleeder" to *Newstopia*: (Really) fake news in Australia'. *Popular Communication*, 10(1–2): 27–39.

Harrington, S. (2013) 'Tweeting about the telly: Live TV, audiences, and social media'. In: Weller, K., Bruns, A., Burgess, J., Mahrt, M. and Puschmann, C. (eds.) *Twitter and Society*. Peter Lang, New York, pp. 237–47.

Harris, S. K. (2015) 'Networked erasure: Visualizing information censorship in Turkey'. *Convergence The International Journal of Research into New Media Technologies*, 21(2): 257–78.

Hartley, J. (2012) *Digital Futures for Cultural and Media Studies*. Wiley-Blackwell, Malden, MA.

Hartley, J. and Green, J. (2006) 'The public sphere on the beach'. *European Journal of Cultural Studies*, 9(3): 341–62.

Hasinoff, A. A. (2012) 'Sexting as media production: Rethinking social media and sexuality'. *New Media & Society*, 15(4): 449–65.

Heemsbergen, L. J. (2015) 'Designing hues of transparency and democracy after WikiLeaks: Vigilance to vigilantes and back again'. *New Media & Society*, 17(8): 1340–57.

Hermida, A. (2010) 'Twittering the news: The emergence of ambient journalism'. *Journalism Practice*, 4(3): 297–308.

Hermida, A. (2014) *Tell Everyone: Why we share and why it matters*. Doubleday, Toronto.

Hermida, A., Lewis, S. C. and Zamith, R. (2014) 'Sourcing the Arab Spring: A case study of Andy Carvin's sources on Twitter during the Tunisian and Egyptian revolutions'. *Journal of Computer-Mediated Communication*, 19(3): 479–99.

Herrman, J. and Notopoulos, K. (2013, 6 April) 'Weird Twitter: The oral history'. *BuzzFeed*. Retrieved from http://www.buzzfeed.com/jwherrman/weird-twitter-the-oral-history#.qeLzlRp3a

Higgie, R. (2015) 'Playful politicians and serious satirists: Comedic and earnest interplay in Australian political discourse'. *Comedy Studies*, 6(1): 63–77.

Higgin, T. (2013) '/b/lack up: What trolls can teach us about race'. *Fibreculture*, 22: 133–51.

Highfield, T. (2011) *Mapping intermedia news flows: Topical discussions in the Australian and French political blogospheres*. PhD thesis, Queensland University of Technology, Brisbane. Retrieved from http://eprints.qut.edu.au/48115/

Highfield, T. (2012) 'Talking of many things: Using topical networks to study discussions in social media'. *Journal of Technology in Human Services*, 30(3–4): 204–18.

Highfield, T. (2013) 'National and state-level politics on social media: Twitter, Australian political discussions, and the online commentariat'. *International Journal of E-Governance*, 6(4): 342–60.

Highfield, T. (2015a) 'News via Voldemort: Parody accounts in topical discussions on Twitter'. *New Media & Society* (online first).

Highfield, T. (2015b) 'Tweeted joke lifespans and appropriated punch lines: Practices around topical humor on social media'. *International Journal of Communication*, 9: 2713–34.

Highfield, T. and Bruns, A. (2012) 'Confrontation and cooptation: A brief history of Australian political blogs'. *Media International Australia*, 143: 89–98.

Highfield, T., Harrington, S. and Bruns, A. (2013) 'Twitter as a technology for audiencing and fandom: The #eurovision phenomenon'. *Information, Communication & Society*, 16(3): 315–39.

Highfield, T. and Leaver, T. (2015) 'A methodology for mapping Instagram hashtags'. *First Monday*, 20(1). Retrieved from http://firstmonday.org/ojs/index.php/fm/article/view/5563/4195

Hinde, N. (2015, 21 January) 'Did Instagram ban this account because of a photo showing women's pubic hair?' *The Huffington Post (UK)*. Retrieved from http://www.huffingtonpost.co.uk/2015/01/21/instagram-ban-the-bush_n_6508694.html

Hindman, M. (2009) *The Myth of Digital Democracy*. Princeton University Press, Princeton, NJ.

Hjorth, L. and Burgess, J. (2014) 'Intimate banalities: The emotional currency of shared camera phone images during the Queensland flood disaster'. In: Goggin, G. and Hjorth, L. (eds.) *The Routledge Companion to Mobile Media*. Routledge, London, pp. 499–513.

Holton, A. E. and Lewis, S. C. (2011) 'Journalists, social media, and the use of humor on Twitter'. *Electronic Journal of Communication*, 21(1–2). Retrieved from http://www.cios.org/EJCPUBLIC/021/1/021121.html

Hopkins, J. and Thomas, N. (2011) 'Fielding networked marketing: Technology and authenticity in the monetization of Malaysian blogs'. In: Araya, D., Breindl, Y. and Houghton, T. J. (eds.) *Nexus: New intersections in internet research*. Peter Lang, New York, pp. 139–56.

Houghton, T. J. and Chang, Y.-C. (2011) 'Haxorz: Alternative perspectives on the "computer underground"'. In: Araya, D., Breindl, Y. and Houghton, T. J. (eds.) *Nexus: New intersections in internet research*. Peter Lang, New York, pp. 213–37.

Howard, P. N. and Hussain, M. M. (2011) 'The role of digital media'. *Journal of Democracy*, 22(3): 35–48.

Howard, P. N., Agarwal, S. D. and Hussain, M. M. (2011) 'When do states disconnect their digital networks? Regime responses to the political uses of social media'. *Communication Review*, 14(3): 216–32.

Hubbard, B. (2015, 10 January) 'Jihadists and supporters take to social media to praise attack on *Charlie Hebdo*'. *New York Times*. Retrieved from http://www.nytimes.com/2015/01/11/world/europe/islamic-extremists-take-to-social-media-to-praise-charlie-hebdo-attack.html

Hughey, M. W. and Daniels, J. (2013) 'Racist comments at online news sites: A methodological dilemma for discourse analysis'. *Media, Culture & Society*, 35(3): 332–47.

Jackson, N. and Lilleker, D. (2009) 'Building an architecture of participation? Political parties and Web 2.0 in Britain'. *Journal of Information Technology & Politics*, 6(3): 232–50.

Jane, E. A. (2014) '"Your a ugly, whorish, slut": Understanding e-bile'. *Feminist Media Studies*, 14(4): 531–46.

Jarrett, K. (2009) 'Private talk in the public sphere: Podcasting as broadcast talk'. *Communication, Politics & Culture*, 42(2): 116–35.

Jarvis, J. L. (2014) 'Digital image politics: The networked rhetoric of Anonymous'. *Global Discourse*, 4(2–3): 326–49.

Jenkins, H. (2006) *Convergence Culture: Where old and new media collide*. New York University Press, New York.

Jenkins, H. (2012) '"Cultural acupuncture": Fan activism and the Harry Potter Alliance'. *Transformative Works and Cultures*, 10. Retrieved from http://journal.transformativeworks.org/index.php/twc/article/view/305/259

Jenkins, H., Ford, S. and Green, J. (2013) *Spreadable Media: Creating value and meaning in a networked culture*. New York University Press, New York.

Jenson, J., Taylor, N., de Castell, S. and Dilouya, B. (2015) 'Playing with our selves'. *Feminist Media Studies*, 15(5): 860–79.

Jericho, G. (2012) *The Rise of the Fifth Estate: Social media and blogging in Australian politics*. Scribe, Melbourne.

Jethani, S. and Raydan, N. (2015) 'Forming persona through metrics: Can we think freely in the shadow of our data?' *Persona Studies*, 1(1): 76–93.

Jin, S. V., Phua, J. and Lee, K. M. (2015) 'Telling stories about breastfeeding through Facebook: The impact of user-generated content (UGC) on pro-breastfeeding attitudes'. *Computers in Human Behavior*, 46: 6–17.

Johnson, A. (2014, 3 October) 'Cartographies of disaster'. *reform (Medium)*. Retrieved from https://medium.com/re-form/cartographies-of-disaster-24fe711d04e6

Johnson, A. (2015) 'Decrowning doubles: Indexicality and aspect in a Bahraini Twitter parody account'. *Al-'Arabiyya*, 48: 61–83.

Jung, S. (2012) 'Fan activism, cybervigilantism, and Othering mechanisms in K-pop fandom'. *Transformative Works and Cultures*, 10. Retrieved from http://journal.transformativeworks.com/index.php/twc/article/view/300

Juris, J. S. (2012) 'Reflections on #Occupy Everywhere: Social media, public space, and emerging logics of aggregation'. *American Ethnologist*, 39(2): 259–79.

Kalviknes Bore, I.-L. and Hickman, J. (2013) 'Continuing *The West Wing* in 140 characters or less: Improvised simulation on Twitter'. *Journal of Fandom Studies*, 1(2): 219–38.

Kang, J. C. (2015, 4 May) '"Our demand is simple: Stop killing us": How a group of black social-media activists built the nation's first 21st-century civil rights movement'. *New York Times*. Retrieved from http://www.nytimes.com/2015/05/10/magazine/our-demand-is-simple-stop-killing-us.html

Karppi, T. (2013) '"Change name to No One. Like people's status": Facebook trolling and managing online personas'. *Fibreculture*, 22: 278–300.

Katz, E. and Lazarsfeld, P. F. (1964) *Personal Influence: The part played by people in the flow of mass communications*. Free Press, New York.

Kaufmann, M. (2015) 'Resilience 2.0: Social media use and (self-)care during the 2011 Norway attacks'. *Media, Culture & Society*, 37(7): 972–87.

Keen, A. (2007) *The Cult of the Amateur: How today's internet is killing our culture*. Doubleday, New York.

Keim, N. and Clark, J. (2009) 'Field report: Building social media infrastructure to engage publics'. Retrieved from http://www.cmsimpact.org/future-public-media/documents/field-reports/public-media-20-field-report-building-social-media-infra

Kelly, J. and Etling, B. (2008) *Mapping Iran's Online Public: Politics and culture in the Persian blogosphere*. Berkman Center for Internet & Society, Cambridge. Retrieved from http://cyber.law.harvard.edu/publications/2008/Mapping_Irans_Online_Public

Kent, L. (2014, 15 November) 'G20 Brisbane: German Chancellor Angela Merkel stops by Caxton Street bars, takes selfies'. *ABC News (Australian Broadcasting Corporation)*. Retrieved from http://www.abc.net.au/news/2014-11-15/german-chancellor-angela-merkell-stops-by-brisbane-pubs/5893476

Kirkland, S. (2015, 13 January) '#JeSuisNico trends after Nicolas Sarkozy was caught sneaking to front of Paris march'. *BuzzFeed*. Retrieved from http://www.buzzfeed.com/samkirkland/je-suis-nico#.is2oj69jE

Klausen, J. (2015) 'Tweeting the jihad: Social media networks of Western foreign fighters in Syria and Iraq'. *Studies in Conflict & Terrorism*, 38(1): 1–22.

Kligler-Vilenchik, N. and Thorson, K. (2015) 'Good citizenship as a frame contest: Kony2012, memes, and critiques of the networked citizen'. *New Media & Society* (online first).

Knuttila, L. (2011) 'User unknown: 4chan, anonymity and contingency'. *First Monday*, 16(10). Retrieved from http://firstmonday.org/ojs/index.php/fm/article/view/3665/3055

Koziol, M. (2015, 3 August) 'Bronwyn Bishop "Speaker's resignation" tweet comes back to bite Tony Abbott'. *The Sydney Morning Herald*. Retrieved from http://www.smh.com.au/federal-politics/political-news/bronwyn-bishop-speakers-resignation-tweet-comes-back-to-bite-tony-abbott-20150803-giqg1l.html

Kushin, M. J. and Kitchener, K. (2009) 'Getting political on social network sites: Exploring online political discourse on Facebook'. *First Monday*, 14(11). Retrieved from http://firstmonday.org/ojs/index.php/fm/article/view/2645/2350

Kwak, H., Lee, C., Park, H. and Moon, S. (2010) 'What is Twitter, a social network or a news media? Categories and subject descriptors'. *Proceedings of WWW 2010*, pp. 591–600.

Langlois, G. and Elmer, G. (2013) 'The research politics of social media platforms'. *Culture Machine*, 14. Retrieved from http://www.culturemachine.net/index.php/cm/article/view/505/531

Larsson, A. O. (2014a) 'Everyday elites, citizens, or extremists? Assessing the use and users of non-election political hashtags'. *MedieKultur*, 56: 61–78.

Larsson, A. O. (2014b) 'Online, all the time? A quantitative assessment of the permanent campaign on Facebook'. *New Media & Society* (online first).

Larsson, A. O. and Kalsnes, B. (2014) '"Of course we are on Facebook": Use and non-use of social media among Swedish and Norwegian politicians'. *European Journal of Communication*, 29(6): 653–67.

Larsson, A. O. and Moe, H. (2012) 'Studying political microblogging: Twitter users in the 2010 Swedish election campaign'. *New Media & Society*, 14(5): 729–47.

Lavender, P. (2012, 17 November) 'Obama, McKayla Maroney are not impressed (photo)'. *The Huffington Post*. Retrieved from http://www.huffingtonpost.com/2012/11/17/obama-mckayla-maroney-_n_2150140.html

Leaver, T. (2008) 'Watching Battlestar Galactica in Australia and the tyranny of digital distance'. *Media International Australia*, 126: 145–54.

Leaver, T. (2013) 'Olympic trolls: Mainstream memes and digital discord?' *Fibreculture*, 22: 216–33.

Leavitt, A. (2013) 'From #FollowFriday to #YOLO: Exploring the cultural salience of Twitter memes'. In: Weller, K., Bruns, A., Burgess, J., Mahrt, M. and Puschmann, C. (eds.) *Twitter and Society*. Peter Lang, New York, pp. 137–54.

Lee, Y.-O. (2015) 'The fragile beauty of peer-to-peer activism: The public campaign for the rights of media consumers in South Korea'. *New Media & Society* (online first).

Lehti, L. (2011) 'Blogging politics in various ways: A typology of French politicians' blogs'. *Journal of Pragmatics*, 43(6): 1610–27.

Lemish, D. (2004) '"My kind of campfire": The Eurovision Song Contest and Israeli gay men'. *Popular Communication*, 2(1): 41–63.

Lerman, K. and Ghosh, R. (2010) 'Information contagion: An empirical study of the spread of news on Digg and Twitter social networks'. *Proceedings of 4th International Conference on Weblogs and Social Media*. Retrieved from http://arxiv.org/abs/1003.2664

Lewis, S. C., Holton, A. E. and Coddington, M. (2014) 'Reciprocal journalism: A concept of mutual exchange between journalists and audiences'. *Journalism Practice*, 8(2): 229–41.

Lexpress.fr. (2015, 8 January) '*Charlie Hebdo*: des hashtags contre l'islamophobie'. *L'Express*. Retrieved from http://www.lexpress.fr/actualite/societe/charlie-hebdo-des-hashtags-contre-l-islamophobie_1638762.html

Li, D. and Walejko, G. (2008) 'Splogs and abandoned blogs: The perils of sampling bloggers and their blogs'. *Information, Communication & Society*, 11(2): 279–96.

Lievrouw, L. A. (2011) *Alternative and Activist New Media*. Polity, Malden, MA.

Lilleker, D. G. and Malagon, C. (2010) 'Levels of interactivity in the 2007 French Presidential candidates' websites'. *European Journal of Communication*, 25(1): 25–42.

Lin, A. (2015, 9 January) '#JeSuisAhmed pays tribute to killed French policeman'. *SBS News*. Retrieved from http://www.sbs.com.au/news/article/2015/01/09/jesuisahmed-pays-tribute-killed-french-policeman

Lindgren, S. (2013) *New Noise: A cultural sociology of digital disruption*. Peter Lang, New York.

Lindgren, S. (ed.) (2014) *Hybrid Media Culture: Sensing place in a world of flows*. Routledge, Abingdon.

Lindgren, S. and Lundström, R. (2011) 'Pirate culture and hacktivist mobilization: The cultural and social protocols of #WikiLeaks on Twitter'. *New Media & Society*, 13(6): 999–1018.

Lingel, J. and Bishop, B. W. (2014) 'The GeoWeb and everyday life: An analysis of spatial tactics and volunteered geographic information'. *First Monday*, 19(7). Retrieved from http://firstmonday.org/ojs/index.php/fm/article/view/5316/4095

Lingel, J. and Golub, A. (2015) 'In face on Facebook: Brooklyn's drag community and sociotechnical practices of online communication'. *Journal of Computer-Mediated Communication*, 20(5): 536–53.

Liu, S. B. and Palen, L. (2010) 'The new cartographers: Crisis map mashups and the emergence of neogeographic practice'. *Cartography and Geographic Information Science*, 37(1): 69–90.

Lobato, R. and Thomas, J. (2015) *The Informal Media Economy*. Polity, Cambridge.

Loken, M. (2015) '#BringBackOurGirls and the invisibility of imperialism'. *Feminist Media Studies*, 14(6): 1100–1.

Lotan, G., Graeff, E., Ananny, M., Gaffney, D., Pearce, I. and boyd, d. (2011) 'The revolutions were tweeted: Information flows during the 2011 Tunisian and Egyptian revolutions'. *International Journal of Communication*, 5: 1375–405.

Lovink, G. (2008) *Zero Comments: Blogging and critical internet culture*. Routledge, New York.

Loza, S. (2014) 'Hashtag feminism, #SolidarityIsForWhiteWomen, and the other #FemFuture'. *Ada: A Journal of Gender, New Media, and Technology*, 5. Retrieved from http://adanewmedia.org/2014/07/issue5-loza/

Lyon, D. (2014) 'Surveillance, Snowden, and big data: Capacities, consequences, critique'. *Big Data & Society*, 1(2): 1–13.

mac Suibhne, E. (2015, 29 April) 'Baltimore "looting" tweets show importance of quick and easy image checks'. *Medium*. Retrieved from https://medium.com/@Storyful/baltimore-looting-tweets-show-importance-of-quick-and-easy-image-checks-a713bbcc275e

Macha, N. (2014, 16 June) '54 days in prison and counting for Ethiopia's Zone 9 bloggers'. *Global Voices*. Retrieved from https://globalvoicesonline.org/2014/06/16/54-days-in-prison-and-counting-for-ethiopias-zone-9-bloggers/

MacKinnon, R. (2008) 'Blogs and China correspondence: Lessons about global information flows'. *Chinese Journal of Communication*, 1(2): 242–57.

Maddock, J., Starbird, K., Al-Hassani, H., Sandoval, D. E., Orand, M. and Mason, R. M. (2015) 'Characterizing online rumoring behavior using multi-dimensional signatures'. *CSCW '15*. ACM, New York, pp. 228–41.

Manivannan, V. (2013) 'Tits or GTFO: The logics of misogyny on 4chan's Random – /b/'. *Fibreculture*, 22: 109–32.

Manning, H. and Phiddian, R. (2015) 'Nearly all about Kevin: The election as drawn by Australian cartoonists'. In: Johnson, C. and Wanna, J. (eds.) *Abbott's Gambit: The 2013 Australian Federal Election*. ANU Press, Canberra, pp. 161–87.

Markham, T. (2014) 'Social media, protest cultures and political subjectivities of the Arab Spring'. *Media, Culture & Society*, 36(1): 89–104.

Marwick, A. E. (2015) 'Instafame: Luxury selfies in the attention economy'. *Public Culture*, 27(1): 137–60.

Marwick, A. E. and boyd, d. (2011a) 'I tweet honestly, I tweet passionately: Twitter users, context collapse, and the imagined audience'. *New Media & Society*, 13(1): 114–33.

Marwick, A. E. and boyd, d. (2011b) 'To see and be seen: Celebrity practice on Twitter'. *Convergence: The International Journal of Research into New Media Technologies*, 17(2): 139–58.

Massanari, A. L. (2015) *Participatory Culture, Community, and Play: Learning from reddit*. Peter Lang, New York.

Matias, J. N. (2015, 28 June) 'Were all those rainbow profile photos another Facebook study?' *The Atlantic*. Retrieved from http://www.theatlantic.com/technology/archive/2015/06/were-all-those-rainbow-profile-photos-another-facebook-experiment/397088/

Matias, J. N., Johnson, A., Boesel, W. E., Keegan, B., Friedman, J. and DeTar, C. (2015) *Reporting, Reviewing, and Responding to Harassment on Twitter*. Women, Action, and the Media. Retrieved from http://womenactionmedia.org/twitter-report

McCombs, M. (2005) 'A look at agenda-setting: Past, present and future'. *Journalism Studies*, 6(4): 543–57.

McCombs, M. and Shaw, D. L. (1972) 'The agenda-setting function of mass media'. *Public Opinion Quarterly*, 36: 176–87.

McCosker, A. and Johns, A. (2013) 'Productive provocations: Vitriolic media, spaces of protest and agonistic outrage in the 2011 England riots'. *Fibreculture*, 22: 171–93.

McDonald, S. (2014, 25 April) 'Apocalyptic error puts the F in AFR'. *Guardian*. Retrieved from http://www.theguardian.com/world/australia-news-blog/2014/apr/25/apocalyptic-error-puts-the-f-in-afr

McElroy, K. (2015) 'Gold medals, black Twitter, and not-so-good hair: Framing the Gabby Douglas controversy'. *#ISOJ: International Symposium on Online Journalism*, 1(1). Retrieved from https://isojjournal.wordpress.com/2015/04/15/gold-medals-black-twitter-and-not-so-good-hair-framing-the-gabby-douglas-controversy/

McEnery, T., McGlashan, M. and Love, R. (2015) 'Press and social media reaction to ideologically inspired murder: The case of Lee Rigby'. *Discourse & Communication*, 9(2): 237–59.

McKee, A. (2003) *Textual Analysis: A beginner's guide*. Sage, London.

McNair, B. (2006) *Cultural Chaos: Journalism, news and power in a globalised world*. Routledge, Abingdon.

Meese, J. (2014) ' "It belongs to the internet": Animal images, attribution norms and the politics of amateur media production'. *M/C Journal*, 17(2). Retrieved from http://journal.media-culture.org.au/index.php/mcjournal/article/viewArticle/782

Meese, J. (2015) 'User production and law reform: A socio-legal critique of user creativity'. *Media, Culture & Society*, 37(5): 753–67.

Meier, P. (2012) 'Crisis mapping in action: How open source software and global volunteer networks are changing the world, one map at a time'. *Journal of Map & Geography Libraries: Advances in Geospatial Information, Collections & Archives*, 8(2): 89–100.

Meikle, G. (2002) *Future Active: Media activism and the internet*. Routledge, New York.

Meikle, G. (2012) ' "Find out exactly what to think – next!": Chris Morris, *Brass Eye*, and journalistic authority'. *Popular Communication*, 10(1–2): 14–26.

Meikle, G., Wilson, J. and Saunders, B. (2008) 'Vote / citizen'. *M/C Journal*, 11(1). Retrieved from http://journal.media-culture.org.au/index.php/mcjournal/article/viewArticle/20

Meraz, S. (2007) 'Analyzing political conversation on the Howard Dean candidate blog'. In: Tremayne, M. (ed.) *Blogging, Citizenship, and the Future of Media*. Routledge, New York, pp. 59–81.

Meraz, S. (2011) 'The fight for "how to think": Traditional media, social networks, and issue interpretation'. *Journalism*, 12(1): 107–27.

Meserko, V. M. (2014) 'Going mental: Podcasting, authenticity, and artist–fan identification on *Paul Gilmartin's Mental Illness Happy Hour*'. *Journal of Broadcasting & Electronic Media*, 58(3): 456–69.

Messina, C. (2007, 22 October) 'Twitter hashtags for emergency coordination and disaster relief'. *Factory City (blog)*. Retrieved from http://factoryjoe.com/blog/2007/10/22/twitter-hashtags-for-emergency-coordination-and-disaster-relief/

Miazhevich, G. (2015) 'Paradoxes of new media: Digital discourses on Eurovision 2014, media flows and post-Soviet nation-building'. *New Media & Society* (online first).

Miller, B. (2015) '"Dude, where's your face?" Self-presentation, self-description, and partner preferences on a social networking application for men who have sex with men: A content analysis'. *Sexuality & Culture*, 19(4): 637–58.

Milner, R. M. (2013) 'Hacking the social: Internet memes, identity antagonism, and the logic of lulz'. *Fibreculture*, 22: 62–92.

Miltner, K. M. (2014) '"There's no place for lulz on LOLCats": The role of genre, gender, and group identity in the interpretation and enjoyment of an Internet meme'. *First Monday*, 19(8). Retrieved from http://firstmonday.org/ojs/index.php/fm/article/view/5391/4103

Miltner, K. M. and Baym, N. K. (2015) 'The selfie of the year of the selfie: Reflections on a media scandal'. *International Journal of Communication*, 9: 1701–15.

Moe, H. (2012) 'Who participates and how? Twitter as an arena for public debate about the data retention directive in Norway'. *International Journal of Communication*, 6: 1222–44.

Monroy-Hernández, A., Kiciman, E., boyd, d. and Counts, S. (2012) 'Narcotweets: Social media in wartime'. *Proceedings of the Sixth International AAAI Conference on Weblogs and Social Media*, pp. 515–18.

Monroy-Hernández, A., boyd, d., Kiciman, E., De Choudhury, M. and Counts, S. (2013) 'The new war correspondents: The rise of civic media curation in urban warfare'. *CSCW 13: Proceedings of the 2013 Conference on Computer-Supported Cooperative Work*, pp. 1443–52.

Monterde, A. and Postill, J. (2014) 'Mobile ensembles: The uses of mobile phones for social protest by Spain's indignados'. In: Goggin, G. and Hjorth, L. (eds.) *The Routledge Companion to Mobile Media*. Routledge, Hoboken, NJ, pp. 429–38.

Morozov, E. (2011, 7 March) 'Facebook and Twitter are just places revolutionaries go'. *Guardian (Comment Is Free)*. Retrieved from http://www.guardian.co.uk/commentisfree/2011/mar/07/facebook-twitter-revolutionaries-cyber-utopians

Morozov, E. (2013, 5 February) 'Why social movements should ignore social media'. *New Republic*. Retrieved from http://www.newrepublic.com/article/112189/social-media-doesnt-always-help-social-movements

Morstatter, F., Pfeffer, J., Liu, H. and Carley, K. M. (2013) 'Is the sample good enough? Comparing data from Twitter's Streaming API with Twitter's Firehose'. *Proceedings of the 7th International AAAI Conference on Weblogs and Social Media*, pp. 400–8.

Mortensen, M. (2015) 'Conflictual media events, eyewitness images, and the Boston Marathon bombing (2013)'. *Journalism Practice*, 9(4): 536–51.

Mowlabocus, S. (2010) *Gaydar Culture: Gay men, technology and embodiment in the digital age*. Ashgate, Burlington, VT.

Munger, M. C. (2008) 'Blogging and political information: Truth or truthiness?' *Public Choice*, 134(1–2): 125–38.

Murthy, D. (2015) 'Twitter and elections: Are tweets, predictive, reactive, or a form of buzz?' *Information, Communication & Society*, 18(7): 816–31.

Nahon, K. and Hemsley, J. (2013) *Going Viral*. Polity, Cambridge.

Nakamura, L. (2008) *Digitizing Race: Visual cultures of the internet*. University of Minnesota Press, Minneapolis.

Nakamura, L. (2012) 'Queer female of color: The highest difficulty setting there is? Gaming rhetoric as gender capital'. *Ada: A Journal of Gender, New Media, and Technology*, 1. Retrieved from http://adanewmedia.org/2012/11/issue1-nakamura/

Nakamura, L. (2014) '"I WILL DO EVERYthing that am asked": Scambaiting, digital show-space, and the racial violence of social media'. *Journal of Visual Culture*, 13(3): 257–274.

Nakamura, L. and Chow-White, P. A. (eds.) (2012) *Race After the Internet*. Routledge, New York.

Nooney, L. and Portwood-Stacer, L. (2014) 'One does not simply: An introduction to the special issue on internet memes'. *Journal of Visual Culture*, 13(3): 248–52.

Novak, A. N. and Khazraee, E. (2015) 'The stealthy protestor: Risk and the female body in online social movements'. *Feminist Media Studies*, 14(6): 1094–5.

Oboler, A. (2012) 'Aboriginal memes & online hate'. Online Hate Prevention Institute. Retrieved from http://ohpi.org.au/reports/IR12-2-Aboriginal-Memes.pdf

Olszanowski, M. (2014) 'Feminist self-imaging and Instagram: Tactics of circumventing censorship'. *Visual Communication Quarterly*, 21(2): 83–95.

Oravec, J. A. (2012) 'The ethics of sexting: Issues involving consent and the production of intimate content'. In: Heider, D. and Massanari, A. L. (eds.) *Digital Ethics: Research and practice*. Peter Lang, New York, pp. 129–45.

Orsini, L. R. (2011, 31 August) 'Protesting loud with silence'. *The Daily Dot*. Retrieved from http://www.dailydot.com/news/tumblr-members-silent-protest/

Owens, J. (2015, 17 March) 'No protection for bloggers from metadata laws rules George Brandis'. *The Australian*. Retrieved from http://www.theaustralian.com.au/business/media/no-protection-for-bloggers-from-metadata-laws-rules-george-brandis/story-e6frg996-1227265808805

Page, R. (2012) 'The linguistics of self-branding and micro-celebrity in Twitter: The role of hashtags'. *Discourse & Communication*, 6(2): 181–201.

Papacharissi, Z. (2010a) *A Private Sphere: Democracy in a digital age*. Polity, Cambridge.

Papacharissi, Z. (2010b) 'The virtual public sphere 2.0: The internet, the public sphere, and beyond'. In: Chadwick, A. and Howard, P. N. (eds.) *The*

Routledge Handbook of Internet Politics, 2nd edn. Routledge, New York, pp. 229–45.

Papacharissi, Z. (2015) *Affective Publics: Sentiment, technology, and politics.* Oxford University Press, Oxford.

Papacharissi, Z. and de Fatima Oliveira, M. (2012) 'Affective news and networked publics: The rhythms of news storytelling on #egypt'. *Journal of Communication*, 62: 266–82.

Park, H. W. and Jankowski, N. W. (2008) 'A hyperlink network analysis of citizen blogs in South Korean politics'. *Javnost – the Public*, 15(2): 57–74.

Paßmann, J., Boeschoten, T. and Schäfer, M. T. (2013) 'The gift of the gab: Retweet cartels and gift economies on Twitter'. In: Weller, K., Bruns, A., Burgess, J., Mahrt, M. and Puschmann, C. (eds.) *Twitter and Society*. Peter Lang, New York, pp. 331–44.

Penney, J. (2011) 'KEVIN07: Cool politics, consumer citizenship, and the specter of "Americanization" in Australia'. *Communication, Culture & Critique*, 4(1): 78–96.

Petersen, L. N. (2014) 'Sherlock fans talk: Mediatized talk on tumblr'. *Northern Lights*, 12: 87–104.

Phillips, L. (2015, 13 January) 'Lost in translation: *Charlie Hebdo*, free speech and the unilingual left'. *Ricochet*. Retrieved from https://ricochet.media/en/292/lost-in-translation-charlie-hebdo-free-speech-and-the-unilingual-left

Phillips, W. (2015) *This is Why We Can't Have Nice Things: Mapping the relationship between online trolling and mainstream culture*. The MIT Press, Cambridge, MA.

Poell, T. and Borra, E. (2012) 'Twitter, YouTube, and Flickr as platforms of alternative journalism: The social media account of the 2010 Toronto G20 protests'. *Journalism*, 13(6): 695–713.

Poell, T. and Darmoni, K. (2012) 'Twitter as a multilingual space: The articulation of the Tunisian revolution through #sidibouzid'. *NECSUS: European Journal of Media Studies*, 1(1). Retrieved from http://www.necsus-ejms.org/twitter-as-a-multilingual-space-the-articulation-of-the-tunisian-revolution-through-sidibouzid-by-thomas-poell-and-kaouthar-darmoni/

Poell, T., de Kloet, J. and Zeng, G. (2014) 'Will the real Weibo please stand up? Chinese online contention and actor-network theory'. *Chinese Journal of Communication*, 7(1): 1–18.

Portwood-Stacer, L. and Berridge, S. (2015) 'Feminist hashtags and media convergence'. *Feminist Media Studies*, 15(1): 154.

Postigo, H. (2012) 'Cultural production and the digital rights movement: Framing the right to participate in culture'. *Information, Communication & Society*, 15(8): 1165–85.

Potts, L. and Harrison, A. (2013) 'Interfaces as rhetorical constructions: reddit and 4chan during the Boston Marathon bombings'. *Proceedings of the 31st ACM International Conference on Design of Communication*, pp. 143–50.

Poulaki, M. (2015) 'Featuring shortness in online loop cultures'. *Empedocles: European Journal for the Philosophy of Communication*, 5(1–2): 91–6.

Pramlady (2015, 21 March) 'IKEA named their new pillow cover Putin'. *reddit /r/mildlyinteresting*. Retrieved from http://www.reddit.com/r/mildlyinteresting/comments/2ztnd5/ikea_named_their_new_pillow_cover_putin/

Press Association (2014, 22 May) 'Polling staff told to stop people taking selfies'. *Guardian*. Retrieved from http://www.theguardian.com/politics/2014/may/21/polling-staff-stop-selfies-local-european-elections

Procter, R., Vis, F. and Voss, A. (2013) 'Reading the riots on Twitter: Methodological innovation for the analysis of big data'. *International Journal of Social Research Methodology*, 16(3): 197–214.

Quodling, A. (2015, 22 April) 'Doxxing, swatting and the new trends in online harassment'. *The Conversation*. Retrieved from http://theconversation.com/doxxing-swatting-and-the-new-trends-in-online-harassment-40234

Ramsey, D. X. (2015, 10 April) 'The truth about Black Twitter'. *The Atlantic*. Retrieved from http://www.theatlantic.com/technology/archive/2015/04/the-truth-about-black-twitter/390120/

Reger, J. (2014) 'The story of a slut walk: Sexuality, race, and generational divisions in contemporary feminist activism'. *Journal of Contemporary Ethnography*, 44(1): 84–112.

Reilly, P. (2015) 'Every little helps? YouTube, sousveillance and the "anti-Tesco" riot in Stokes Croft'. *New Media & Society*, 17(5): 755–71.

Renninger, B. J. (2015) ' "Where I can be myself ... where I can speak my mind": Networked counterpublics in a polymedia environment'. *New Media & Society*, 17(9): 1513–29.

Rentschler, C. A. (2014) 'Rape culture and the feminist politics of social media'. *Girlhood Studies*, 7(1): 65–82.

Ringrose, J., Harvey, L., Gill, R. and Livingstone, S. (2013) 'Teen girls, sexual double standards and "sexting": Gendered value in digital image exchange'. *Feminist Theory*, 14(3): 305–23.

Rodríguez-Amat, J. R. and Brantner, C. (2014) 'Space and place matters: A tool for the analysis of geolocated and mapped protests'. *New Media & Society* (online first).

Rodríguez Ortega, V. (2013) 'Spoof trailers, hyperlinked spectators & the web'. *New Media & Society*, 16(1): 149–64.

Rogers, R. (2013a) 'Debanalizing Twitter: The transformation of an object of study'. In: Weller, K., Bruns, A., Burgess, J., Mahrt, M. and Puschmann, C. (eds.) *Twitter and Society*. Peter Lang, New York, pp. ix–xxvi.

Rogers, R. (2013b) *Digital Methods*. The MIT Press, Cambridge, MA.

Romano, A. (2015, 3 March) 'It's a bird! It's a weasel! It's a bunch of Weasel Pecker memes'. *Mashable*. Retrieved from http://mashable.com/2015/03/03/weasel-pecker-memes/

Rosenberg, A. (2015, 13 January) 'How "Harry Potter" fans won a four-year fight against child slavery'. *Washington Post*. Retrieved from http://www.washingtonpost.com/news/act-four/wp/2015/01/13/how-harry-potter-fans-won-a-four-year-fight-against-child-slavery/

Ross, K., Fountaine, S. and Comrie, M. (2015) 'Facing up to Facebook: Politicians, publics and the social media(ted) turn in New Zealand'. *Media, Culture & Society*, 37(2): 251–69.

Ross, N. (2012, 19 January) 'Hash Wednesday: 80 best #FactsWithoutWikipedia tweets'. *ABC News (Australian Broadcasting Corporation)*. Retrieved from http://www.abc.net.au/technology/articles/2012/01/19/3411201.htm

Rothrock, K. (2015, 10 April) 'The Kremlin declares war on memes'. *Global Voices*. Retrieved from https://globalvoicesonline.org/2015/04/10/russia-the-kremlin-declares-war-on-memes/

Russell, A. (2007) 'Digital communication networks and the journalistic field: The 2005 French riots'. *Critical Studies in Media Communication*, 24(4): 285–302.

Russell, A. and Echchaibi, N. (eds.) (2009) *International Blogging: Identity, politics, and networked publics*. Peter Lang, New York.

Ryall, J. (2015, 8 February) '#ImStickingWithTony hashtag is the real winner in the Australian leadership crisis'. *Mashable*. Retrieved from http://mashable.com/2015/02/08/imstickingwithtony-abbott/

Sainty, L. (2015, 14 April) 'People are angry about Woolworths' Anzac Day website'. *BuzzFeed*. Retrieved from http://www.buzzfeed.com/lanesainty/people-are-mad-about-woolworths-anzac-day-website#.yxZOREpRz

Salter, A. and Blodgett, B. (2012) 'Hypermasculinity and dickwolves: The contentious role of women in the new gaming public'. *Journal of Broadcasting & Electronic Media*, 56(3): 401–16.

Sanyal, P. R. (2015, 31 March) 'Another blogger hacked to death: Is free thinking becoming fatal in Bangladesh?' *Global Voices*. Retrieved from https://globalvoicesonline.org/2015/03/31/another-blogger-hacked-to-death-is-free-thinking-becoming-fatal-in-bangladesh/

Sarkeesian, A. (2015, 20 February) 'Anita Sarkeesian's guide to internetting while female'. *Marie Claire*. Retrieved from http://www.marieclaire.com/culture/news/a13403/online-harassment-terms-fight-back/

Sauter, T. and Bruns, A. (2014) 'Tweeting the TV event, creating "public sphericules": Ad hoc engagement with SBS's *Go Back To Where You Came From* – Season 2'. *Media International Australia*, 152: 5–15.

Schifferes, S., Newman, N., Thurman, N., Corney, D., Göker, A. and Martin, C. (2014) 'Identifying and verifying news through social media'. *Digital Journalism*, 2(3): 406–18.

Schmidt, J. (2007) 'Blogging practices: An analytical framework'. *Journal of Computer-Mediated Communication*, 12(4): 1409–27.

Schmidt, J. (2013) 'Twitter and the rise of personal publics'. In: Weller, K., Bruns, A., Burgess, J., Mahrt, M. and Puschmann, C. (eds.) *Twitter and Society*. Peter Lang, New York, pp. 3–14.

Senft, T. M. (2013) 'Microcelebrities and the branded self'. In: Hartley, J., Burgess, J. and Bruns, A. (eds.) *A Companion to New Media Dynamics*. John Wiley, Malden, MA, pp. 346–54.

Senft, T. M. and Baym, N. K. (2015) 'What does the selfie say? Investigating a global phenomenon'. *International Journal of Communication*, 9: 1588–606.

Shah, N. (2015) 'Sluts "r" us: Intersections of gender, protocol and agency in the digital age'. *First Monday*, 20(4). Retrieved from http://firstmonday.org/ojs/index.php/fm/article/view/5463/4415

Sharma, S. (2013) 'Black Twitter? Racial hashtags, networks and contagion'. *New Formations*, 78: 46–64.

Shaw, A. and Benkler, Y. (2012) 'A tale of two blogospheres: Discursive practices on the left and right'. *American Behavioral Scientist*, 56(4): 459–87.

Shaw, F. (2012a) '"Hottest 100 Women": Cross-platform discursive activism in feminist blogging networks'. *Australian Feminist Studies*, 27(74): 373–87.

Shaw, F. (2012b) 'The politics of blogs: Theories of discursive activism online'. *Media International Australia*, 142: 41–9.

Shaw, F. (2013a) 'Still "Searching for Safety Online": Collective strategies and discursive resistance to trolling and harassment in a feminist network'. *Fibreculture*, 22: 93–108.

Shaw, F. (2013b) '"Walls of Seeing": Protest surveillance, embodied boundaries, and counter-surveillance at Occupy Sydney'. *Transformations*, 23. Retrieved from http://transformationsjournal.org/journal/issue_23/article_04.shtml

Shaw, F., Burgess, J., Crawford, K. and Bruns, A. (2013) 'Sharing news, making sense, saying thanks: Patterns of talk on Twitter during the Queensland floods'. *Australian Journal of Communication*, 40(1): 23–39.

Shearlaw, M. (2015, 13 January) 'What made the Paris attack more newsworthy than Boko Haram's assault on Baga?' *Guardian*. Retrieved from http://www.theguardian.com/world/2015/jan/13/-sp-what-makes-one-massacre-more-newsworthy-boko-haram-charlie-hebdo

Shifman, L. (2012) 'An anatomy of a YouTube meme'. *New Media & Society*, 14(2): 187–203.

Shifman, L. (2014a) *Memes in Digital Culture*. The MIT Press, Cambridge, MA.

Shifman, L. (2014b) 'The cultural logic of photo-based meme genres'. *Journal of Visual Culture*, 13(3): 340–58.

Shirky, C. (2011) 'The political power of social media'. *Foreign Affairs*. Retrieved from http://www.foreignaffairs.com/articles/67038/clay-shirky/the-political-power-of-social-media

Sinanan, J., Graham, C. and Zhong Jie, K. (2014) 'Crafted assemblage: Young women's "lifestyle" blogs, consumerism and citizenship in Singapore'. *Visual Studies*, 29(2): 201–13.

Singer, J. B. (2005) 'The political j-blogger: "Normalizing" a new media form to fit old norms and practices'. *Journalism*, 6(2): 173–98. Retrieved from http://jou.sagepub.com/cgi/content/abstract/6/2/173

Singleton, B., Fricker, K. and Moreo, E. (2007) 'Performing the queer network: Fans and families at the Eurovision Song Contest'. *SQS Journal*, 2(2). Retrieved from http://www.helsinki.fi/jarj/sqs/sqs2_07/sqs22007singletonetal.pdf

Smyrnaios, N. and Rieder, B. (2013) 'Social infomediation of news on Twitter: A French case study'. *NECSUS. European Journal of Media Studies*, 2(2): 359–82.

Soon, C. and Cho, H. (2011) 'Flows of relations and communication among Singapore political bloggers and organizations: The networked public sphere approach'. *Journal of Information Technology & Politics*, 8(1): 93–109.

Splichal, S. (2009) '"New" media, "old" theories: Does the (national) public melt into the air of global governance?' *European Journal of Communication*, 24(4): 391–405.

Stache, L. C. (2015) 'Advocacy and political potential at the convergence of hashtag activism and commerce'. *Feminist Media Studies*, 15(1): 162–4.

Starbird, K., Maddock, J., Orand, M., Achterman, P. and Mason, R. M. (2014) 'Rumors, false flags, and digital vigilantes: Misinformation on Twitter after the 2013 Boston Marathon bombing'. *iConference 2014 Proceedings*, pp. 654–62.

Stevenson, A. J. (2014) 'Finding the Twitter users who stood with Wendy'. *Contraception*, 90(5): 502–7.

Sullivan, J. (2012) 'A tale of two microblogs in China'. *Media, Culture & Society*, 34(6): 773–83.

Sunstein, C. (2008) 'Neither Hayek nor Habermas'. *Public Choice*, 134(1–2): 87–95.

Tapia, A. H., LaLone, N. and Kim, H.-W. (2014) 'Run amok: Group crowd participation in identifying the bomb and bomber from the Boston Marathon bombing'. In: Hiltz, S. R., Pfaff, M. S., Plotnick, L. and Shih, P. C. (eds.) *11th International ISCRAM Conference*. Pennsylvania State University, University Park, pp. 265–74.

Terrell, J. (2014) 'The Harry Potter Alliance: Sociotechnical contexts of digitally mediated activism'. In: McCaughey, M. (ed.) *Cyberactivism on the Participatory Web*. Routledge, New York, pp. 41–61.

Thomas, K. (2013) 'Revisioning the smiling villain: Imagetexts and intertextual expression in representations of the filmic Loki on Tumblr'. *Transformative Works and Cultures*, 13. Retrieved from http://journal.transformativeworks.org/index.php/twc/article/view/474/382

Thorson, K., Driscoll, K., Ekdale, B. et al. (2013) 'YouTube, Twitter and the Occupy movement: Connecting content and circulation practices'. *Information, Communication & Society*, 16(3): 421–51.

Thrift, S. C. (2015) '#YesAllWomen as feminist meme event'. *Feminist Media Studies*, 14(6): 1090–2.

Thurman, N. and Walters, A. (2013) 'Live blogging – digital journalism's pivotal platform? A case study of the production, consumption, and form of Live Blogs at Guardian.co.uk'. *Digital Journalism*, 1(1): 82–101.

Tiidenberg, K. (2015) 'Boundaries and conflict in a NSFW community on Tumblr: The meanings and uses of selfies'. *New Media & Society* (online first).

Tiidenberg, K. and Gómez Cruz, E. (2015) 'Selfies, image and the re-making of the body'. *Body & Society* (online first).

Tolentino, J. (2015, 27 March) 'Your beautiful, feminine period stains are against Instagram guidelines'. *Jezebel*. Retrieved from http://jezebel.com/your-beautiful-feminine-period-stains-are-against-inst-1694044070

Tomkinson, S. and Harper, T. (2015) 'The position of women in video game culture: Perez and Day's Twitter incident'. *Continuum Journal of Media & Cultural Studies*, 29(4): 617–34.

Tong, J. and Zuo, L. (2014) 'Weibo communication and government legitimacy in China: A computer-assisted analysis of Weibo messages on two "mass incidents"'. *Information, Communication & Society*, 17(1): 66–85.

Tremayne, M. (ed.) (2007) *Blogging, Citizenship, and the Future of Media*. Routledge, New York.

triple j (2015, 26 January) '8 hilarious but totally true reasons you won't hear "Shake It Off" in the Hottest 100'. *Triple J Feed*. Retrieved from http://www.abc.net.au/triplej/musicnews/s4168284.htm

Tsing, A. L. (2011) *Friction: An ethnography of global connection*. Princeton University Press, Princeton, NJ.

Tufekci, Z. (2013) ' "Not this one": Social movements, the attention economy, and microcelebrity networked activism'. *American Behavioral Scientist*, 57(7): 848–70.

Tufekci, Z. (2014) 'Big questions for social media big data: Representativeness, validity and other methodological pitfalls'. *ICWSM '14: Proceedings of the 8th International AAAI Conference on Weblogs and Social Media*. AAAI, Ann Arbor, MI, pp. 505–14.

Tufekci, Z. and Wilson, C. (2012) 'Social media and the decision to participate in political protest: Observations from Tahrir Square'. *Journal of Communication*, 62(2): 363–79.

Twitter. (n.d.) 'Filtering notifications and mentions for verified users'. *Twitter Media / Best Practices*. Retrieved from https://media.twitter.com/best-practice/filtering-mentions-for-verified-users

Tynan, L. (2008) 'Blogging and citizen journalism'. In: Bainbridge, J., Goc, N. and Tynan, L. (eds.) *Media and Journalism: New approaches to theory and practice*. Oxford University Press, South Melbourne, pp. 409–16.

'Utegate, as told by LOLCATS' (2009, 30 June) *Lolpolz*. Retrieved from http://dailylolz.lolpolz.com/2009/06/coming-soon.html

Vagianos, A. (2015, 21 January) 'Instagram admits they "don't always get it right" when it comes to nudity'. *The Huffington Post*. Retrieved from http://www.huffingtonpost.com/2015/01/21/instagram-pubic-hair-censorship-sticks-and-stones_n_6515654.html

Valtysson, B. (2013) 'Democracy in disguise: The use of social media in reviewing the Icelandic Constitution'. *Media, Culture & Society*, 36(1): 52–68.

van der Nagel, E. (2013) 'Faceless bodies: Negotiating technological and cultural codes on reddit gonewild'. *Scan: Journal of Media Arts Culture*, 10(2). Retrieved from http://scan.net.au/scn/journal/vol10number2/Emily-van-der-Nagel.html

van der Nagel, E. and Frith, J. (2015) 'Anonymity, pseudonymity, and the agency of online identity: Examining the social practices of r/Gonewild'. *First Monday*, 20(3). Retrieved from http://firstmonday.org/ojs/index.php/fm/article/view/5615/4346

van der Nagel, E. and Meese, J. (2015, 27 February) 'reddit tackles "revenge porn" and celebrity nudes'. *The Conversation*. Retrieved from http://theconversation.com/reddit-tackles-revenge-porn-and-celebrity-nudes-38112

van Dijck, J. (2013) *The Culture of Connectivity: A critical history of social media*. Oxford University Press, New York.

van Dijck, J. and Poell, T. (2013) 'Understanding social media logic'. *Media and Communication*, 1(1): 2–14.

Vanbremeersch, N. (2009) *De la démocratie numérique*. Seuil, Médiathèque, Paris.

Varnali, K. and Gorgulu, V. (2015) 'A social influence perspective on expressive political participation in Twitter: The case of #OccupyGezi'. *Information, Communication & Society*, 18(1): 1–16.

Vis, F. (2013) 'Twitter as a reporting tool for breaking news: Journalists tweeting the 2011 UK riots'. *Digital Journalism*, 1(1): 27–47.

Vis, F., Faulkner, S., Parry, K., Manykhina, Y. and Evans, L. (2013) 'Twitpic-ing the riots: Analysing images shared on Twitter during the 2011 UK riots'. In: Weller, K., Bruns, A., Burgess, J., Mahrt, M. and Puschmann, C. (eds.) *Twitter and Society*. Peter Lang, New York, pp. 385–98.

Vivienne, S. and Burgess, J. (2012) 'The digital storyteller's stage: Queer everyday activists negotiating privacy and publicness'. *Journal of Broadcasting & Electronic Media*, 56(3): 362–77.

Vogt, N. (2015) 'Podcasting: Fact sheet (State of the news media 2015)'. Retrieved from http://www.journalism.org/2015/04/29/podcasting-fact-sheet/

Walker Rettberg, J. (2008) *Blogging*. Polity, Cambridge.

Walker Rettberg, J. (2009) ' "Freshly generated for you, and Barack Obama": How social media represent your life'. *European Journal of Communication*, 24(4): 451–66.

Walker Rettberg, J. (2014) *Seeing Ourselves Through Technology: How we use selfies, blogs and wearable devices to see and shape ourselves*. Palgrave Macmillan, Basingstoke.

Wall, M. (2005) ' "Blogs of war": Weblogs as news'. *Journalism*, 6(2): 153–72.

Wall, M. (2015) 'Citizen journalism: A retrospective on what we know, an agenda for what we don't'. *Digital Journalism*, 3(6): 797–813.

Warner, M. (2002) 'Publics and counterpublics'. *Public Culture*, 14(1): 49–90.

Watson, M. (2015, 18 April) 'Angry young Labor members have launched a pretty excellent meme war against the Greens'. *Junkee*. Retrieved from http://junkee.com/angry-young-labor-members-have-launched-a-pretty-excellent-meme-war-against-the-greens/55279

Webb, L. M. (2015) 'Shame transfigured: Slut-shaming from Rome to cyberspace'. *First Monday*, 20(4). Retrieved from http://firstmonday.org/ojs/index.php/fm/article/view/5464/4419

Weller, K., Bruns, A., Burgess, J., Mahrt, M. and Puschmann, C. (eds.) (2013) *Twitter and Society*. Peter Lang, New York.

Wheeler, B. (2014, 21 May) 'Voters advised not to take selfies in polling booths'. *BBC News*. Retrieved from http://www.bbc.com/news/uk-politics-27486392

White, A. and Di Stefano, M. (2014, 15 December) 'Outrage as bystanders take selfies at Sydney siege'. *BuzzFeed*. Retrieved from http://www.buzzfeed.com/alanwhite/outrage-as-bystanders-take-selfies-at-sydney-siege

Wilken, R. and Goggin, G. (eds.) (2015) *Locative Media*. Routledge, New York.

Williams, M. E. (2015, 27 March) 'Instagram has a problem with women: Bloody accident photos are fine, but periods are "inappropriate"?' *Salon*. Retrieved from http://www.salon.com/2015/03/27/instagram_tries_to_fix_its_period_problem/

Wilson, J. (2011) 'Playing with politics: Political fans and Twitter faking in post-broadcast democracy'. *Convergence: The International Journal of Research into New Media Technologies*, 17(4): 445–61.

Wilson, J. (2014) 'Kevin Rudd, celebrity and audience democracy in Australia'. *Journalism*, 15(2): 202–17.

Wilson, J. (2015, 26 March) 'After the onions, there's no longer any doubt. Tony Abbott is a "loose unit"'. *Guardian (Comment Is Free)*. Retrieved from http://www.theguardian.com/commentisfree/2015/mar/26/after-the-onions-theres-no-doubt-tony-abbott-is-a-loose-unit

Wolff, R. (2015, 20 April) 'Hillvetica: A short, strange trip'. RickWolff.com. Retrieved from http://rickwolff.com/hillvetica/

Woods, H. S. (2014) 'Anonymous, Steubenville, and the politics of visibility: Questions of virality and exposure in the case of #OPRollRedRoll and #OccupySteubenville'. *Feminist Media Studies*, 14(6): 1096–8.

Wright, S. (2012) 'Politics as usual? Revolution, normalization and a new agenda for online deliberation'. *New Media & Society*, 14(2): 244–61.

Yalkin, C., Kerrigan, F. and vom Lehn, D. (2013) '(Il)Legitimisation of the role of the nation state: Understanding of and reactions to Internet censorship in Turkey'. *New Media & Society*, 16(2): 271–89.

Yanoshevsky, G. (2009) 'L'usage des vidéoblogs dans l'élection présidentielle de 2007. Vers une image plurigérée des candidats'. *Mots. Les Langages du Politique*, 89: 57–68.

Yardi, S., Romero, D., Schoenebeck, G. and boyd, d. (2010) 'Detecting spam in a Twitter network'. *First Monday*, 15(1). Retrieved from http://firstmonday.org/ojs/index.php/fm/article/view/2793/2431

Yep, G. A., Olzman, M. and Conkle, A. (2012) 'Seven stories from the "It Gets Better" project: Progress narratives, politics of affect, and the question of queer world-making'. In: Lind, R. A. (ed.) *Produsing Theory in a Digital World: The intersection of audiences and production in contemporary theory*. Peter Lang, New York, pp. 123–41.

Yeshua-Katz, D. and Martins, N. (2013) 'Communicating stigma: The pro-ana paradox'. *Health Communication*, 28(5): 499–508.

York, J. C. (2011, 1 February) 'Egypt: A voice in the blackout, thanks to Google and Twitter'. *Global Voices*. Retrieved from http://globalvoicesonline.org/2011/02/01/egypt-a-voice-in-the-blackout-thanks-to-google-and-twitter/

Young, S. (2011) *How Australia Decides: Election reporting and the media*. Cambridge University Press, Cambridge.

Zappavigna, M. (2014) 'Enjoy your snags Australia … oh and the voting thing too #ausvotes #auspol: Iconisation and affiliation in electoral microblogging'. *Global Media Journal (Australian Edition)*, 8(2). Retrieved from http://www.hca.uws.edu.au/gmjau/?p=1139

Zappavigna, M. (2015) 'Searchable talk: The linguistic functions of hashtags'. *Social Semiotics*, 25(3): 274–91.

Zimmer, M. and Proferes, N. (2014) 'A topology of Twitter research: Disciplines, methods, and ethics'. *Aslib Journal of Management*, 66(3): 250–61.

Zimmerman, J. (2015, 1 July) 'Can a rainbow heart transform how we deal with internet trolls?' *Guardian*. Retrieved from http://www.theguardian.com/commentisfree/2015/jul/01/rainbow-heart-transform-internet-trolls

Zittrain, J. L. (2014) 'Reflections on internet culture'. *Journal of Visual Culture*, 13(3): 388–94.

Zook, M., Graham, M., Shelton, T. and Gorman, S. (2010) 'Volunteered geographic information and crowdsourcing disaster relief: A case study of the Haitian earthquake'. *World Medical & Health Policy*, 2(2): 7–33.

Zuckerman, E. (2008) 'Meet the bridgebloggers'. *Public Choice*, 134(1–2): 47–65.

Zuckerman, E. (2012, 8 March) 'Unpacking Kony 2012'.... *My Heart's in Accra (blog)*. Retrieved from http://www.ethanzuckerman.com/blog/2012/03/08/unpacking-kony-2012/

Index

Hashtags

Main index

Page numbers in *italic* refer to figures